P9-EDA-177

stockhausen

CONVERSATIONS WITH THE COMPOSER

Jonathan Cott

SIMON AND SCHUSTER · NEW YORK

Published by Simon and Schuster
Rockefeller Center, 630 Fifth Avenue
New York, New York 10020

SBN 671-21495-0
Library of Congress Catalog Card Number: 72-93506
Designed by Edith Fowler
Manufactured in the United States of America

1 2 3 4 5 6 7 8 9 10

ACKNOWLEDGMENTS

I would like to thank the following persons who, in various ways, helped make this book possible: Ann Druyan, Linda Healey, Joachim Krist, Michael Marcus, Alice Mayhew, Danny Moses, Joachim Neugroschel, Carol Saltus, Jane Seitz, Mitchell Weber, Margaret Wolf.

Grateful acknowledgment is made to *Rolling Stone* magazine for permission to reprint, in slightly altered form, the conversation with Stockhausen (Part I of this book) which first appeared in the July 8, 1971 issue. Interview © Straight Arrow Publishers, Inc.

Thanks to Werner Scholz and Robert Slotover for permission to use photographs of Stockhausen from their collections.

I am also grateful to Universal Edition, Vienna/London (Sole U.S.A. representative, Theodore Presser Co.), for permission to reproduce material from the following scores:

Kurzwellen: UE 14951, Copyright 1969 by Universal Edition.
Plus Minus: UE 13993, Copyright 1965 by Universal Edition.
Punkte: (1966 version), Copyright 1963, 1964 and 1966 by Universal Edition.
Stimmung: UE 14805, Copyright 1969 by Universal Edition.
Studie II: UE 12466, Copyright 1956 by Universal Edition.

Special thanks to Karlheinz Stockhausen for allowing me to copy and reproduce personal score materials and photographs: *Mantra* notes and score materials © Karlheinz Stockhausen.

contents

introduction

> "The exaltation of the mind derived from things eternal bursting forth in sound."
>
> —St. Thomas

In 1970, when the Free Berlin Network asked Karlheinz Stockhausen for a "concentrated" biographical statement, he wrote the following:

> Karlheinz Stockhausen, born on August 22 (Leo), 1928, at 3:00 A.M., first child of the elementary school teacher Simon Stockhausen from Engelsbruck and his wife Gertrud, née Strupp, from Neurath. Both parents came from a rural background. The mother, bearing three children in just three years and living in utter poverty, began suffering deep depressions and was committed to a mental hospital, where she was officially killed in 1941. The father managed for a few years with housekeepers, marrying one of them, who bore him two more children; he then volunteered for the army in 1939, dying a "heroic death" somewhere in Hungary.
>
> The eldest son entered an "Institute for Teachers' Education" in 1941; from 1944 till the end of the war he worked in a hospital at the front; then he became a field hand on a farm, learning Latin at night; from 1946 to 1947 he attended a "humanistic" *Gymnasium* (high school), got his diploma, was accepted at the State Academy of Music in Cologne in 1947 for Hans-Otto Schmidt-Neuhaus's piano class (he had been studying piano ever since the age of six with the village organist Kloth in Altenberg), studied music education from 1948 to 1951, received his teacher's license summa cum laude, all the while played in Cologne bars almost every night, as well as for dancing classes, toured as an improvisational musician with the magician Adrion for a year, directed an amateur

operetta theater, spent his vacations working in a factory, or as a parking lot attendant, or guarding homes of occupation troops. Prayed a lot.

After getting his teacher's license, he married Doris, spent a year in Paris taking Olivier Messiaen's courses in aesthetics and analysis, having previously composed his first work *Kreuzspiel* (Crossplay), then *Spiel* (Play) for Orchestra, then *Punkte* (Points), etc. Since 1953, he has been associated with the Studio for Electronic Music at the West German Radio Network in Cologne, becoming its artistic director in 1963. In 1953, he composed the first piece of electronic music: *Study I* for sine tones. From 1953 to 1956, he studied phonetics and communication science with Meyer-Eppler at the University of Bonn. He has by now composed forty works. published two volumes of *Texts* with DuMont Schauberg in Cologne, as well as about forty records.* Since 1958, he has spent several months annually on tour and has conducted, played, and commented on his own works in almost all countries of the world. He has lectured and conducted seminars of composition at the International Summer Courses for New Music, Darmstadt, and has taught composition at the Basel Conservatory, at the University of Pennsylvania in Philadelphia, at the University of California, Davis, and has also been an instructor for five years at the Cologne Courses for New Music, which he founded in 1963. He composed *Telemusik* and *Solo* for the Japanese radio network NHK in Tokyo in 1966, and in 1968 lived for some time in Mexico. In 1964, he formed a group, together with a few friends, with which he gave hundreds of concerts of his *electronic instrumental* music, whose final results he called "intuitive music." In 1967, he married Mary Bauermeister.

He has been married twice, has six children, and doesn't belong to any church or party. His friends include Henri Pousseur, André and Diego Masson, Alfred Schlee, Otto Tomek, Pierre Boulez, Ernst Brücher, Aloys Kontarsky, Harald Bojé, Roger Smalley, Hugh Davies, Mesias Maiguashca, Max Ernst, Michael Vetter, Joan Miro, Narayan Menon, Peter Eötvös, Luciano Berio, J. Marks, Sami Karkabe, Leonard Stein, Christoph Caskel, Bengt Hambraeus, Wataru Uenami,

* See appendix for catalog of works and discography. Richard Toop has recently translated the first two DuMont volumes into English; a third volume appeared in 1971.

Alexei Lyubimov, Shin-ichi Matsushita, Toru Takemitsu, and many others.

At the end of February 1971, Stockhausen came to New York City to present two enthusiastically received concerts at Philharmonic Hall and Alice Tully Hall. He and the five members of his Group Stockhausen—who play instruments like the elektronium, tam-tam, 55-chord, and piano—joined the New York Philharmonic Orchestra in a three-hour performance of *Hymnen*, the four-track electronic work which, divided into four sections ("regions"), uses and transforms national anthems like the Marseillaise, the Internationale, and The Star-spangled Banner. Despite minimal rehearsal time, Stockhausen had members of the orchestra respond to and transpose the basic taped materials of the work's Third Region—which was played over enormous loudspeakers on and above the stage—while Group Stockhausen, the composer's own highly trained transformational improvisers, commented on the music of Regions 1, 2, and 4.

In an interview in the *New York Times* two weeks before the concert, Stockhausen talked about the inability of a musician working in a "streamlined factory" situation to respond successfully to the "demands of creative spiritual work . . . he will never transport the public into a spiritual realm." But as the composer pointed out after concluding his second rehearsal with the orchestra: "Being creative is more important than just looking for the outcome of a work. So it's good that when I leave New York the musicians will know the way I work, rather than just have a definite idea only of a piece of music that I've composed. If they've enjoyed themselves during these ten hours of rehearsals, working with me and learning new things, then this is a very creative process. The musicians might later have a different approach to their whole work, and then slowly things might change."

There was a responsive young audience at Philharmonic Hall for the February 25 performance of *Hymnen*. Stockhausen sat at the center of the hall, meditating before the presentation, then working the filters and potentiometer which controlled the sound and balance levels between speakers and musicians. The giant tam-tam, surrounded by speakers and glowing burnished gold, became the visual center for the proliferations of sounds of this amazing work, both heart of the sun and reflecting moon.

In the Malaysian Ma'yong theater, an acting troupe, which is considered to have medicinal powers, is hired during an illness. A shaman, called a *bomor*, purifies all the instruments on stage, lights incense and candles, and strews rice about the platform. The aim is that of social healing, the purification and well-being of the community achieved by means of communion with the divine. And this New York performance of *Hymnen* truly created the same sense of hypostatic ritual, suggesting also those beautiful magnified and highly charged moments of the Indian Kathakali dance, Noh drama, Balinese opera, or, closer to home, the extraordinary "theater" of Robert Wilson's *Deafman Glance*. It is certainly not surprising that Stockhausen's composition *Prozession* implies both the structural "process" and the ritual "procession."

For Stockhausen is a "nature," as Goethe distinguished such an artist from the mere "talent," the former being "more comprehensive, deeper, and broader." Like Narad, the great minstrel in Sri Aurobindo's *Savitri* who warns the heroine of her husband's death in order to push her further on her already highly evolved spiritual path, Stockhausen might be seen as an agent provocateur for the divine. He is exploring all regions of *nada* (sound), knowing it to be an instrument of the spirit in all its ascending (human) and descending (divine) specificities and unities.*

What we usually overlook, however, is the fact that the earliest Western music was not only considered the appropriate medium by which to address God but was used in its physical manifestations of "numbers made audible" as the basis for metaphysical extensions. From Plato and Plotinus to Boethius—with his tripartite structuring of *musica mundana* (the Pythagorean harmony of the universe), *musica humana* (the harmony of soul and body), and *musica instrumentalis* (music as actual "sound")—to Kepler's correlation of musical tones and intervals with planetary move-

* Many Indian treatises have attempted to define the nature of sound, positing the idea of *anāhata*—non-manifest sound. Concerning this, P. B. Mukharji, in an appendix to a work by Swami Pratyagatmananda, has written: "This sound can create, destroy, and recreate manifold universes. Its reach is far greater than the waves one can receive on a radio in Calcutta from places as far away as London, New York, Moscow, or Melbourne. Its ambitions and capacities are measureless. It will bring you news of the vast stellar nebulae and inter-stellar spaces, of all the existing spatial firmaments and possible ones of the future, not to speak of those of the past. It is a potency, presence, possibility, and performance, all at the same time." And he designates four stages of sound's development: nascent static sound (the unifying sound container), visionary sound, cognizing sound (the sound condenser), and selective sound (the converter). The ancient Chinese believed that the *huang chung*—the principal tone of absolute pitch—was a "cosmologic and sacred element" of music and also the foundation of a healthy state: the extinction of a dynasty was ascribed to the failure to secure the true *huang chung*.

ments and astrological functions; from composers of projected "futuristic" works—Ives (*Universal Symphony*), Scriabin (*Mysterium*), and Varèse (*Espace*)—to Sun Ra's Astro-Infinity music, there have been philosophers, theorists, and composers who have understood the cosmic and universal source, the *mana,* of the musical impulse. For Stockhausen, music is a medium by which to discover oneself, and it can, in his words, "become still more open, universal, more cosmically oriented. Sooner or later, when one has achieved this consciousness, one will travel there as a cosmic tourist and by that show that everything exists at once."

"I am electrical by nature. Music is the electric soil in which the spirit lives, thinks, and invents." Stockhausen again? No, this is Beethoven speaking to Bettina Brentano. Composers from Bach and Beethoven to Schönberg, Stravinsky, and especially Webern thought of themselves as vessels of spiritual transformation. And it is in this sense of musical alchemy that Stockhausen is both a preserver and an innovator. Where the above composers were working almost solely within a Western tradition, however, Stockhausen has fostered within himself aspects of a global musical identity. In compositions like *Carré, Telemusik, Stimmung,* and *Mantra,* he has intuitively absorbed Balinese, Japanese, and Indian musical practices; but instead of merely creating a collage of atmospheric "Eastern" quotations, Stockhausen has attempted to mediate between Eastern and Western musical traditions. His development of new time dimensions, his exploration of sounds in space, his mediation of statistical and deterministic elements, his revelation of how one can transubstantiate one musical parameter into another, and his presentation in his compositions of the processes of these changes are all at the service of an integrating conception of art and life.

Most contemporary Western composers seem to look askance at any thaumaturgical attribution or explanation of their musical inspiration and efforts. And yet it was Webern himself who ultimately identified scientific processes and inspired creation: "The further one presses forward, the greater becomes the identity of everything, and finally we have the impression of being faced by a work not of man but of Nature." And Webern also wrote: "I understand the word 'Art' as meaning the faculty of presenting a thought in the clearest, simplest form, that is, the most 'graspable' form. Given this, I cannot conceive of Our Father as being something antithetical to art; rather it is the highest example. For it achieves the greatest 'graspability,' clarity, and directness."

There is certainly something "magical" about thinking that a value-neuter musical "construct" attains its importance and significance merely by the fact of its "autotelic" character. As Frank Kermode has written about twentieth-century poetry criticism: "I do not think the commonplace modern conception of the work of art as some sort of complex image, autotelic, liberated from discourse, with coincident form and meaning, could have evolved—as it clearly did—from Symbolist aesthetic if there had not been . . . a *rapprochement* between poet and occultist." And the notorious fragmentation of contemporary music into factious ideological "camps" cannot disguise the fact that the finest recent compositions—whether by Morton Feldman, Luciano Berio, Stefan Wolpe, Harry Partch, Pierre Boulez, or Elliott Carter—attain to an experience beyond their intricate or incidental structures.

"The spirit will be the music itself," Stockhausen says. "This might have been forgotten, but I think that every composer who has understood that he's only realizing what must be done, as Schönberg said, not what he personally wants to do, transcends self-expression and begins the spiritual spiral through his work. Which means that he starts with the personal, making art as the mirror of himself in order to look in his own mirror. Then the spiral begins to wind up and he realizes that he's no longer the same. Through the *doing* itself, he becomes a better person because he becomes more conscious. So the next time he sees the dying quality of the piece he also notices that he's lifted himself up one winding of the spiral, and now he tries to go beyond the barriers of languages, beyond the Babylonian tower which has split all the people into fragments. And he tries to discover a universal language which is vibration and rhythm—that's what everybody has in common. He wants to become a musician of the world. But the stars, too, are sounding. And where is the end of the spiral? The end is connected to the beginning. The spirit of the universe is never the same—it's moving all the time, it's a curved spiritual universe."

> "A house constitutes a body of images that give mankind proofs of illusions of stability. We are constantly re-imagining its reality; to distinguish all these images would be to describe the soul of the house; it would mean developing a veritable psychology of the house."
>
> —Bachelard

The first part of this book consists of conversations (our talks were all in English) held over a two-day period at the end of February 1971 in between Stockhausen's exhausting schedule of rehearsals with the New York Philharmonic. Instead of an entropic situation developing—words collapsing from fatigue—Stockhausen in fact telescoped, compressed, and distilled his most central concerns in the course of our three and a half hours of discussion. In this sense, Part I serves as an apposite overture to this book.

Part II is an expansion of the earlier themes and ideas, and it is a result of over thirty hours of conversations (late night talks, driving in the car, drinking apple juice and beer in the kitchen, on the train to Donaueschingen) which took place in September 1971 when I was a guest at Stockhausen's home in a beautiful wooded area in Bergishes Land, half an hour's drive from Cologne. Each of the thirteen white-walled, large-windowed rooms of the house—for which Stockhausen made the basic design—is an asymmetrical hexagon, no one room having the same size or view; no ceiling is straight, and only the floors are horizontal. From three to eleven steps lead into another room (many of the rooms are interconnected so that at first you often enter rooms you hadn't expected), and, conversely, every room has a glass door leading outside to different kinds of trees, bushes, and flowers. The effect is that of nature always coming inside and also of an expanse of lightness.

The house is on the slope of a hill, with a forest behind overlooking the valley. All around are various kinds of evergreen bushes, Japanese and Serbian pines, cedars, cypresses, and one especially beautiful hundred-year-old beech. In addition, Stockhausen has planted over one hundred different kinds of trees. "They're democratically arranged now," he tells me. But when he first built the house, hundreds of fir, pine, and birch trees were being strangled by parasitic strangler vines. "It was like a big city," he says. Now, in early autumn, golden leaves blow along the rising lawn; rabbits and deer warily come out of the woods; jays, bullfinches, thrushes, and titmice make nests on the roof; buzzards and hawks glide overhead.

At one point, Stockhausen told me that he once wanted to have steps going from the foot of the hill, *through* the house, and then leading up to the highest part of the slope where a six foot tam-tam would be placed. "That was just an idea," Stockhausen says. "It used to be that you couldn't see the house when you approached it. I wanted to close everything up." But now he's cut see-throughs into the wall of trees and foliage so that there are openings everywhere.

Coming back to the house, I ask Stockhausen what compositions of his are embodied by the design of his home. "It has very much to do with the way I compose serial music," he tells me. "In their larger sections *Gruppen* and *Zeitmasze* are proportioned in a similar way. Each side of a wall has a different length from another, there's that irregularity. It's the permutation of different measures for height, volume, length, and width. . . . *Mantra,* too, would be very close to this house."

"What would a *Stimmung* house be like?"

"Caves, slopes, curving rooms! It would be nestlike . . . moving walls. But this would be insanely expensive."

These views of the composer's home are colored as gently as they are by a visitor's leisured eye as well as by the desires of memory in which reverie stills all activity. In fact, Stockhausen's daily life is far from the quiet "Sunday music" suggested by my description. Until this past year, the composer has spent little time in his home. In 1970, for example—the year he completed *Mantra*—Stockhausen visited and worked in Berlin, London, Bali, Australia, Ceylon, Darmstadt, Warsaw, Baden-Baden, Paris, Vienna, the United States, and Osaka (where he spent four months).

When he is not performing and *is* at home (and not composing sixteen hours a day), Stockhausen is continually busy: teaching at the State Conservatory once a week; checking on every stage in the preparation of his Deutsche Grammophon recordings—from the mixing and the dead grooves to the design of record sleeves; preparing and correcting the printing and publishing of his scores (for many of them he designs and draws the final copy); checking out all of the technical arrangements for every concert tour—from the placement of amps, cables, and electrical circuits to the listing of camera serial numbers for customs and the handling of all correspondence (in June 1972, for example, the composer flew to Iran for two days to meet personally with the sound engineers responsible for the twelve concerts Stockhausen and his musicians gave at the September 1972 Shiraz Festival); preparing performances and—as he did in 1972—spending eight hours a day for three months rehearsing with four choir groups and instrumentalists for a recording and concert tour of *Momente* (December 1972–January 1973); and, finally, overseeing the daily operations and organizing the activities of the WDR Electronic Music Studio, of which he is artistic director.

In addition, Stockhausen often designs new electronic equipment which can be used in the studio and for live performances, his latest invention being the Module 69A—an ingenious electronic device that can rest in one's lap. This device features four inputs for any kind of microphone and other sound sources; several generators for frequency and amplitude modulation; a ring modulator; touch-sensitive finger plates for rhythmetizing sounds; eight potentiometers, any of which can be used for frequency and volume control of all the signals; and a rotation mill, eight keys, and a field of 8x8 output connections with which one can distribute the signals to any of eight channels in a desired configuration. Four of these boxes are being built.

Stockhausen himself lives modestly. He has few possessions and seems to wear only two pairs of light trousers, a couple of white Mexican shirts, and occasionally a Norfolk jacket. His study also exemplifies this simplicity: on a long, slightly angular desk—following the shape of the windows—are placed rulers, pencils, and a telephone. Antique cymbals, bells, and bamboo sticks hang from the ceiling. There's a phonograph and tape machines, a couple of shelves of books, a map of the stars—northern and southern sky—attached to a closet, and a wonderfully rich-sounding but fast-actioned spinet piano next to the desk on which Stockhausen sometimes plays ragtime and folk tunes for his children. On the piano stand is a photo of the composer's youngest child Simon, on the bottom of which is written:

> "We may find when all the rest has failed
> Hid in ourselves the key of perfect change."
> —Aurobindo in *Savitri*

One afternoon while Stockhausen was working inside, I was variously daydreaming and reading—leaves falling over me in the hammock—when I came across an extraordinary passage from Novalis (*The Disciples of Sais*, translated by Michael Hamburger) which seemed to be a perfect description of Stockhausen himself:

> He watched the stars and imitated their courses and positions in the sand. Into the ocean of the air he gazed incessantly; and never tired of observing its clearness, its movements, its clouds, its illumination. He collected stones, flowers, beetles of every kind and arranged them in various patterns in front of him. To men and animals he gave his attention, on the shores of the sea he sat and looked for shells. To his own heart and thoughts he listened intently. He did not know where his longing would lead him. When he had grown up, he wandered about, viewed other countries, other seas, other atmospheres, stones that were strange to him, unknown plants, animals, men; descended into caves, saw how the earth has been built up in shelves and many coloured layers, and pressed clay into curious rock formations. Now he discovered familiar patterns everywhere, only weirdly mingled and combined, and in this way often the strangest objects fell into order in his mind. Soon he looked for analogies in all things, conjunctures, correspondences; till he could no longer see anything in isolation.—All the perceptions of his sense crowded into great variegated images: he heard, saw, touched, and thought at the same moment. He loved to bring strangers together. Now stars were men to him, now men were stars, stones were animals, clouds were plants; he played with the powers and phenomena, he knew just where and how to find this shape and the other, to make them appear; and thus he himself drew tones and passages from the strings.

New York—September 1972

part one

NEW YORK

FEBRUARY 1971

HYMNEN: MUSIC FOR THE POSTAPOCALYPSE

C: I was listening to the Fourth Region of *Hymnen* recently, and the cliché about music being ahead of its time struck me. You said that you were writing music, not for the apocalypse, but for the postapocalypse, for the time of reintegration when people would have to be picking up the pieces. I felt I was listening to *Hymnen* now the way it would sound like then, and it was an extraordinary experience to be immersed in something that you think you're hearing at another time.

S: I know exactly what you mean. I recall a meeting with a young girl after having played *Hymnen* in Mexico City in 1968. She was about twelve years old. And she came to me with her mother because she was shy and afraid of talking straight away. She said, "I have one question, Mr. Stockhausen. Do you think that we have to go through this degree of destruction before we're reborn?" She said it in particular about the Fourth Region. And that young girl touched me in the inner of my being. I said, "I think so." So she must have felt something very important that the music woke up in her.

You see, usually we read about catastrophes that are to come. But I find even talking to very conscious people that they always think in the back of their minds there might be an escape; perhaps they think it's just words and that the scientists who announce these catastrophes do so as an early warning system in order to escape from these crises. They think it might not come. But it will come. And even for the most conscious people, this requires an effort. We have to go through these crises at the end of this century and during the first decades of the next, there is no other way.

"BECOMING CONSCIOUS IS ALREADY BEING ON THE OTHER SIDE."

C: So *Hymnen* in particular might be a work that acts as a kind of physical-psychic therapy to prepare yourself for these necessary awarenesses?

S: Well, I hear it that way. You see, becoming conscious is already being on the other side. You see clearly where we are up to and then death isn't frightening any more. Also a collective death in large groups. Because you feel that our destiny is a universal destiny and not only a terrestrial one, which means that if the whole cosmos were not made for me, my whole life and the whole of existence would have no meaning. I say if I'm born in order to know only America, Japan, Bali, and India but not all the other things, then what are they made for? What are they for?

C: Do you hear from the other side?

S: I have all sorts of sound visions, very often at night in a deep sleep. I wake up and the entire pieces are in me, I've *heard* them. And I have all sorts of visions of events that obviously are in the future because they haven't happened yet. I've had very strong visions coming several times already years ago of a war between Russia and China, not in abstract thoughts but in pictures, pictures and sounds. And I've seen American cities being destroyed, America joining Russia in this big conflict, and the Japanese joining in. And I've seen the situation after this—purifying shock. And I don't know what to do with these pictures, you see, I as a single man cannot yell it out and change the world. I think it has to come.

"WE ARE ALL TRANSISTORS."

C: I had one dream which I associated with *Hymnen*. There were no longer any figures, I couldn't pinpoint myself in relationship to the fragments of people populating the dream, but rather I heard and saw clear massive blocks of sounds and spaces.

S: That's not unusual. We are all transistors in the literal sense. Waves arrive, antennae receive them, and the so-called high fidelity system plays them back as directly as possible without distorting them too much. And a human being is always bombarded with cosmic rays which have a very specific rhythm and structure, and they transform his atomic structure and by that his whole system. And if we're too much involved with our personal ego, desires, interests, people, whatever it is, then these rays become focused on us as individuals with our tiny private problems. But when we more and more forget ourselves—I mean try to make ourselves pure in the state of reception and transmission—then this current passes through. And if you then have a special talent—that you have no merits for, it's just given to you—to work in sound, light, or in gestures as a dancer, then you can use what you have in order to concretize what comes through you, and then that communication is possible. You become a focus. The current goes through you, and then it goes to the others through you.

I've had several letters during the last weeks from very young people in Germany who are literally turned on. They make music in small groups at night in the forest, trying to make the music in harmony with the sound in the forest. And they are really trying to catch waves from distant stars. I want to show you these letters of eighteen-, nineteen-year-olds. I think there's a new generation, a new consciousness. Those guys, what they describe! For example, in the last letter that I got from a young man, he tells how he listened to shortwave sounds over earphones for several hours over a period of several nights. And then one evening he heard the Third and Fourth Regions of *Hymnen*. He listened to them again for four hours, meditating in between the sections and then focusing on the waves. And he said that in the nine megahertz Region all of a sudden he hit a point where he flipped out. He completely went off and had a cosmic trip.

I know this young man. He wasn't on drugs, and he's very brilliant and thinks and speaks very logically. He asked me if I knew about these waves. And I didn't. All I know is that I've come on very strange situations when I've performed with shortwave radios together with other instruments. And I always need at a certain moment to tune in certain shortwaves. Because they're not only the result of interferences from the terrestrial vibrations of all those private and public radio stations, ships, and Morse code stations, but in addition to this new quality which results from these interferences, there are also all the quasar waves. And I'm definitely sure that there are a lot of rhythmetized waves coming from outside of our solar system. These are very important things to deal with. And if young people have such experiences, then I take it as real.

C: In *Kurzwellen* and *Spiral* you have musicians responding to events they receive on shortwave radios, transforming and transposing these events. Wouldn't it be possible to enable players to respond, for example, to you as if you were a transistor?

S: Ah, yes, we've done seven hours of recording in a week's time in Darmstadt in August 1969, and they will all come out in a seven-record Deutsche Grammophon set: *Aus den Sieben Tagen*—From the Seven Days. I'm part of the group that played on these recordings. There were very short texts which had a purifying rather than a suggestive function. They put all of us in a special spiritual state in order to make ourselves open, to use what we *are* as musicians in conjunction with all that we have learned in the context of other music. All this is part of a process through which we realize that we are a vessel, and this vessel then just reflects, responds. And in this manner we've done the very best recordings that I can think of in my whole life, without rehearsing.

Until 1960 I was a man who related to the cosmos and God through Catholicism, a very particular religion that I chose for myself almost as a way of opposing the post-war Sartrean nihilistic attitudes of the established intellectuals. Almost all my colleagues were, and still are, complete nihilists. And then I began to float because I got in touch with many other religions. In Japan I prayed many times to Buddhas just as I've prayed to the Christian god. And then to the gods of the Mayas and the Aztecs in Mexico. I lived for short periods in Bali, Ceylon, and India and felt that the religions were all part of the face of a multifaceted universal spirit, of the total spirit.

In 1968, I came very close to death, to suicide, and giving myself up in that sense. But after that I found a suprareligious way for myself. I didn't think of myself any longer as a member of a particular social group. And from that moment on I became conscious that all my music had these flashlights, in short moments, which at that period in May 1968 revealed themselves to me for seven days and nights without a single break. That was the most fantastic experience up to then because I found out that intuition is not something that just happens to you, like a car accident, but that you can call for it and that you can develop a technique for it. It comes when you need it. And when you play in a group—intuitive music, not written-out music—then you badly need it. Otherwise, you only rely on your mechanics, on what you've studied, learned, and rehearsed many times. But once you've had this it never leaves you. You *know* now, once and forever, that this exists. You *know*, because you haven't thought it or reflected on it, you've experienced it.

People talk about how the individual is finished historically. That's ridiculous. Because I think that very particular discoveries and events can only occur when a man is completely alone—being a vessel in a completely self-responsive, self-responsible activity. And on the other hand we've found this new meaning of the group. And there is feedback between the two. The group cannot develop if there isn't an individual self-discovery developing, on the part of both the individual members and in particular of the one who draws the group together.

PERIODICITY: "GOD BREATHES PERIODICALLY."

C: I gather you're against periodicity in music (the repeated cyclic patterns one finds in, for example, "primitive" trance music, Terry Riley, the bass riffs of rock, Donovan's "The Trip").

S: No, I'm not against it at all. All I think is that periodicity is one aspect, of the very large and the very small. And it should always be shown in a musical activity as being just one aspect of the universe. As you know, we have the large periodicities of the year, of the month or the moon, of the day, and also of the cosmic year. There is a fundamental periodicity of the whole cosmos when it explodes and contracts—it *breathes*, God *breathes* all the time, naturally, periodically, as far as we can think. This is the fundamental of the universe, and all other things are partials of this fundamental—the galactic years and the years of the sun systems, etc. And going down to the atoms and even the particles of the atoms, there is always periodicity. Nevertheless, periodicity is, as I say, like the abstract year, but what changes within the year? Sometimes the snow comes earlier, or later.

Actually, within this periodicity, no day is the same. We shouldn't forget this, that's all. There has been a lot of music where this periodicity becomes so absolute and dominating that there's little left for what is happening within the periods. And there is not enough polyphonic periodicity, as there is in the universe or in our body. There should always be several layers of different periodicities which then produce a very intricate, seemingly aperiodic total result. But when you follow the individual layers, you again find periodicity. Or in very large cycles you sometimes find periodicity, but within these there is a lot of aperiodic movement, and this should never be forgotten. You see, marching music is periodic, and it seems in most marching music as if there's nothing but that collective synchronization, and this has a very dangerous aspect. For example, when I was a boy the radio in Germany was always playing typical brassy marching music from morning to midnight, and it really conditioned the people.

"WE ARE AN ELECTRIC SYSTEM."

C: You've taken what Plato said about music's power to reflect and determine consciousness in a very deep sense.

S: Absolutely! We *are* an electric system—let's forget about our always dying bodies, so to speak, in order to be reborn in a different form. Naturally, as an electric system we're always influenced by the waves that run through us. And the sound waves directly attack the whole skin, not only the eardrums. You can hear through the whole body. I can close my ears and hear very well. Rhythmically, for example. People who have lived with tribal music certainly know that you hear with the body. And what is important is that all the atoms have a rhythm of their own, like a person to whom a name has been given, each of which is quite different as one wave structure from another. All this is modulated by the soundwaves that come through it, because these waves are transformed between the inner ear and the cortex into electric rhythms. It's electricity, and this electricity runs through the whole system. And when the music has stopped, then we are modulated, and to some extent the old periodicities start to regain the rhythms that they had before, but they are *never* the same, no matter what comes through us. We *are* modulated once and forever.

This applies as well to our own bodies. I just told someone yesterday how to get to sleep. Concentrate on specific parts of the body: inside the head and then on the eyes, with eyelids closed, concentrating on the black color and projecting all your thoughts and images. And I said, if this doesn't work, just move inside of your body, starting with the toes, until you're completely in the little toe, then the fourth, third toe, second, first, then slowly go continuously up the leg, then the other leg. Do this with the hand, with both hands, always leading the inner forces to the heart section. And then starting with the head, opening your skull, let the electricity that is always there enter and lead it wherever you want, where you need it. And I told this person who has headaches very often how to get rid of them without pills. Just find out where it's located and then move the electricity in that section of the skull, moving it round many times and very slowly.

C: Do you see a human consciousness being able to relate the technology of the synthesizer to the human structure?

S: Yes. It's an extension of man. It's part of us. It is we. You cannot divide it from us. How can you divide an oyster from its shell? Or let's say a violin player from his violin? Then he's no longer a violin player.

C: Speaking about violin-playing oysters, if you take a fiddler crab from the ocean and place it in a sealed box and remove it to the Midwest, it goes through the same diurnal periodic rhythmic movements, as if the sea were still there, inside itself.

S: Yes. That's what they *are*. It's a vibrating system with a very particular structure of rhythm. That's what we all are when we're talking.

CONVERSATION WITH SUZUKI: ARTIFICIAL VERSUS THE NATURAL

C: But what role does consciousness play in relationship to a machine's functions?

S: Well, we arrive at a very strange discussion now. I have not been able up to now to materialize myself completely within a machine, in an object, though I have been able in a few moments of my life at a very high state of consciousness to identify completely with an animal or with a plant. Maybe others have that power. I don't see any reason why spirit cannot materialize in any form. Maybe one day a spirit will materialize within a machine and do very strange things. [Laughter.]

I once had a discussion with Professor Suzuki, the old Japanese philosopher, he was more than ninety years old—I had a wonderful time in his home, just before he died. He said, "I am not a musical person, I have deaf ears for music and sounds." But, nevertheless, he wanted to know how I made my sounds. He had heard this and that about my work. And I said, "You know, I make the sounds in a very artificial way. I use generators and mix synthetically by recording them on different channels of tapes and then mix them with a potentiometer until I get a sound, and then I cut it with a scissor and splice the tape." And I said, "You see, that's a completely different method, a new method, as opposed to the natural way of producing a sound with your voice."

He looked at me and said, "I cannot understand your language. I cannot understand why you say this is artificial and this is natural." I said, "What do you mean? By using this apparatus and equipment, that's artificial." And he said, "That is quite natural." "Well, OK," I said, "what is not natural?" He said, "It would only be artificial if it went against your inner conviction. You're being completely natural in the way you do it." And then I said, "Wonderful, I'll forget about my Western education, and the way we call things artificial and natural. When we speak about a homunculus we think it's an artificial man that they tried to make in medieval times." He said, "That is quite natural. I don't see anything wrong with it."

You see, he took artificial to be something that is more than merely artful. If something conflicts with our natural feelings and prevents our being at one with ourselves, only then would that be artificial. So a machine, a computer, is a quite natural extension of the brain. It's like producing a baby.

MUSICAL TIME

C: Ever since *Refrain*, *Carré*, *Telemusik*, and *Momente*, you've been approaching and working with different characteristics of musical time in radically new ways. Could you talk about this?

S: When I was in Japan for the first time and experienced the No theater, the sumo fight, gagaku music, or the shomyo temple music, I became aware that the Japanese have a completely different *time* than we Europeans have. The Japanese have a far larger time scale at the bottom, which means they have much slower and longer events than we ever would admit; we'd call them boring or wouldn't experience them for any length. We would never conceive of a music that lasts three days, we would never listen to sounds that, as single sounds, one after another, last longer than ten seconds. And the same is true for the very fast events. There is not very much in the middle region of time. But at the very fast and the very slow regions they have more octaves, so to speak, than we do.

I had composed *Kontakte* and *Carré* long before I went to Japan. And in *Carré* already a new experience of time came into my music because of a very specific, personal experience. I was flying every day for two or three hours over America from one city to the next over a period of six weeks, and my whole time feeling was reversed after about two weeks. I had the feeling that I was visiting the earth and living in the plane. There were just very tiny changes of bluish color and always this harmonic spectrum of the engine noise.

At that time, in 1958, most of the planes were propeller planes, and I was always leaning my ear—I *love* to fly, I must say—against the window, like listening with earphones directly to the inner vibrations. And though theoretically a physicist would have said that the engine sound doesn't change, it changed all the time because I was listening to all the partials within the spectrum. It was a fantastically beautiful experience. And I really discovered the innerness of the engine sounds and watched the slight changes of the blue outside and then the formation of the clouds, this white blanket always below me. I made sketches for *Carré* during that time, and thought I was already very brave in going far beyond the time of memory, which is the crucial time between eight- and sixteen-second-long events. When you go beyond them you lose orientation. You don't recall exactly if it was fourteen or eighteen seconds, whereas you'd never make that mistake below that realm of memory.

At that time, for example, I wrote articles about what would happen to a man who sat in a dark prison cell for a long time hearing just one sound, a door slamming, then nothing again for a year, then another door slamming. What I meant by that was that there would have been one sound which lasted a year, because the prisoner wouldn't have thought of any other sound, *that* was the sound for a year. And like this, we can imagine eternity, an eternal duration. And that led me then to the concept of *moment form*, where I said that a moment lasts not just an instant—according to our time system a fraction of a second or a few seconds—but it can last an eternity if it isn't changing.

A TONE'S INNER LIFE

C: One of the things I thought about when listening to *Hymnen* was that of the idea of a *moment* of time. It seems as if you sometimes freeze a moment of time—stop it on its horizontal direction to look at it vertically, which you can only do paradoxically in a horizontal way, so that you enable the listener to get inside that moment, to see it from the inside.

S: This concerns the microworld of the sound, and I became aware of this very early in my work. Making a sound for a given composition, synthetically in a studio, demands that you listen very carefully to the inside of the sound that you're synthesizing, to all the partials, though you don't intend these partials to be heard as individual partials, but rather to use them to achieve a unified sound event. This has led me then in *Kontakte* and in *Carré* to sections where I simply stop the time which is cut rhythmically or by musical sections. I present a given sound spectrum for a rather long time so that you can follow the individual changes within the layers. It's like microscopic analysis.

Because I think that every sound has an inner life. And you can enlarge this in the way you listen to it if the shape of a given sound doesn't move too fast away from you; this then allows you the possibility to listen vertically and not to expect that only harmonic or rhythmic change will be significant.

In *Zeitmasze*, which is a very simple piece for woodwinds, I hold a chord for a while and then let one instrument after another come out, through crescendo-decrescendo dynamics. At the beginning it sounds like a unified sound, and then you become aware that it consists of components, because the individual components come out and go away again. Or, in *Hymnen*, I suddenly let a component become active rhythmically, but with very fast vibrations while the others remain calm, and then another becomes active. It's always like that in nature: something that's flying or moving catches your attention much quicker than something that doesn't move.

JAPANESE CULTURE: IMITATION AND TRANSFORMATION

C: How do you see your relationship as a German composer to the musical and spiritual awarenesses you arrived at in Japan and Bali?

S: You see, once you've achieved a certain independence from the natural forces and your heritage, you can become someone who also discovers within himself the Balinese and the Japanese. That's why it's wrong to say, "He's influenced by the Japanese." What I've actually experienced is that I came to Japan and discovered the Japanese in me. I immediately wanted to become that "Japanese," because it was new to me that I could live like that. And I wish I could have been able to identify with the Japanese 100 percent for a while in order to have developed this person within me. I only ate Japanese food, and I dressed like the Japanese—in the old-fashioned way, I mean—and that gives you different behavior, a different feeling, different thoughts, different timing.

Now people say that the Japanese are the great imitators of our time, that they imitate us. When I play with my friends, in *Kurzwellen*, for example, or when we do intuitive music together, the first step is always that of imitating something and the next step is that of transforming what you're able to imitate. The best musician is one who can immediately play what he has heard, either on the radio—any tune—or who can immediately find the pitch of a bird and play that, too. But then the next step after you're a wonderful imitator is that of transforming what you imitated before. You first absorb and then transform it, and this is very important.

So, I always say the Japanese are way ahead of the rest of the world, the least provincial—they have a natural advantage because they're people of an island which was cut off for three hundred years from the rest of the world, even forcibly, by the militaristic generals who ruled the country. But there is that fantastic, almost spongelike facility of absorbing other cultures now. And I say they're not only imitators, you will see, they are very strong people who chose their traditional culture and their whole daily life, which has become *so* cultured, more so than in any Western country. Eating, making love, walking, dressing, making your home—this all has become highly cultured. It's not that art has been separated from the daily life; the daily life has become art. The tea ceremony is still a real ceremony of quietness and concentration and even meditation. So the conventional and the creative aspects always merge. What I mean is that the Japanese, after having swallowed the so-called Western culture and technology, will be the first to become universal people.

C: You yourself seem to have become a universal composer.

S: Having been cut off from the world, as a boy from farmer's stock, for a long period of my life, I wasn't educated like most of my colleagues in high schools. Culturally and in my home I was living in a very close, small world. When I was twenty-three, I became an intellectual in the extreme for several years because everything was all new to me. Until I was twenty-one or twenty-two, I hadn't much of an idea about what music was like. I played some music that I had heard on radios, but we didn't even have a record player at home, we had nothing. Well . . . there was no home, that's the real explanation.

I'm a very curious person by nature, everything that's new and unfamiliar to me is a challenge. I was already in the music conservatory, and I was, I think, one of the two or three students during a five-year student period who was interested in and informed about contemporary music after the war. And only I was really informed about Schönberg's work, because there were no scores available, you had to copy them by hand. I have a natural gift for picking up new things. And then I was invited to many different countries, and I enjoyed that very much, walking through the villages, living in people's homes and picking up the culture. And always naturally having the strong desire to create a new world out of everything I found.

AN APPLE ON THE MOON: THE KNOWN OBJECT IN A NEW WORLD

I have never accepted any found object or any style. I wanted to erase any recognizable element in my own music for ten years. I was the most abstract abstract composer. Now, since I've gone into these new realms of consciousness and cut myself off from the past, from memory, from the preformed world—the recognizable has become very mysterious, very magical. If you found an apple on the moon, that would make it even more mysterious. You see, I finally felt strong enough to create a new world in which a known object doesn't become stronger than you. The great danger is that if you make a citation in music, literature, or in painting and you quote something which, because it's old, is stronger, then there's a natural tendency for it to wipe out the new things which you haven't heard or seen before—they're weak, you've seen them only once so you can't remember them.

But what's important is that when you have something very precise—a precise formula that everybody recognizes—and you wish to put it into a world which is new, then the basic problem of composition begins again. How much time and space do you give to new things with respect to the known phenomena? So you should give much less of what is known, in proportion to what is new, in a given context in order to create a balance between the two: let's say two or three seconds of a well-known motif or theme is enough to balance forty, fifty, or even more seconds of unfamiliar, new sound formulas. And the new sound formulas must also be very sharp, not only background or sustained notes and chords or clusters. You see, a cluster is a very imprecise thing, it's just a band of sound. And if from within a cluster you bring out a precise melody, it will stick in your mind forever because the cluster isn't strong, it's just a background. So we should be very careful about background patterns in music because as soon as a musical formula enters which is more precise, the background becomes a background. In *Punkte*, for example, there's *only* background. That's very important. If it's only background, it's not background anymore—it's a textural music, and you listen into the sound. It's not that there's something put on top which immediately removes all the rest to a secondary function in order to give an atmosphere—something like a sauce around a piece of meat.

FOREGROUND-BACKGROUND TECHNIQUE

The foreground-background technique, in music as in painting, has been used for several hundred years. We've had the accompaniment—the basso ostinato, or just the parallel lines to a melody, or the homophonic style where you have chords adding harmonic accents that give shape and color to a melody—but all this has no individual function as in music of three-, four-part polyphony. You see, we've gone through almost two centuries of background and foreground technique—the motive, the theme, and something further removed that is together with it. And that's why, starting with *Kontra-Punkte* in 1951, I stopped dealing with that problem. I didn't want any background any more, but everything was now of equal importance.

And in my most recent piece *Mantra* there's a formula, a mantra, but there's nothing that's accompanying it or giving a background to it—there's nothing but a mantra which is repeated 156 times, in all kinds of enlargements and compressions over sixty-two minutes. There are several layers sometimes. Let's say one mantra as an expansion takes two minutes, and in the meantime you have five or six other mantra transpositions which take a much shorter time. Naturally then only if you'd follow that layer of the slow mantra would you follow it completely. But then you'd lose a lot of the rest.

C: If you're using the mantra as a kind of musical material, is it possible to meditate on it? And wouldn't working with a mantra in this way suggest a "dramatic" quality not usually associated with mantras?

S: I think identifying with a sound *is* meditation. A musical meditation is when you completely become the sound. I'm using the mantra as a living being. I want to expand the traditional concept of the mantra which says you are in one state in order to reach a point where we can go through many, many different states with one mantra. We should go in and out in these realms of consciousness, these rooms of consciousness, *completely* freely. The greatest thing would be if I could discover the whole world within me and be one after another, from moment to moment, a different being, so that one being within me comes to the top and then another. No, I don't want to go away from dramatic forces, from the static, the dramatic, the epic—nowadays I even want to compose pieces where you have one layer which is completely static and another which is then moving with a clear direction toward a climax and a third layer which is epic, like telling you something but not aiming at a certain end—narrative. There are three basic qualities of musical formation: the lyrical, which is the instant, the here and now; the dramatic, which is development, with precise beginning and ending, climaxes, high points and low points; and epic, which is the juxtaposition of different moments, as in a variation form or the traditional form of the suite—that's an epic form, you can always add a new section, a new chapter so to speak. There's no strong directionalism as in a dramatic form, but it's also not static; within a given moment it goes somewhere, it describes some event. And I want all the three.

C: So you would have to listen to your music differently from the way you'd listen to John Cage or rock music or Balinese music?

S: I would say so. You have to switch very quickly when you listen to my music and to change with the music from one character to another. Like a person who, very dramatic at a given moment, then becomes completely quiet, meditative, and then outgoing.

C: In a sense it's like Beethoven's last quartets.

S: *Very* right. In his last pieces, composition becomes the subject, it's no longer a theme or a motive used in a materialistic way.

He says: This can happen, and then he doesn't follow it up for long. There's a long bridge which lasts much longer than the head of a fugue, which he just exposes, finishes, and then he goes somewhere else. That's like flying, flying around the globe, or going through all the different aspects of our soul. And from the most quiet to the most excited, from the most abstract to the most concrete, from quotes to newly invented moments—yes, that is the best example.

TIMBRE COMPOSITION: "THE MATERIAL ITSELF MUST BE PART OF THE CREATIVE ACT."

C: I know, especially after listening to *Stimmung*, that you believe that timbre can be used not simply as just one of many musical characteristics but as the basis of an entire piece of music. You've talked about "different atmospheres, different degrees of timbre" and of "very precise degrees of brightness or of speed."

S: I say, nowadays, the material itself must be part of the creative act. Which means that when I start a new piece, the selection of either a preformed sound source, an instrument, or sound material must be already organized or structured—the way the whole piece will be structured. That gives you the guarantee that the material and the form are one. You no longer form a given material, you also create the material, you make your own sounds. That's the same as what's happening in the synthetic industry—they can now make any material from a basic, how can I say it, unqualified material by working on the molecular structures chemically. And the great dream is that you can make different beings rise by going into the cell structure, into the nucleus. The discovery of the DNA code, for example, focuses on how you can create different species of beings by starting from the very smallest particles and their components. That's why we are all part of the spirit of the atomic age. In music we do exactly the same.

I made the first synthetic sounds in 1951 under very primitive conditions. The sounds are synthesized from sine waves, let's say, or from pulses. You make a sound with an inner life because you intend to use it in a particular composition, and you don't want just to make the material and later on press it into a form, you see what I mean? That would simply add a few new samples to our traditional instrumental sound world. What I'm interested in is to see how form and material become completely one. Like architecture, its form will change with completely new material. There's a feedback between the material that you create and the way you form this material in larger forms.

There are always two aspects. You can use timbre in a completely hedonistic way, just to enjoy, more or less, a given sound, as in rock music. You can listen to timbre and hear the "new sounds." But after two years they're out of fashion because you've gotten used to them. And you've never been able to understand these new sounds as making something clear to you, within a given composition. There wasn't that firm relationship between the material and the forming. That's why the electric guitar for me isn't better than a trumpet. I got used to the electric guitar sound as well as the trumpet sound, so what? Or any electric organ, or playing Bach with a synthesizer, so what? That doesn't change a thing. It's just old wine in new bottles. What changes the whole situation is if this timbre has its illuminating force. And that's why I always say a given timbre, or a given combination of instruments, should never be repeated.

STIMMUNG: MELODIES, RHYTHMS, AND CHORDS OF TIMBRE

We will learn that there are chords of timbre, melodies of timbre, Schönberg says it. Rhythms of timbre. You will hear my work *Stimmung*, which is nothing for seventy-five minutes but one chord—it never changes—with the partials of natural harmonics on a fundamental, the fundamental itself isn't there, the second, third, fourth, fifth, seventh, and ninth harmonics, and nothing but that. And then timbral changes of these fundamentals. And the timbres are precisely notated with the international phonetic alphabet and numbers. So when I sing, let's say [sings a single pitch with many inflections] you can focus on each partial very precisely. With two breaths I could make the whole vowel circle, and I've written the numbers up to the twenty-fourth harmonic and the singers needed six months just in order to learn precisely how to hit the ninth harmonic, or the tenth, eleventh, thirteenth, up to the twenty-fourth. You see, that's a real composition with timbres where the timbres are rhythmetized the way we formally rhythmetize pitches. It's a wonderful technique to learn because you become so conscious of the different parts of the skull which are vibrating. If you met the singers, you'd see how as human beings they've changed. They're completely transformed now that they've sung it more than a hundred times since the World Fair in Osaka.

C: How do you control the choices you make in your individual works and also in your "collective intuitive music" in works such as *Kurzwellen* and *Opus 70?*

PERIODICITY VERSUS FREE PLAY

S: Whenever I have to make a decision I have to completely identify, innerly, with what is happening, with the forces, and I have to become each force one after another, as a being together with other forces. So I will identify with one force—let's say a sound which is fortissimo in a certain register—with respect to the other forces which are surrounding it, before, afterwards, at the same time. And if I feel that my being that sound is simply covering the others, erasing them, or making them become completely unimportant, then I might only accept that situation if at a later or earlier moment I give to those other elements, which here have been hit on their heads so to speak, their own rights—so they can rise to an upper level. But I would never accept a situation where one force is completely thrown out and is there in vain, only decoratively.

C: Do you deal with performers in the same way?

S: Yes. And I use the potentiometer to give every musician his chance to come through and to balance things out. If someone, because he's playing on his own for a long time, is unconsciously wiping out the rest, then I take him back a little. In my process planning works there are symbols, plus and minus or equal signs, or a sign that tells someone all of a sudden to give a cue, and the others play synchronously with him for a given number of events until they are all free again. The sound itself should always renew itself—the sound and the context of the sound. But the forces, so to speak, are partly precontrolled by me because there are a given number of transformation signs for each musician, and I know that no matter what each wants, when everybody has minus signs within a given area, the sound will go down, one by one, and it will become softer, less segmented, no matter what the individual desire of the musician is. You see, I have an overall control over tendencies, but at a given moment what occurs—the given combination of sounds, vertically and horizontally—surprises me, and should be surprising.

That's what I said before in a completely different context. I think periodicity and control is the principle of the universe on a large scale, and free play is the principle of the universe on a smaller scale. On an individual level I'm very meticulous. We have a pejorative word, *kleinlich*, which means a person who's . . . petty? Yes. I'm terribly petty about certain things. Let's say if there's dirt in a corner, I can be terrible. Or concerning the preciseness of presetting a plan for a tour, I have to make sure that every screw and every electric contact has been discussed first by letter. I have to be sure that these little things are really controlled. So I'm a terribly petty person about petty things. But in large things I'm very generous.

I shouldn't be in a mood before I'm performing. I meditate before I start to play, I pray. When I start playing I have learned to forget about myself. It hardly ever happens nowadays that while I'm working I'm thinking of something else for even a fraction of time. The moment I start playing I'm gone, and I am the sounds and I am the process, and you can't ask me—I can't give you any answer—what has happened. When it's over, then I fall back, like from a session of laughing gas, into thinking and becoming aware of my environment.

"PLAY THE VIBRATION IN THE RHYTHM OF YOUR SMALLEST PARTICLES."

C: In a piece of yours entitled *Aufwärts* (a text from *From The Seven Days*) you instruct your musicians as follows: "Play a vibration in the rhythm of your smallest particles; then play a vibration in the rhythm of the universe. Play all the rhythms that you can distinguish today between the rhythm of your smallest particles and the rhythm of the universe—one after the other—and each one for so long until the air carries it on."

S: The musician would probably make an artificial approach if he thought, "Do I have it already, or don't I?" But it would work quite naturally if he had gone through many meditations, meditating on the cells, molecules, and if possible, even the smaller particles of the atoms of his body. This suggests a futuristic piece. You see, not everything I do can be completely solved nowadays. It's what I think musicians will have reached as a state when they are in *total* meditation and through that meditation have reached the power of penetrating into the subconscious matter of their bodies.

You see, I can go, as I've said before, into certain parts of my body, and sometimes I have a very precise experience of the body's individual cells. And it will take some time, until I can penetrate into the molecules, and bring the electric juice that's me, the electric structure, into these molecule structures and conduct them the way I want, make them collaborate. I have for example already been able sometimes to feel the precise moment when bacteria or viruses enter into me. I sometimes have trouble with my right ear, and—this seems again to be beyond the realm of normal discussion—I've had moments when I could chase viruses out of my ear. Literally chase them out—I felt the moment when they were leaving or when I killed them. And I had gone to doctors and found out what they were doing there, and by trying to change the chemical structure within, I threw them out.

Well, I can do this spiritually, too. These are a few examples of what I expect by discovering one by one consciously the vibrations of your smallest particles. The smallest particles, for a certain musician who's very physical, may be just his limbs, his arms, his legs, and his fingers, because he's not able to penetrate into the cells or the molecules, so to speak, and their components, their particles. And then he will play very physical music. In fact there are other texts in the same cycle of pieces where I actually say, "Play the vibration of the rhythm of your limbs."

RHYTHMS OF THE UNIVERSE

C: But if you feel this vibration and want to play it, won't the vibration that's needed to manifest it on an instrument alter the original impulse?

S: No. You just concentrate on the vibration and that acts immediately on the vibrations of the instrument. Hold the bow on the violin, and you will see what happens. And that is a constant process. All you know is that you have to make audible this concentration . . . like thinking aloud.

And the other extreme concerns that of the rhythms of the universe. Some of our musicians, especially the most intellectual, Kontarsky, for example, said, "I can't do anything with that instruction. What shall I do with it, the rhythm of the universe?" I said, "Have you never had any dream experience of the rhythm of the universe, have you never been flying in between stars, have you never had a direct experience of the rotation of the planets, let's say of our own planet, or of the other planets of our solar system? Must these rhythms necessarily be slow?" All these questions came up in discussions. And he said, "No, no, no, I have no such experience, I'm sorry." And then I said, "Well, at least you have one possibility, because you're a very visual person, you read a lot, your education is visual, and your thinking is visual. What about the constellations of the stars?" He said, "Oh, wonderful!" I said, "Well, just one more suggestion. Think of the interval constellations of Webern's music. And then combine them with the constellations of the stars. Let's say you think of Cassiopeia or the Big Dipper." And from that moment on that player became the most precise member of our group for performances of such intuitive music. Kontarsky really played the bones—transforming the visual proportions into rhythmic and pitch proportions. And then, as these were very precise geometrical figures in our performance, the others were playing the smallest vibrations that they could produce with their fingers on the chords. I said, "Go to the heartbeat, go to the pulse, try to dive." And I showed them one thing: when you close your eyes . . . yes, let's do that, and no figures, just the dark. I don't have the dark at this moment, I have spots of gold within the dark. I see spots. And now there is, you see . . .

C: I see the tip of a candle.

S: Get rid of the candle. Nothing, just nothing. And there, I see millions of small spots of dust, moving. Like clouds. Goldish dust.

COLORS OF MEDITATION: VIOLET-RED AND GOLD

C: There are convex rainbow shapes, very thin, and energy centers of orange going whoosh . . .

S: Breathing? Moving? Right. I have the same. Now if I were playing an instrument, these little particles immediately suggest a pattern within the sound that I'm producing [makes noise reproducing the pattern]. And I've discovered that when there are very good moments when we are performing or when I'm listening to other music, then it becomes just red-violet, no shape, it's all just like a curtain. And when this starts breathing, very slowly—it's between the heartbeat and breathing beat—it starts breathing like that and then I'm absolutely sure that it's good. In a pitch-black room, too, the violet always comes. Only after a while do you get to the next step after violet, a goldish color, and then you may be sure that the cosmic juice is flowing into you. The new musician must very consciously do all these exercises and play in these different states of spirit.

You'll be amazed, when you hear the recordings of *Aufwärts*, by the quality, the newness, and the lack of clichés, far beyond my personal imagination. And that's what I call intuitive music, when a player, through a certain meditative concentration, becomes a wonderful instrument and starts resonating. Because I think the music is always there. The more open you are, the more you open yourself to this new music by throwing out all the images, all the automatic brain processes—it always wants to manifest itself.

BRAIN-WAVE MUSIC

C: Do you know of the recent experiments with brain-wave music?

S: That always reminds me too of the experiments that they do with rats. I had a friend in Los Angeles who said, "We're doing very interesting acoustical research now with rats, stimulating pulses or picking up brain waves from animals and transforming them into audible sound." And I attended a concert in which David Tudor, together with a composer at Davis, California, where I taught for six months, were performing a piece with "brain waves." The performance, in the beginning, seemed to be very magic-like, a table-lifting society, and it seemed to promise quite a lot because of the way they were watching and looking at each other. The speakers' cardboard membranes were pushing the air, and these pulsations—a kind of colored low noise—were produced by the performers' brain waves. It's the same effect as if air were being pumped into a tire. So what? There's a certain periodicity which becomes more or less irregular, maybe interesting for doctors.

You see, years ago in Paris I was present at an event at which the French sculptor Schoeffer, together with Pierre Henry, made a construction for light and sound on the Eiffel Tower, where the humidity of the air, the speed of the wind, and the temperature all were analyzed, turned into sound information, and were heard through large speakers: the different parameters of the sound were conducted by the natural forces. Well, this is then simply a translation of what you experience anyway if you're attentive. They did it on the Eiffel Tower, and naturally at that height you were not—well, you couldn't hear the sounds anyway, the wind was blowing, it was wild [makes whooshing sound]. And people walking underneath really paid no attention to the musical structure. It was just like wind chimes, somehow nice.

MUSICAL ATOMIZATION

You see, so many composers think that you can take any sound and use it. That's true insofar as you really can take it and integrate it and ultimately create some kind of harmony and balance. Otherwise it atomizes. And we've had enough atomization. It atomizes us and then we're depressed when we go home. You can include many different forces in a piece, but when they start destroying each other and there's no harmony established between the different forces, then you've failed. You must be capable of really integrating the elements and not just expose them and see what happens.

Ultimately the way you compose the notes is the way you want to compose people, so to speak. On paper, every note is like a person. I must give it enough space and time, and if there isn't enough time at one spot, then I must give it more time at a later point. This isn't symbolism. This doesn't represent specific people, but *forces*. People to me are forces. And then when people listen to this music they will become what the music is.

SPATIAL MOTION

C: Would you say something about spatial motion in your music?

S: Apply everything we have said about timbre to space. We're used to sounds which have been fixed to objects that have produced sounds, like instruments or human voices. And we have lost the ability to fly like birds, to make flying sounds in a concert hall. That's why there's the stage and the people who are all sitting. And the movement of the sound has no importance whatsoever. The sound travels in the hall by itself, bangs against the walls and hits the ears, but the sound source is never traveling. It's only in a forest that you can still experience this, where birds are flying. With the airplane this has come back, and with modern traffic, where a car is passing by and the sound makes the typical Doppler effect, or whatever. We still have a lot of cities where it's essential in the center of the city that you hear if the car's approaching from your back so that you can jump away. There it becomes important that you know where the sound's coming from. Every animal and hunter, naturally, is very attentive to where sounds are coming from.

OSAKA WORLD'S FAIR: THE SPHERICAL HALL

Every sound moves the molecules of the air and needs its space. That's why it's so bad to have speakers, for example, where one membrane is supposed to give space at a given moment to all the different sound waves before they're emitted into the air. There should practically be for every sound a different area where this sound lives and also enough space where it can travel. So that's why when there's a high temperature in the room, the sound can't travel anywhere, it's too thick. What's important is that for the first time in the history of mankind we have the means to make sound travel. Which means real stereophony, putting speakers everywhere in a hall. And up to now this has hardly been the case. If we have speakers, we have them on the stage, and it causes a lot of problems—four or eight speakers in the four corners of a room, high enough that they don't hit the backs of the heads of the people who are sitting in front of the speakers. For the first time I had this new experience at the World's Fair in Osaka where I, together with an architect, constructed this completely spherical hall which seated 550 people on a sound-transparent platform in the middle of the sphere, and there were speakers everywhere. There were several devices that I designed by which I was able to make the sound travel.

Let's say someone was singing in a microphone, the microphone was connected to a control desk, and I had a sound mill which had one input and fourteen outputs, so I could put the fourteen outputs on any of these fifty speakers which surrounded the audience which was on a platform in the middle of the sphere.

So I could make complete circles around the people, not only horizontal circles, but vertical circles, below-above, below-above. Or spiral movements of all different loops. I pushed the buttons of different connections, and I turned the sound mill, a very simple device with fourteen contacts, smoothing out the connections between the different contacts. And then I moved the mill, like a coffee mill that moves the sound with the maximum speed that I can create with my hand—up to six or seven revolutions a second. And you can draw a polyphony of two different movements, or let one layer of sound stay at the left side, then slowly move up to the center of the room, and then all of a sudden another layer of sound will start revolving like mad around you in a diagonal circle. And the third spatially polyphonic layer will just be an alternation between front-right and back-left, or below me and above me, below me and above me, alternating. This polyphony of spatial movements and the speed of the sound become as important as the pitch of the sound, the duration of the sound, or the timbre of the sound.

CHANGING PERSPECTIVES

And that really brings us into the space age of music; but that space I have described is the space of a direct physical experience, and by going through this experience we arrive at a new inner space. It's not the outer space, it's the inner space. We talk about outer space, flying with a rocket. You see, that's something else, because you're watching these balls—to begin with the two balls, the moon and the earth, you can't see the other ones yet, we haven't reached that far. But that's the next step: I mean there is a direct relationship between our desire to expand our consciousness of the outer and the inner—it's the same. And in music it's also the same. We want to expand ourselves through the experience of moving sound and to see what happens to us. Because then we will move with the sound and fly, too. We are no longer sitting in the chair, innerly. We no longer have a fixed position or one perspective in listening to music, as we do in music where you have a tonal center or where you have a certain meter, as in rock music. There you are centered. That's your chair. There you sit. And everything else is related to that position where you're sitting. And also what you're listening to is fixed in space. But the moment that starts moving, you start moving with the sounds. But you might be moving with a different layer than some of the musicians, so your perspective changes. You have a mobile perspective, and no longer the classical one. You're no longer related to one tempo. You no longer have a specific inner fixed harmonic perspective to which you refer all the other sound, noise, pure tone, bird tones, clusters, and so on and so forth, but you change the perspective, according to what's predominating for a certain while in the music that you're listening to. Then this becomes the new center, then all of a sudden a cluster may become the center. And the sound that is purer or broader than a cluster slowly replaces it. It's like a change of perspective, as in painting. Klee announced this for the first time, and I don't see any paintings yet which really follow this great discovery of showing in one painting one object which is seen from five, six or seven different perspectives at the same time—the multiple perspective within one composition.

"FIRST YOU MUST MAKE THE MUSIC, AND THEN THE MUSIC CHANGES YOU."

First you must make the music, and then the music changes you. That's the feedback. That's a spiral. But it always changes. Having an idea of something—there the idea comes in. And doing something that you are not yet. The idea of flying: I can't fly yet, but God, how shall I fly? They've thought for thousands of years how they could regain that power they didn't know they once had. They saw that the birds were able to fly, and they had the idea of imitating them. And then, you see, they developed the possibility of how to fly. They tried, they fell on their noses many times. In music it's the same. I do new compositions, and I am not yet what the music is. Then one day, all of a sudden, I can make it. I find the means, something within me works it out. And then when I listen to it [whistles like a bird flying] I become the way the music is. I become a multiple being, a being which changes perspective, I become more flexible, I no longer have that one standpoint. I change my standpoint all the time. And then by changing, being changed by what I've done, what I do changes more—I demand more. I can't tell you any longer what is music and me in such a process. I change the music, the music changes me. You cannot separate the music from me any longer, and you cannot separate the music from the listener any longer. The listener becomes the music. And by that the music is influenced by the listener because he changes the music. What is the music? I don't know.

part two

KÜRTEN, GERMANY

SEPTEMBER 1971

> "Even in dreams when all thinking has become quiescent, the hearing nature is still alert. It is like a mirror of enlightenment that is transcendental of the thinking mind because it is beyond the consciousness sphere of both body and mind. In this Saha world, the doctrine of intrinsic, Transcendental Sound may be spread abroad, but sentient beings as a class remain ignorant and indifferent to their own Intrinsic Hearing."
>
> —*Surangama Sutra*

THE SLEEPERS AND THE WAKING

C: Heraclitus wrote: "The waking have one world in common; sleepers have each a private world of his own."

S: This opposes an experience I've described in an aphorism: "When I'm lying by your side awake, you have only half of me; but when I'm sleeping at your side, you have me completely." In sleep all the gates of the body are open, and you slip in and out. A lot of people, some pleasant, others impolite, enter and play with you.

C: Heraclitus means by "waking" what you mean by "sleeping."

S: Ah, yes, I've used the word "sleeping" in a different context—as when Jesus told his disciples: Don't sleep—three times in the Garden of Gethsemane—in order to keep open the connections with the divine, bringing every action and thought home into a total agreement. Otherwise you're like a baby who dies without its mother's nurture. Very few people can stay totally alone, having complete confidence in God.

I'm not speaking, as you know, about the old God. I always say we should name God, even if we know it's only a name. Musicians always sing out what's important; and we should name but never stop naming, finding God everywhere, in all forms.

Some people think I'm naïve when I speak out about this essential experience of finding contact with the divine. I was born a Catholic. Already before the last war my father had to leave the church because of the pressure of the Nazi party, and I witnessed many contradictions that occurred within him because of this. At the end of 1940 he put me into a state school where religion was completely suppressed, and I could only pray at night. For most people, war washes away the connection of man to the divine; people become very physical living so close to death. When I was sixteen I was in an ambulance crew that helped get the heavily wounded to the hospital. And I saw trees cluttered with pieces of human flesh, after the strafing by the planes. And it's hard to imagine the sexual behavior in the midst of dying bodies at the hospital. I have no illusions about people who give up God.

HITLER, SRI AUROBINDO, AND GANDHI

C: Do you think people would go to war if they had a high enough spiritual consciousness?

S: I think they would—if you had to go to war to get rid of a state like the German state under Hitler. I give my support to someone like Aurobindo who sent his brothers to Europe in order for them to learn how to make bombs to blow up bridges and trains of the English occupation army in India. He could have talked until he died, and nothing would have changed. Aurobindo was strongly opposed to Gandhi who was against the English entering the war, after Chamberlain had been so weak with Hitler. And Aurobindo said if the dark forces come—though they, too, are part of the divine and have their purpose—still you make a stand. There's that real divine freedom where you can say no to God. Hitler would have enjoyed Gandhi's passive resistance; that's just what he wanted. Hitler was obsessed by the devil. Now they're trying to make him sound more like a human being, a man who had his outrages once in a while and who wasn't really well informed.

It's difficult making general statements that are very personal. I have no illusions about the dark forces. After the war I worked as a pianist in bars, during the height of the black market. I got cigarette butts when everyone left, made new cigarettes out of them, and traded them for butter. Everyone was cheating each other, and, in fact, they were the most sentimental. They asked to hear their favorite songs, and they all wanted to be on the side of doing something beautiful, but God knows what mysteries there are in the devilish forces. They have to play that role to shake things up, to wipe things out. As in nature.

I would never be an army general. I am clearly opposed to people who deny the divine. . . .

C: But most authoritarian leaders say that God's on their side.

S: But these are words. I want to see how they act. They have to realize what they're talking about. If they behave like pigs and at the same time have the word God in their mouths, then that's the most devilish attitude. I want to see what they support, recommend, and deny. I want to see if they just want to oppress people, to tell them what to think and believe: I want to see their state of consciousness. . . . If someone like Hitler came to power again, I'd leave—even before, because I've got a lot of premonitions in such matters.

"THE SPIRIT WILL BE THE MUSIC ITSELF."

I think the ultimate goal of a creative person is to transform his whole existence as a person into a medium that's more timeless, more spiritual. All my energy goes into the music; and it's not really my music. I don't ultimately know what my music has to do in this world and what it means. Because it must be filled with new meanings, with other people, other spirits. I'm commissioned, so to speak, by a supernatural power to do what I do. I think the spirit, as a personal spirit, will be the music itself, so I don't have to take care of it anymore: it begins to have its own life, and sometimes when I meet it again, I hardly recognize it.

DREAMING *TRANS*

C: Dreams have often provided solutions to specific problems. When Niels Bohr, for example, was trying to analyze the structure of the atom, he had a dream one night in which he saw the sun and the planets whirling around it, and at that point he knew how to go about his work. A better example is that of Elias Howe, who invented the sewing machine. He'd been putting thread at the top of the needle so that when it descended, the thread got twisted up. One night he dreamt he was attacked by warriors with long spears, at the tips of which were little eyes. He woke up and realized he should put the threads at the bottom of the needle.

Many composers, too, have written about how they've received ideas and actual musical materials in dreams: Tartini, Mozart, Saint-Saëns, Stravinsky, Kagel.

S: There are two different kinds of dreams which we can distinguish. One I've had many times since the beginning of my work. In serial construction you very often have complicated problems of combining the different parameters which, while you're preparing the composition, are notated in numbers. When you've reached a dead end in pitch construction, it's because you've had to obey rules which you have made too strict. For example, the major seventh as well as the minor ninth—the upper as well as the lower one—have to occur before a pitch can jump out of its octave two octaves higher or lower. This is one of the many rules. And then you reach a point where the row makes such a jump impossible for a specific pitch. I remember that very often when I'd worked until late at night, I gave up; the brain continued working on the problem during my sleep, and I knew the solution next morning.

This is one aspect and I don't think this is what you really meant. You were speaking about the possibility of anticipating in a dream a complete new work: you hear and see it. This has happened in *Telemusik* for the general form plan and now in *Trans*. In the case of *Trans*, for example, I was busy doing different things; and completely unexpectedly, during the night of December 10, 1970, I dreamt an entire piece. Next morning I only had a very short time before going to an appointment to quickly write down a few notes about that dream. And I have this page in front of me. It says: "Dreamt orchestral work"—the date's on top—"orchestra sits in series." I saw two rows of string players in front from the extreme left to the extreme right of the stage sitting in a straight line without music desks. There was a second row a little bit above the first, and the heads of the musicians there appeared between those of the first row. And they all played synchronously, and extremely slow and loud, a very dense sound wall—a chromatically dense closed wall. I wrote: "This sound wall opens with different intervals at periods of about twenty seconds, allowing music behind this wall to come through—brass and woodwinds mixed—and I hear low instruments that are the fundamentals; in timbres they're colored like organ mixtures. With each low melodic line of one of the lower instruments there are several instruments in parallel, playing softer and coloring this low sound."

THE SOUND WALL AND THE WEAVING CHAIR

And then I've written here: "At the same time I hear the sound of a weaving chair." God knows how I came to that idea, I've never thought about the sound of a weaving chair; perhaps it dates back to my childhood. It's also very similar to the sounds of a train switch—my uncle was a train switchman. Also, I was in Bali in 1970, and there I visited a place, a small room where about twenty young girls between the ages of about nine and fourteen were weaving clothes. And they had these old wooden weaving chairs. I heard this noise in the dream, every twenty seconds, a shuttle of a weaving chair passing loudly through the hall from the left to the right, shooting through the air. And with each shuttle sound the string players were beginning the next upward movement of their bows, all synchronously, and then in the middle of the duration between two shuttle sounds, they started a downward motion. Another shuttle sound, and they played a new note. The first shuttle sound opens the chromatically dense wall at a certain interval, closes it with the next sound. It opens, it closes. I knew it should last at least half an hour—always these periodic shuttle sounds and the string players changing the notes.

In the dream I also saw a curtain in front of the audience, which is quite unusual for an orchestral piece, I've never seen that before. It was completely dark in the hall, the curtain very slowly opened from the middle. And through the curtain you saw the first string players in the center, looking like figures in a wax museum, moving only their right hands, slowly. The curtain opened little by little, and you saw the string but not the wind players; they had to be covered, I couldn't see them. The entire string orchestra appeared in a red-violet light . . . very foggy. The next morning I asked: Where did I get the red-violet light? And then I realized it was exactly the same light I've seen several times in meditation when you close your eyes and chase away all thoughts and pictures so that you have just the dark and then a lighter gray with many little spots floating around—the light particles—then changing slowly to a red-violet light.

It's a warm light, actually; and I might say in parentheses that the closest thing to it I've seen in daylight is when I flew over the North Pole from Copenhagen to Tokyo. It was a night flight . . . very early morning . . . I couldn't see the sun, but the entire ice floe underneath was changing very very slowly from black to gray into this red-violet light. All you could see was, like an enormous brain, gray-bluish veins where the ice obviously was broken . . . but long, very long . . . there were no clouds. And then this light became brighter and brighter and turned slowly through all the colors of the spectrum, ultimately into a more yellowish red. So the meditation's violet-red and this color that I saw in nature over the North Pole come very close to the light in my dream. You also see it sometimes over the ocean in the evening when the sun's just set behind the horizon . . . the last days in summertime when it sinks very slowly . . . it's those last moments when you have that red-violet light. In another dream I once saw a very precise hexagonal form, and it was breathing very slowly like a heart in exactly this red-violet light. This was a very important dream, though I didn't know why until now: this hexagon came up to me very slowly; moving away, coming again . . . three times . . . and it was finished. And as I've mentioned to you before, when our group performed *Prozession, Kurzwellen,* or *From the Seven Days,* when I saw that light, I absolutely knew how good it was. There was something in the air which was absolutely good. This seems very mystical, but when this has occurred for long periods during a concert, the performance is always extraordinary. And when it's recorded, I can check it. So it's not just some idiocy I'm talking about.

C: What you've just said reminds me that the highest frequency in the color range is extreme violet, which is twice the frequency of the lowest, extreme red.

S: It's very interesting. There's that violet that turns into a very aggressive bluish violet which I feel is very distractive. Whereas the violet I'm talking about seems to be completely interwoven with reddish light spots that have this more yellowish tint, like the very bright roses you see in front of the house here. Quite a few of the roses turn into this blue-violet, and they're cold. Whereas this yellowish red of warm flames is quite different.

Anyway, why was this color in my dream foggy? I saw what I couldn't realize in reality . . . I saw it moving upward. Like in the early spring or autumn here in the morning, I saw a violet mist rising . . . like tobacco smoke also, a little . . . not too thick. And in the dream, this was the light through which you could just see the musicians.

HEARING THROUGH TRANS

Immediately in the morning I wrote down a few possibilities. I hadn't dreamed the exact notes of the opening. In the background I heard music which was floating rather than jumping, in intervals, the wind sounds continuously going up and down. Whereas the string sounds in front were completely immobile, straight sounds, very loud and sustained, without any vibrato. And in the dream I felt: Why can't I hear what's behind this? There was something very precise going on in the back of the orchestra, but I couldn't hear it because there was always that strong loud wall in front of me. It's funny, I knew there were people behind and I could have intellectually thought of solving this problem when I worked the piece out by using speakers, since you don't see the musicians in back anyway. But no, there had to be the people there.

C: When did you decide to complete *Trans?*

S: I told this dream to my friend Dr. Tomek who is in charge of the music department of the Southwest German Radio. I mentioned to him that I'd dreamed a new piece and would like to realize it. About a month later he said: I see a possibility of doing it this year in Donaueschingen, would you have time to work it out? At that point I'd already made other arrangements, but I agreed. I did it in an incredibly short time. I was composing in one room and next door were two people who virtually took the pages from my table every day and immediately started copying the score. Every four days we sent what we had to the publisher to make the material. I was up at nine in the morning, and we stayed up until three or four o'clock. For two months. And at the end I had a very elaborate score of 120 pages.

C: You were following the instructions of your dream.

S: Nevertheless, when I was working out the piece, I had a lot of freedom in determining the individual melodic structures within each period, between the two sounds of the weaving chairs. The first string wall seems to be most important during the piece, but it's the music behind this wall that took so much time to compose; it's very precisely calculated in all its rhythmic details and pitch constructions. That reminds me: I told my assistant about the weaving chair, and he mentioned that he knew a woman in a small village in southern Germany who had a wooden weaving chair. And he went there that next Sunday and recorded the shuttle sounds.

Dr. Tomek immediately arranged to make an experimental setup of *Trans* at the television station in Baden-Baden. At first they didn't know what to do at all. They thought of taking one of those transparent curtains that are sometimes used in theaters to project a colored mist during certain scenes, and they demonstrated this a month later, showing me all different kinds of violet lights. And they were completely astonished when I said: No, that's not it, it should be a little more red, there shouldn't be those dark edges. They said, It really doesn't matter. But I was keeping to what I'd seen in the dream.

And I remember that when I gave a concert in New York that February—it was at Alice Tully Hall—and when I saw the carpet on the floor, I just laughed, I was happy. And I asked the hall manager for a piece of this carpet. When you looked at it from a distance of about two yards, it came closest to the color of my dream. He gave me a piece, and I sent it to Baden-Baden. The preselected lamps were already of that color. So we found the color approximately, not completely, because it wasn't misty or mysterious enough.

TRANSPERSONAL MUSIC

C: Why did you decide to call the piece *Trans?*

S: I can't tell you. I've thought it over many times. I told several people about that dream because it preoccupied me, really. The first title that came to me was *Musik für den nächsten toten—Music for the Next to Die.* And I told it to two of my friends, and they said: No, listen, everyone will say that's a kind of strange funeral music. And so I tried other titles: one which I liked very much was *Beyond—Jenseits* in German. In French it's very beautiful: *Au Delà*—what is on the other side. We say: He's in the *Jenseits,* he has died. And *Jenseits* also means "across the border."

C: You mentioned that unlike many of your recent compositions, which were related in a way to a particular person, *Trans* was transpersonal.

S: They were personal because the human came in. In *Momente,* for example, the part of the solo soprano is a real portrait of Mary—of her giggling and ways of laughter and singing and whistling. And in *Stimmung,* although it's very transcendental, there's a lot of direct reference to the way I feel about Mary, about my wonderful experience of this female being. As a partner. Whereas *Trans,* as far as I know, has nothing to do with my life, my personal life—I don't know what it has to do with. It seemed as if I were writing a piece that would be like the *Tibetan Book of the Dead*: music that would help people dying, music for the moment after they've died for the beginnings of their journeys.

C: So it really is transpersonal music.

S: Completely. And it has something to do with the beyond, with what's on the other side—that *there* is the real music, you see: *there* is the composed music with all its configurations, very meaningful, full of relationships and mysteries.

C: The novelist and critic Michel Butor once described his compositional procedures: "Before I set off on a journey, a detailed geographical map of the region (which is still vague) I intend to visit must be plotted out in my head. In the case of a novel, this is the moment at which my plan is finalized. If I intend to write an essay, on the other hand, it is the point when, after reading and rereading the text so many times, everything starts to become obscure and ideas fail me. It's terribly disturbing. The only way I can escape from the trap I have laid for myself is by writing. Luckily enough, I soon glimpse the end of the path along which I've struck out and my text unwinds like a skein of wool. It almost seems that I'm reading my own text or rather that my writing is a correction of the whole book."

I'm struck by the "skein of wool," applied to the weaving idea in *Trans.* But also, if you substitute "composing" for "writing" here—so that composing is in a sense a *correction*—you find a wonderful analogy to the way you've described the composition of *Trans.*

S: It is a strange function, actually; and Butor's very right —still thinking you're a composer because you're literally executing something with all your technique and developing a new technique in order to realize this. But really it's as if someone else had given me a work. The score was written so quickly, and when I sat down very tired in the early evening after I'd stopped composing for a while, I'd sit and look at the early pages and admire how nicely the copyists had drawn them. But I couldn't make sense of it. It looked completely strange to me. And I said to the copyists: I can't understand that I've written this. Just a moment. How does it work?

I'd never before composed a piece in such a fashion. I got up in the morning and knew I had to complete another section, sometimes two sections that day, otherwise the performance would never take place. So I couldn't think twice about what I was doing. I took a bath, did my meditation, and during this time things were occurring. I never questioned anything that came into my mind with regard to *Trans:* never, is it good, not good, right, not right, I never had any doubts. I just did it. Because it depended on the first decisions that came to me in the morning which then determined the overall plan for a whole section. And then the minor decisions I was able to make during the course of the day's work. Or sometimes late in the evening. I'd think that next morning I'd have to start the next section. And then for five or ten minutes I went outside in the dark, without wanting anything . . . empty . . . and things would come, very faintly. So I'd think: Tomorrow I'll do a three-part superimposition. The whole overall plan was made during the first week, providing for the central note, the durations, for how many orchestral groups would play, even for the number of beats per section. So with these few given characteristics, I heard the next section and I composed it.

TRANSCENDENTAL SOUND

C: In one of the most elaborate and beautiful of the Buddhist sutras—the *Surangama Sutra*—each of the disciples describes to Buddha the process by which a particular sense activity became the channel leading to the attainment of samadhi. With Buddha's blessing, one of the disciples states that emancipation can be most surely attained by means of Transcendental Hearing. Here are selections from three stanzas: "Some time when you are reflecting upon your Transcendental Hearing, a chance sound suddenly claims your attention and your mind sets it apart and discriminates it and is disturbed thereby. As soon as you can ignore the phenomenal sound the notion of a Transcendental Sound ceases and you will realize your Intrinsic Hearing. . . . As soon as this one sense perception of hearing is returned to its originality and you clearly understand its falsity, then the mind instantly understands the falsity of all sense perceptions . . . for they are all alike illusive and delusive visions of unreality, and all the three great realms of existence are seen to be what they truly are, imaginary blossoms in the air. . . . All the Brothers in this Great Assembly . . . should reverse your outward perception of hearing and listen inwardly for the perfectly unified and intrinsic sound of your own Mind-Essence, for as soon as you have attained perfect accommodation, you will have attained the Supreme Enlightenment."

S: There's something fantastic about these three texts. They are like musicians, always speaking about listening and hearing. I'm sure that in our society, if you had statements made by people who might have gone as far as these people, all the terms would become visual.

C: The attainment of Intrinsic Hearing suggests the blocking out of just those phenomenal materials a composer needs to use.

S: But think of the situation in which you hear completely *new* music when you begin to block out the sound images, the music that's surrounding you, or the music that you've composed or heard before yourself? I think it's very close to what he's saying. Except that the person who's written this isn't in the position and doesn't need to write music. I *have* to function as a music maker, and that's something different. I'm not in the situation of finding or trying to find enlightenment myself, but rather to make music for the world, for the people. That's a great difference. I have to realize, to concretize something.

Coming back to *Trans*, there are a lot of things happening which people seeing and hearing it for the first time might think are gimmicks. And I must confess that I didn't attend to all of the details which have resulted in certain problems. For instance, during rehearsals, they found that the string players were unable to hold the left arm quietly for as long a time as is required. So they've constructed special chairs with wooden handrests for the thirty violin and viola players on which they can rest their left elbows. And as for the right hand, they've discovered that after three or four minutes a musician has to stop for at least one or two periods of twenty seconds so that the muscles can loosen up again.

Now this has led to a fantastic choreography that I hadn't expected. In the dream I saw them bowing continuously, but the final result is quite different. The double basses are at the edges, left and right, then come the cellos, the viola players, and then the violins—from the two sides to the center. I've now choreographed it so that you see, for example, a group of six instruments stopping at the right side, holding the tip of the bow still on the highest string for some time, and then starting again. Another group in the middle stops, then a third one at the left side—and starts again. So that now there's activity and inactivity changing the picture. You can see, polyphonically, mobility against immobility. And this only came about because the orchestra members said that they couldn't bow all the time.

Then I wondered where I should put the papers with the notes, because in the dream I didn't see any stands, they would have hidden the bodies. My solution was to make little papers about six inches high and four inches long. I tried writing out the eighty or eighty-one notes for each string player on such a small piece of paper. And I suggested gluing them with Scotch tape on the violins so that they'd stand up right in front of the players' eyes. They tried this, but found out that most of the string players wear glasses and couldn't see. They suggested drawing a very large card and putting it on the floor in front of the players. That would have been bad because you wouldn't be able to see into the musicians' eyes anymore, they'd all be bent forward. So finally we decided to attach these little sheets of paper to the scrolls of the violins and violas and connect them with a wire so that they stood up. And now the musicians can see perfectly.

DESCRIPTION OF TRANS: FOUR EVENTS

When I was making the overall time and formal plan for *Trans*, I felt that something should happen during the piece which would jump out of this completely homogeneous situation, and it led me to four scenes which I've also seen and heard as complete picture and sound visions. I can't tell you why they are this and not another way. Or why there are no others. For example, there's one scene after about two-and-a-half minutes of the first main section. From the right side behind the curtain, a percussion player enters like a soldier with the rhythms of the wind players and takes a few steps in slow march movement. He then stands in front of the viola player, makes a sharp turn to the right with his back to the public: at his left side he's carrying what we call a Basel drum, like a medieval marching soldier. You still see these drums at the Basel carnival. He hits his drum once very loudly, together with the sound of the weaving chair, and at this moment the first viola player jumps up and starts a solo which is extremely virtuoistic, like a little wound-up toy instrument. Do you know those little percussion players which have a motor inside and start drumming like mad? That's the way the viola player starts, making pizzicatos, going up and down very fast, mixed into arco sounds. And then the drummer, after having struck his one beat, turns to the right and marches away. The violist only plays for about twenty-two seconds; then comes the next shuttle sound, and he stares into the air in the direction from which the shuttle sound was coming . . . and then looks slowly down, becoming almost immobile, like all the other players, as if nothing's happened.

C: This reminds me in a way of an E. T. A. Hoffmann story.

S: It's more surreal, very strange. Then a little later a stagehand, carrying a music stand with a theater light, walks in—clumsy, a bit stupid—and brings the light to the first cello player, who's sitting on the right side. When the first viola player performed the solo I mentioned before, the first cellist had to stop and stare completely amazed at the viola player sitting next to him. With the next shuttle sound he continued playing. But when the stagehand comes in now and brings a light stand to him, it's as if he's being given his own chance. Together with the shuttle sound the stagehand switches the light on, and like cello players of traditional music the solo cellist begins performing a fairly slow melody, but a real melody with sweeping movements. He's very happy doing this. And all of a sudden, together with the next shuttle sound, the stagehand turns off the light; the cellist can't see anymore and stops. With the following shuttle, the light's put on again and he continues. Again a shuttle, and the stagehand switches the light off very quickly. The cellist, looking surprised, plays a few more phrases of his solo, stares at the stagehand who's rushing off the stage, rises out of his chair a bit in the direction where the stagehand's disappeared, while repeating the last two notes several times. And then with the next weaving chair sound . . . it's as if nothing's happened.

There's another moment exactly in the middle of the piece when the first violinist, who sits exactly in the center of the string players, suddenly, like a canary, starts making flageolet sounds, always upward bow movements. He repeats the same note fifteen, sixteen times; and hearing this, each string player, one after the other, stops playing. They move their heads very slowly a bit forward and stare at him, as if eyes could tell him he's doing something crazy . . . he looks straight up at the ceiling—that's what I saw. I mean I haven't invented these things, I don't know why it has to be done this way. You see only the whites of his eyeballs and hear this canary-like whistling. So these forty people all staring at him. Do you feel what it's like? And then an embarrassed silence and the next weaving chair sound comes in *cla-cla-clah!* and they all move immediately backward as if a voice from outer space had asked them, What are you doing? They all stare straight ahead again as if nothing had happened, called back to order, so to speak.

Then there's the fourth event. At the left side of the stage, there's a four-yard-high platform, with a ramp leading up to it just behind the string players. You can feel it, but you don't know why it's there. And about three minutes before the end of the piece, there's a section for the wind instruments when everything becomes very dense and complicated and moves upward; it's a gnashing orchestral sound. You see a trumpet player appearing out of the dark on top of the platform with his trumpet. He looks like a ghost up there, without the lower part of his body; he makes a little jerk with his head and, with the next shuttle sound, begins an incredibly hair-raising solo. [Imitates.] And he makes mistakes; you hear them because he's trying to repeat a note at certain times and misses it. He makes furious comments to himself with glissandos. You feel like laughing, but it's a strange laughter. It's like someone coming to bring a message, but nobody knows what it means, as if there were a fire or as if the trumpet player were giving the signal for an attack before a battle. But the string players just continue their slow movement. And then the brass players in the back, one by one, catch up with his tempo and double it synchronously. What he plays is completely integrated into what the others play, and for the first time you hear the string players making a few accents synchronously with him. After that the solo ends with a few of the lowest possible sounds of the trumpet—loud, flutter-tongued, spluttering sounds spit into the trumpet—and then he walks away.

Finally comes what's for me, and I'm sure for any listener, the most breathtaking moment in the whole piece when, without any reason, the whole orchestra stops, and there's a general pause. It's like a stop-motion image in a movie: all of a sudden, *baff!* you hear the weaving chair sound and the orchestra completely stops; there's no sound for twenty seconds, which is a very long time in a piece where something like this hasn't happened yet. There's total silence. After twenty seconds you have just one shuttle shooting through the air—*karraak!*—and then another twenty seconds of silence . . . nothing happens. With the next weaving chair sound, the music continues, and in the background all four groups of the wind players begin slowly to play one simple melody with very subtle chordal harmonization. After twenty-five minutes, all the string players are suddenly playing a very simple melody completely synchronously and calmly with the wind players in the back. Then with the next shuttle sound, again there's the totally closed chromatic wall. The wind players stop, and the curtain slowly closes.

VISUAL EVENTS AND SOUND: KONTAKTE AND ORIGINALE

C: Excepting *Originale*, this seems to be your first work which has a complex choreographed visual aspect.

S: It's not really complex, but at every moment the visual events are related to the sound. . . . But even in *Kontakte*, there are a few moments: for instance, after the public enters and it's quiet in the hall, the pianist stands up and walks to the tam-tam which is standing alone with the gong at the center of the stage. He takes a long metal knitting needle out of his pocket, touches the tam-tam at its upper edge and very slowly moves the needle all around it, making the sound: *ssschhhoouuu*. It's like turning on the wheel of the world . . . moving a wheel very slowly. This sound then continues in the speakers. Exactly the same sound. . . . He walks back to the piano and just when he reaches it, still half standing, he hits a chord with both hands in the lowest and highest registers, together with the percussion player and the sound in the speakers. And then he sits down.

And at another important point the percussion player leaves his instruments and goes to the gong and begins to beat it furiously from the back, from the front, at all edges, with different beaters. Then a little later, the pianist leaves his instrument and goes to the tam-tam; and they both play, first each player by himself, and afterward each gives the other cues and they play synchronously together with the tape. The one who came second leaves first, and the one who came first leaves last. . . . Yes, I think these few moments have a tremendous importance if they're well done. It's very beautiful to see the pianist playing more and more of those percussion instruments—the cowbells at his left side and the antique cymbals in front of him. At another point, both musicians play clusters of Indian bells, one after another and then together. There are also on both sides the twelve brown bamboo sticks suspended with strings. And when you hit them together with one sharp movement, it's really like a pistol shot; it's terrifically loud. But also when you slightly move them aleatorically with all the fingers irregularly, then you have this fantastic wood chime sound. I found them in a market in Los Angeles, and I immediately decided to use them in *Kontakte*. And it looks marvelous to see these effects.

In *Originale*, of course, I used the term "musical theater" to describe the action of producing sound as a theatrical event. You compose an entire composition in which the production of the sound is the action, but at the same time you look for ways of creating sounds that theatrically make sense in terms of their sequence and superimposition.

"Judge then of thy Own Self: thy Eternal Lineaments explore,
What is Eternal & what Changeable, & what Annihilable.
The Imagination is not a State: it is the Human Existence itself."

—William Blake

C: When you've been asked why, in your collective intuitive music, one needs a leader or a center, you've responded by asking several questions in return: "Why does a spiritual group need a guru? Why has an atom a nucleus? Why is every planet not a sun?" You seem to be suggesting an operative law in nature.

RELATIVITY AND DETERMINISM

S: The music reflects more general occurrences and complications. Relativity has entered the field of music as it has all the other fields. Determinism was a strict prescription in the form of musical instructions to the performer; he had to perform what was written, and there was only a very small range of variability left to his discretion. When I was studying music, the highest ideal of the good interpreter was to be faithful to the score. Then, one by one, scores were written in which statistical processes became very important. I started doing this in 1954, highly influenced by my teacher Meyer-Eppler who was teaching communication science at the University of Bonn where aleatoric processes in statistics, primarily in mathematics but also in sociology and physics, played a strong role.

In the seminars at that time, we were making artificial texts by cutting up newspapers into one-, two-, three-syllable units, sometimes going to the extreme and cutting up individual letters. We'd shuffle them like cards, make new artificial texts, and then study the degree of redundancy. Naturally, the more you cut down a given text, the less redundant would be the result of the new chance-produced text.

The Heisenberg uncertainty principle is based on this hypothetical behavior of the components of the atom. That was the main thing in the air at the end of the forties and beginning of the fifties. We worked with micro theories in communication science; Shannon was very important as a mathematician—Markoff, too. And I simply transposed everything I learned into the field of music and for the first time composed sounds which have statistical characteristics in the given field with defined limits. The elements could move, and later on this was also expressed in the scores. In the beginning I used the deterministic notation for indeterminate textures—I didn't know how to notate it.

CAGE, POLLOCK, MATHIEU

C: Did you know about Cage's work at this time?

S: Important things always happen in parallels somehow. Because in '55, Eppler said that there was a similar movement in America, and that it was also philosophically dealing with Eastern thinking, but we had no clear example of what was going on except in painting. I saw Pollock's paintings for the first time then and it seemed to me that a composer like Cage was even living in proximity to painters who did tachistic painting or abstract expressionist painting—Kline, de Kooning, Pollock, and Motherwell, in a different way—in which the action of the painting itself, the traces of brush movements, are what we call aleatoric—the term Meyer-Eppler taught us which referred to the indeterminate behavior of wave structure. The aleatoric result of such an action resulted in completely new textures.

I think this interest actually came from Paris. I remember one interesting event there. A ship went floating down the Seine, and on the ship was a large canvas. Over the Seine the painter Mathieu had stretched a wire on which were attached plastic bags of color. He held a rifle, and when the ship passed under these bags he'd shoot, the colors dripped, and everybody applauded. That was the painting, and he would sign it afterward. (Or I saw photographs showing Mathieu, wearing a helmet like a football player, running with a dripping brush against a canvas.) At that time, too, Tinguely was making the first automatic electric drawing device. This was a machine with a slot in which you put money, and then a metal arm was electrically put into vibration and started drawing on a paper turning underneath. I saw the results of these interests later in America.

Coming back to the point of our discussion, the relativity that entered determinism gave more and more aleatoric tasks to the performer. Some intellectuals who are thinking only politically have related this idea to that of the freedom of the individual. Thus, the reasoning goes, the individual is exploited when he performs completely determinate music and simply fulfills the order, so to speak, does exactly what's written—the performer becomes like an altar boy, an acolyte, just a very faithful realizer. Whereas when a musician is asked, let's say, to play a note anytime between two time limits, from a beginning to an ending cue, then they'd say, "Well, you see, here he makes his own decision." This has come of the extreme in my text *From the Seven Days* where almost nothing is prescribed, and the musician only reads a text I have written which doesn't even describe the music but puts him into a particular state in which he can concentrate on certain centers of orientation; the listening process is centered in such a way that a certain system of feedback between the musicians can be actualized. Some musician friends have reproached me, saying that this represents an exploitation of the musician's personal intuitive or creative ability. I said, "Fine, then make your own music."

Many people have taken extreme positions in this matter, for or against. Some are saying, "Wonderful, now the rigid system of the deterministic music is becoming flexible, allowing for more freedom." But I've said from the beginning that it's better not to use the word "freedom." This new situation allows a *choice*, and I think choice is the only thing which gives dignity to the human being. Many persons believe that choice represents freedom, whereas one can also think that the man who decides faithfully to perform a score the way it's written is also very free, because he's free to decide. I've never felt any problem in playing a piece which is completely determinate. I'm free to do it or not. I often love to do something where my person disappears and isn't very important—it brings about qualities that are very beautiful. Real freedom is to say yes to something, no matter what one chooses, but it can't be abstractly defined. As they say, all the people in Russia are unfree; but I really doubt it, because I'm sure that many people agree with what they're doing.

PIANO PIECE XI; STIMMUNG

C: Persons have pointed to certain of your works—particularly *Piano Piece XI*, *Originale*, and the realization procedures in *Mikrophonie I*—to show where your music first started becoming less deterministic.

S: The basic principle underlying my whole attitude when I compose is the following: What occurs within single sounds in the micro-musical region is enlarged. *Piano Piece XI* is nothing but a sound in which certain partials, components, are behaving statistically. There are nineteen components, and their order can be changed at random, except that once you choose a connection from one element to the next, the following element is always influenced by the previous one. I have indicated the main characteristics: how loud and how fast it should be, if it's staccato or legato. As soon as I compose a noise, for example—a single sound which is nonperiodic, within certain limits—then the wave structure of this sound is aleatoric. If I make a whole piece similar to the ways in which this sound is organized, then naturally the individual components of this piece could also be exchanged, permutated, without changing its basic quality.

C: This would be true of *Stimmung* as well.

S: Yes, there's a form scheme which determines the sequence of the chords, and each singer has eight or nine (three have eight, three have nine) so-called models. These fifty-one models can be organized in any order according to my plan. I've determined that for each section one of the six singers is the leader, which means that he brings a new model into the context and he has a choice of eight or nine models. The character of the models changes according to the context because of what's done with each model. Sometimes it's completely imitated by the others when the score indicates that they have to "identify" with the leader; sometimes a singer has to continue the previous model without paying respect to the new one (these are the two extremes); or disturbing or varying the pitches and the periodic pulse of the new model. This depends on the order of the models, but once it has been chosen for a given performance then all the instructions work out what has to be done with these models. It's in all my works. Even in the early completely predetermined compositions, there's a lot of randomness in different degrees.

C: Ligeti once wrote an article in which he talked about "global categories" involving interrelationships of "register, and density, distributions of various types of movement and structure," and of the "compositional design of the *process* of change."

MAKING A SOUND TEXTURE

S: Ligeti lived at my house after the Hungarian Revolution. This was at the time when I was composing *Gruppen* for three orchestras, and I showed him the relative variability within what I called *Gruppen*'s time fields. For example, within a given interval —for what I call a certain musical complex or texture—I'd determined a spiral movement. All the instruments that were participating, according to a predetermined number, had to go in irregular but directionally upward movements; spiraling insofar as they rise and then come down again; go a bit higher, come down again, then go still higher until, reaching the top pitch, they start again from the bottom. So what you hear is a *band*, as I call it.

This is a simple transposition of what I'd done in earlier pieces like *Gesang der Jünglinge*, for example, making sound bands, also with aleatoric transpositions, with generators. Let me describe how we've gone about making a sound texture of twenty seconds' duration. I sat in the studio with two collaborators. Two of us were handling knobs: with one hand, one of us controlled the levels and, with the other hand, the speed of pulses from a pulse generator which were fed into an electric filter; a second musician had a knob for the levels and another for the frequency of the filter; and the third one would manipulate a potentiometer to draw the envelope—the shape of the whole event—and also record it. I drew curves—for example: up down, up-down up-down up-down, up, which had to be followed with the movement of a knob (let's say for loudness) for the twenty-second duration. And during these twenty seconds, another musician had to move the knob for the frequency of the pulses from four to sixteen pulses per second in an irregular curve that I'd drawn on the paper. And the third musician had to move the knob for the frequency of the filter following a third curve.

So, everyone had a paper on which different curves were drawn. We said, "Three, two, one, zero," started a stopwatch . . . we'd all do our curves, individually produce one sound layer which was the product of our movements; and this resulted in an aleatoric layer of individual pulses which, in general, speeded up statistically. But you could never at a certain moment say, "*This* pulse will now come with *that* pitch." This was impossible to predetermine. Then we'd make a second, third, fourth, fifth layer—the number of layers was also determined—and I'd synchronize them all together and obtain a new sound. At that time I very often used the image of a *swarm* of bees to describe such a process. You can't say how many bees are in the swarm, but you can see how big or how dense the swarm is, and which envelope it has. Or when birds migrate in autumn, the wild geese sometimes break formation, flying in nonperiodic patterns. Or think of the distribution of the leaves on a tree; you could change the position of all the leaves and it wouldn't change the tree at all.

And I told Ligeti about these new discoveries, the statistical processes that I had been exploring for three years. And he caught on. What he showed me were string quartets that he'd written before in the style of Bartok's quartets. He particularly liked the statistical aspect of music—although for me it was only one aspect—because I saw in his scores all these *ostinato* movements that occur so many times in Bartok as well. Bartok will have an *ostinato* formula of three, four, or five sounds which are repeated over and over again, sometimes transposed upward or downward. It's like pattern composition, pattern painting, or the weaving methods of Near Eastern carpets. More highly developed decorative art uses this kind of repetitive pattern work. And Ligeti continued working in this fashion, avoiding all the gestalten, the clearly defined figures. Whereas in the beginning I said that we shouldn't fall into the trap of composing only statistical structures while not considering the relativity of these structures—which implies the importance, in one and the same composition, of composing a whole scale between the individual—the indivisible—and the dividual—the divisible—which means between gestalt and texture. There are such marvelous examples in Paul Klee's *The*

Thinking Eye in which you see a fish as a gestalt; but looking at its gills, you find a statistical, aleatoric texture.

STATISTICAL CHARACTERISTICS

C: What exactly is this statistical, aleatoric structure?

S: It's a random distribution of elements within given limits. Only statistics can measure it. A noise is nothing but a statistical distribution of waves which, within limits, are nonperiodic. Unlike a vowel, which has a periodic wave, a voiceless consonant's waves have a statistical, chance distribution which is irregular within given limits; there's a higher and lower frequency limit, and inside, like air molecules, there's an entropic situation—an almost even distribution. If there's a tendency, then it's a directional statistical one—going upward or downward, becoming thinner, thicker, brighter, or darker.

In 1954 I gave a radio talk in which I analyzed Debussy's *Jeux* according to statistical characteristics. I spoke of "masses" of sound, their average densities, about trends in sound blocks that would move upward or downward. I tried not to mention that Debussy might have been thinking of waves in *La Mer* or of certain gestures in *Jeux*. I didn't mention this, though they have the same characteristics. I analyzed it on a purely abstract level.

Parameters, which I had previously used only for the description of individual sounds, I now introduced for whole complexes of sounds, or masses of sounds. A mass has a certain density, it has certain tendencies, it has shape; and we must make a clear differentiation between the gestalt and the texture. My body, for instance, is composed of cells, the cells of molecules, the molecules of atoms, and the atoms of even smaller particles; nevertheless, my body has a gestalt which is different from yours, and naturally there's a very subtle relationship between the texture and the form, the shape.

The whole aim of meditation is nothing but that of penetrating with the electric current into the smallest particles of your body, bringing the light energy into the most unconscious and even subconscious layers, because that ultimately stops the process of death. Physical death wouldn't be an absolute necessity if we were able to penetrate with what we call consciousness, if we were able to lead the electric current, which is always available outside of ourselves, into the body and into all the limbs and their particles.

But coming back to statistics: you see, traditionally you had to compose individual tones and melodies, then two melodies, and then melodies of melodic sequences; in classical music, you always made symmetrical—two plus two, four plus four, and eight plus eight—periods in order to build up a musical entity. And the most important principle was that you should always hear everything—every individual tone—so that one wrong note in a chord was immediately noticeable. In statistical compositions, however, the individual components enter into textures that have their own overall characteristics and become new units which are treated like sounds, but they have an inner life, which is composed. What is characteristic of statistical compositions, as of aleatoric compositions in general, is that you can exchange the position of elements within given limits at random and it doesn't change the characteristics. Like changing the position of the tree's leaves. You can say: "This is a beech tree," even if all the leaves have changed their position. I'll come back to this idea in a minute.

The pianist Kontarsky recently told me that Ligeti spoke of being fed up with his works up to now—he wants to compose clear melodies. I heard him at Darmstadt and he spoke like a man who weaves clothes, talking about *threads* and how the characteristics of threads were like certain textures, more or less dense, and about how they could be superimposed or intermingled, etc. He was obsessed by this one aspect, like a painter who created only monochrome or statistical paintings or used only dripping methods. If Pollock or Kline had continued for another twenty years just doing one kind of painting they wouldn't have been able to stand it. Some artists think that they'd have to regress in order to reintegrate figures—clearly definable, individual events. They don't understand what a wonderful thing for the widening of consciousness it is, having found the new relativity and statistical methods, to see that the figure itself in such a context can become even stronger and more mysterious as it's made relative and put into relationship with the statistical events. Let's not fall into one aspect, but always mediate and enlarge consciousness rather than just replace one thing with another and thereby remain on the same level of consciousness.

My personal approach to these problems has been a scientific one. A contemporary physicist couldn't do any important work without taking these new discoveries into account, and it's natural that the music reflects this. As the word says, a musical "composition" means *putting sounds together*. You can put them together at any speed, density, or distribution in a given time and space field of the audibility range. You can produce a structure and relate it to any natural event. You could, for instance, distribute sounds the way the leaves on a tree are distributed.

THE TREE OF SOUND

C: What would a tree *sound* like?

S: The height of the tree would have to be related to a certain parameter, let's say the maximum loudness. The individual branches would be in the loudness curve—what we call the envelope. You could draw this curve exactly in the shape of a tree. If you take pitch, then you'd have all sorts of *glissandos* going up and down in drawing the tree's outer shape. If you take rhythm, then you could consider the height of the tree as equal to the length of your sound; and wherever there's a branch, you'd have small layers going higher or lower, starting at certain points of this total duration.

Look out the window. You can ask about the differences between this fir tree and that beech tree. First the shape, the general outline which I've already described as a curve shows the difference. What's within this curve? How is it filled? With a certain texture: I see green needles on one side . . . yellow-brown leaves . . . color spots. Very soon the beech will lose all its leaves, but not the fir tree. So there's another aspect of the beech tree—no leaves. I only see the branches, and still they have a characteristic texture and gestalt. The statistic, the aleatoric, always applies to the small elements within larger gestalten.

If I now approach this tree, the closer I come, the more the gestalt disappears—I can't see it anymore. If I approach a branch—a new unity. This next unit—the branch—has elements with aleatoric distribution: the leaves of the smaller branches. Then I come to an individual leaf: again I have an individual gestalt. In this way I recognize that what, from a perspective of a distance of fifty yards, were statistical elements have now become individual ones. And I see that within the individual leaf, the distribution of the veins seem to be statistical. So I take a microscope and again see individuality. Then in a sharper microscope the cells of the leaf will dissolve into many, many components—again statistics—they're floating around like the molecules of the air.

INDIVIDUAL FIGURES AND MULTIPLICITIES

This is what I do in music. I go into the deepest possible layer of the individual sound. There's always this change from the clear gestalt that you can grasp in just one listening to a piece—the very simple subdivisions and blocks. And if you dive into one block you discover multiplicity. In the multiplicity—"dividuality"—you discover individual figures again. Each individual figure has aleatoric components around itself, it becomes a nucleus of a new entity. Deeper and deeper.

C: How deep do you want to go?

S: Endless. As in nature. I want to go as deep as I can. In *Kontakte,* I composed every sound from individual pulses which I spliced on tape. I made loops of one rhythm with individual electric pulses that I recorded on tape with a duration of one second, for example—and sped the rhythms up a thousand times—it took a whole day. I let the loop run until I had four hours of sound. I sped that up at the tape recorder's highest possible speed, and then got four octaves higher, another four octaves higher finally another two octaves, so that in the evening I finally had about fifteen seconds; it had about 1,000 cycles per second. And one cycle of the 1,000 cycles per second was my original rhythm.

C. So you went from the smaller to the larger. Let's say you took the 1,000-cycle-per-second sound and wanted to analyze that. Would you wind up with the original components or with something else?

S: With something else, because a lot has gone out of the roof, which means the amplifier permits only up to 20,000 cycles, so everything from the beginning up to 20,000 is, God knows, somewhere. And new periods come up which are *groups* of periods. You can speed up such a sound more and more and always have sound, because when these periods of the pulses are grouped together, what you lose in the high frequential regions you gain in the low ones, always new fundamentals, so to speak, come up, as long as the sound is periodic. If it's not periodic, then you get noise. But new periods always come up from the bottom. That's why I've sometimes spoken in seminars about the possibility that the whole universe might have just one fundamental. Every 83 billion years we have an "ylem," which is an initial explosion. And the universe expands and then contracts again. After another 83 billion years it explodes again. There's periodicity, but within the periodicity you find the aleatoric distribution of the stars and the components of the universe. This slowest frequency would be the fundamental of the universe.

RUSSIA AND AMERICA: PREPLANNING VERSUS RANDOMNESS

Once in Poland, I was asked about these problems by some Russian interviewers, and I said, "In Russia you have a deterministic system, a 'preplanning' society. It's overplanned, and that's why it doesn't work. America, until recently, was considered the opponent of this system, emphasizing improvisation and living from day to day. Now, this has changed, and both systems are approaching each other with enormous speed and very soon you won't be able to see any differences anymore." They asked me about freedom in the aleatoric music and determinism in the capitalistic system. They took it politically again. I said that what seemed best to me was the fusion and the synthesis of the two. Certain things should be preplanned and deterministic. The overall structures should be clear and shouldn't move too much. But in the detail, you should leave more randomness, leave it up to the individual, to the moment's intuition. Then they saw that statistics or deterministics are two sides of the same coin, it's just how you look at it. The example of the tree shows it very clearly. It's just a question of your perspective and the sharpness of the analytical mind. The sharper the elements of analysis become, the more chance you have to penetrate through the next wall where you meet the same problem again, only on a smaller level.

THE ESSENCE OF SOUND

C: A Buddhist sees through the veils of illusion. Is it equally possible to approach the hypostasis, the essence of sound?

S: I'm much too small. But I've begun to understand it now. There's a wonderful book called *Star Maker* [by Olaf Stapledon], given to me by an American student of mine. I haven't read all of it, but he's described how the author tells of a period of a cosmic explosion in which everything is sound. Not the way we describe the materialistic forms—planets, suns, and galaxies—but a complete explosion of sounds. He lets his fantasy run wild, it's wonderful. When I'd heard for the first time about this new symbiotic theory of the universe, I imagined that there certainly must be an alternating of sound and silence. The whole universe in every second expansion would only exist in holes of negative forms. It's as difficult to imagine this as it is for most people to imagine a sequence of silences.

SUBJECT-OBJECT PERCEPTION: NON-ARISTOTELIAN LOGIC

C: In the clichéd situation where a tree falls in a forest and no one's around to hear it, how do you answer the question of whether there's in fact a sound?

S: That Aristotelian way of thinking which enables you to talk about the object without talking about the subject is finished. It's becoming a special case in a much vaster way of thinking. You should take a look at Gothard Guenter's *Idea and Chart of a Non-Aristotelian Logic* (*Idee und Grundriss einer nicht-Aristotelishen Logik*). He shows the possibility of a post-Hegelian, and, by that, a post-Aristotelian way of thinking in at least a three-dimensional and *n*-dimensional logical system where you no longer have this simple opposition between object and subject. There's no perception without the perceived and no perceived without the perception. People always think they're in the world, but they never realize they are the world. They are identical with what they see and hear, whether they like it or not. The sounds that I hear are me. I become the sound, otherwise I'd never hear it. The air that I inhale is me because this air is my life, that's what I am. I'm a machine in so far as I'm ventilating and burning oxygen. Of course, I'm not all the air, and not all the air is me, but the air that comes into me is me. The sounds that come into me are me, and the same with all the electric waves and thoughts that come into me.

C: Then how do you make a value judgment about what sounds please you or not, if they're all you?

S: We're talking about ourselves all the time. It's very interesting when the soul through aesthetic judgment reveals itself. It's a wonderful confession when someone says, "I don't like this."

C: In a sense he's saying: "I don't like myself or a part of myself."

S: Exactly. What you don't like, you don't like in yourself. You haven't been able to integrate it yet. Understanding is becoming.

THE INTEGRATION OF ALL SOUNDS

C: Aren't there some things you don't want to integrate? Like the record you told me you just received and didn't care for at all.

S: It's difficult, isn't it, but ultimately I want to integrate everything. Yes, that's what the concept of God is. If I were not God, then what's the point, and if God were not me . . . I'm just a particle. Like my finger is a part of my body. My finger doesn't really know why I'm eating, talking to you, but it's somehow aware of the total. It functions very well. Of course, sometimes it doesn't, and I get an infection. We shouldn't all try to be like superman who can eat anything. I perfectly accept my limits, but my consciousness tries or wants constantly to enlarge: to be born in such a way that it wouldn't disturb me anymore; I'd just blow and the sound would fly away. Then I'd also have to have the means to integrate it so that it would belong to me perfectly and wouldn't disturb me. If I had galactic dimensions in my person, this noise wouldn't bother me at all; I probably wouldn't even hear it; it wouldn't interest me. But since I'm born in this body and with the mind's limitations—these limitations are good actually—if I don't want to expose myself to something, I go away.

MUSIC OF THE SPHERES

C: You talked about how you could analyze the structure of a tree, how you could perceive its gestalt—what about persons who in states of raised consciousness think they can hear the sounds of the tree?

S: Every object in the world, down to the smallest atom, produces waves which can be transformed into acoustic waves. Most of the time they're much too fast or slow and can't be heard with our ears. My cochlea are limited in frequency to a range of 20 to 16,000 or 17,000 cycles per second. They're also limited as regards softness and loudness. If I take a microphone with enormous amplification then I discover a completely new sound world. Everything makes sounds. Every star makes enormous sounds. You'd have to put the waves of these rotations into an atmosphere where there's air, where air molecules can transform them into lower vibrations so that they're identical to the construction of our body. There's a music of the spheres all the time, but these sounds would make the worst pollution you can imagine, it would be too loud.

THE ACOUSTICAL GARBAGE MACHINE: THE SOUND SWALLOWER

I think one of the most important roles for the musician now should be that of informing other people how the sounds that go through their bodies, their electric system, form them enormously and that, as with food, one should become aware of what one takes in. The knowledge of the nutritional values of food isn't that advanced in Western societies. And we know much less about the sounds. This is critical, because sounds go into all of the body's pores and cells directly—not just through the ears—everywhere. And people should become more conscious of what kinds of sounds they want and don't want to be exposed to. They should become selective and know what's good for them and what's not. The function of the composer then is not just to compose new music, but to make space for the new music. We want to clean the air to make people become aware of the sounds they produce. I'm referring not only to traffic sounds, but even to talking, dogs barking, or idiotic parrots screeching Jacko-Jacko-Jacko! We must really have a good disposal system for acoustical garbage. The people want Muzak, I'm told, but I'm not really sure what they want. They don't think about it, they just take it passively, and they don't know how to defend themselves.

I don't know how to realize this technically, but I once made a design for a Sound Swallower. In each kitchen you have a Garbage Disposal Unit—*Müll Schlucker* in German! And I want such things in public places. You put up hidden microphones everywhere; imagine this: the sounds picked up by the microphones are analyzed by a computer for their wave structure. Then the negative of this wave is produced by a generator, and this negative wave is almost simultaneously emitted into the air through special speakers. You'd hear nothing, because every sound is immediately matched with its negative. This would make silence, first of all, so that people would become aware of *possible* silence, something that never happens in a crowd. It's like in a fairy tale. You're on the street talking to your friend, and all of a sudden he recognizes that you're just moving into a silent area and he tries to say something but you don't hear anything. Then people could go to the corner and do anything they liked. You'd also have a tiny switch with which to turn the sounds on and off. People could acoustically piss and shit in special acoustical toilets, but they wouldn't be bothering anyone else with their acoustic garbage.

C: Do you imagine this happening to people just walking down the street?

S: How wonderful! Wouldn't it be marvelous?

C: What would it be for most persons to walk without hearing anything? The sensory deprivation might drive them mad.

S: Originally, religion always provided a lot of silence in its ceremonies. For hours people would sit and make no noise or sound; it's most beautiful. . . . I don't mean absolute silence; there's nothing absolute. First of all, produce an empty field; before culture begins you must have space. You see, I think it would be better for consciousness to be developed so that we don't need these drastic technical means. But something must be done. The more people come together, the more urgent the acoustical garbage service becomes in order to show people how to get rid of noises and sounds they haven't chosen themselves and don't want.

THE POWER OF SOUND WAVES

People in advertising and politics know very well what sounds do to the masses. Oh yes. The Khmer people in Cambodia moved thirty- and forty-ton stones, with elephants pushing and people pulling on ropes. Trumpet blowers who periodically blew very sharp signals had an important function, helping to synchronize thousands of people pulling at the rope in order to move such stones even one inch. Sounds can do anything. They can kill. The whole Indian mantric tradition knows that with sounds you can concentrate on any part of the body and calm it down, excite it, even hurt it in the extreme. There are also special mantras, naturally, that can lift the spirit of a person up into supernatural regions so that he leaves his body.

This information must be taught in schools; it's more important than writing and arithmetic. We must know what the waves do to us—all the waves, most of the waves have no names, cosmic rays constantly bombarding and penetrating our bodies. The astrologists have an elaborate knowledge of what certain constellations of other planets do to the human body. Our bodies are preconditioned, having been born under certain influences of the stars, which are enormous magnets, that's just what they are. So the magnetic field of a person is predetermined by certain magnetic constellations. When you record something on a tape recorder what else do you do but magnetize very small elements of metal which are on the tape, and these molecules are ordered in certain patterns that, when they're reproduced, make sound.

People should use sounds for very particular things: to heal, to stir up certain abilities which are asleep. Originally with church and tribal music, the making of the sound itself brought you into the state of trance and meditation, adoration or ecstasy. This has disappeared, and all we have now is the more or less mocking attitude of a concertgoer or someone with his radio or tape recorder who uses music as an acoustical tapestry or, at best, something to identify with, a particular emotion that's dominating him at the moment. But a new function of sounds, of certain constellations of sounds composed by persons who had this more subtle knowledge of what sounds do to man, might suggest records made for very particular purposes.

STIMMUNG

If I knew more about this then I would compose a number of items for a record, and on the cover I'd tell what each item was made for, what it should be used for.

I thought of experimenting on myself to discover what certain sequences of sound events do to me when I concentrate on particular centers of the body, then make this music available in several takes on the record so that they can be used with a very specific purpose in mind. The way it affects me will also affect others sooner or later because I don't think I'm so much different from other people. . . . With *Stimmung*, this is already the case. I'm not speaking so much about a therapeutic quality, although from all the performances we've given I have seen and felt people's responses, especially at the Osaka World's Fair where *Stimmung* was performed seventy-two times. Many persons came up and thanked us for the experience, but they were actually thanking themselves for having let themselves be transported to a state they normally don't reach. We knew when we were good—it didn't happen all the time. When we did succeed, then more persons would come afterward to express their astonishment.

A LETTER FROM JAPAN

October 30, 1970

Dear Mr. Stockhausen:

EXPO '70 GERMAN PAVILION—
STOCKHAUSEN ELECTRONIC MUSIC REPORT

Please find enclosed a mere sample of the many hundreds of clippings regarding your excellent Stockhausen Electronic Music presented at the Osaka World Exposition (Expo '70) from March 14 to September 13, 1970.

During this period approximately 9,800,000 Japanese and other visitors went to the German Pavilion of whom about 40% listened to the German music at the dome Music Auditorium. Therefore, millions of Japanese and other persons visiting the Expo '70 from the world heard your new electronic music.

All the leading Japanese newspapers—*Mainichi, Asahi, Yomiuri, Sankei, Nihon Keizai, Japan Times,* etc.—gave excellent reports of the Stockhausen electronic music. *Yomiuri* wrote the Stockhausen electronic music is a "must" for music lovers. *Asahi* wrote Stockhausen electronic music opens an entirely new future for the world of music. *Mainichi* wrote Stockhausen electronic music is the climax of music at the German Pavilion. *Nihon Keizai Shimbun* writes music lovers have great interest in the German Pavilion. *Sanyo Shimbun* writes electronic music by Stockhausen is the center of attention for music lovers. *Shizuoka Shimbun* writes at the German Pavilion, people ranging from high school boys and girls to old people came to listen to electronic music. *Shimane Shimbun* writes the German Pavilion Music Auditorium features new pioneering electronic music techniques. Both *Mainichi Shimbun* and *Asahi Shimbun* write that Stockhausen new electronic music revolutionizes music of tomorrow, and makes a great contribution to modern music.

Our public opinion survey at the Expo made in cooperation with the Video-Research Company, Japan's leading market research company, reported that the German Pavilion was the No. 4 most popular pavilion at the Japan World Exposition (after the USA, USSR and French pavilions). At the German Pavilion, the biggest attractions of Japanese and other visitors before entering the pavilion were electronic music and industrial exhibits. When polled after they visited the German Pavilion and other foreign pavilions at the exit of the Expo '70, they reported the Stockhausen electronic music and the multi-vision motion pictures (both futuristic) created their deepest impressions at the German Pavilion.

Sankei Shimbun survey of Japanese opinion in September 1970 showed that 12 Japanese liked to one who was not impressed by the German Pavilion. Of those who liked the German Pavilion, their greatest reasons were the futuristic multi-vision movies in Hall A, Stockhausen electronic music in the Music Auditorium, medical exhibit of the human heart in Hall C.

Japanese and other visitors polled in public opinion surveys said they were disappointed in the Australian, Korean, Swiss, Canadian, British, Brazilian Pavilions with a big and wonderful outside, but nothing worth seeing inside. They also expressed disappointment in the American Pavilion saying the Moon Stone was just a stone like any stone you can see on the road or anywhere, but at least they can tell their friends that they saw the Moon Stone. The biggest disappointment was in the Scandinavian Pavilion with a beautiful outside and nothing worth visiting inside. The best pavilion outside with the gardens the visitors liked was the German Pavilion Gardens of Music.

As you can see by the enclosed sample clippings, which are only a part of the clippings on Stockhausen electronic music, Crown Princess Michiko and many other VIPs who heard your music expressed great interest and derived inspiration from your music. I am one of these people, and I think your electronic music appealing to the inner man—similar to my socioatomic (total social science) adrenocorticotrophicastrogenisotope (ACTHAI) theory of public relations and PR dynamic diplomacy for which I got my Ph.D. from Tokyo University—has much to contribute to the welfare of mankind in the modern world of frustration. It has been an honor to hear your electronic music and for having known you, and I hope to have the pleasure of meeting you when I visit Germany at the end of 1970 or early in January 1971.

With best wishes for your continued success in your important pioneering electronic music, and assuring you my fullest cooperation at all times, I remain

Sincerely yours,

Dr. Dr. Yoshitaka Horiuchi, President
Head of International Relations and Public Relations Studies
at Waseda University Graduate School
Former Diplomat and cabinet minister level official
at the Ministry of International Trade and Industry

"The mesh of the universe is the universe itself."
—Teilhard de Chardin

C: Debussy once wrote that "in all compositions I endeavor to fathom the diverse impulses inspiring them and their inner life. Is this not much more interesting than the game of pulling them to pieces like curious watches?" Could you say something more about the idea of "inner life" in your compositions?

A SOUND'S INNER LIFE; SOUND ENVELOPES

S: As early as 1954–55, I spoke of a single sound which might last several minutes with an inner life, and it would have the same function in the composition as an individual note once had. And by that, the dimensions of the music, the expansions of musical duration, have changed considerably. In statistical composition you need much more time to let such a sound—with an inner development, with all its particles—become clear, to spread it out in time and in the space of the frequencies. And the changes of the volume of such sounds with an inner life are completely different. Since the early fifties, we've been thinking of what we call envelopes of sounds, I mean the dynamic curves. Originally the envelope was a result of producing the sound on an instrument almost automatically. The piano key hits a little hammer which strikes the string, and then the string resonates; it has its own resonating curve. Even a violin sound has a very specific attack and, as we say, a body and a decay. This is also true for wind instruments. It all depends on the physical production of the sound —by breath, or by scratching or plucking a string. And there are a lot of noise factors in the beginning of every sound. When a string, for example, is first scratched with a bow, you don't yet have a periodic wave. So the particular kind of dynamic curve of such a sound is, to a large extent, given by way of the production of the sound. But with the electronic media you can make any envelope. This fact led me immediately to the technique of using, in a given composition, a limited number of very characteristic envelopes—as you can see them in the score of my electronic *Study II*, for example [see Fig. 1]—starting with the maximum and decreasing in loudness, but decreasing in one, two, three, four, or five subdivisions. Rhythm is involved immediately insofar as we subdivide the overall dynamic curve of a sound; and we have then to say when the envelope falls in amplitude, when it's raised again, etc. Another form would be that of starting with the minimum and increasing the loudness with several subdivisions of the envelope.

There are these basic forms: maximum at the beginning, maximum at the end, maximum at the center, maximum at the beginning and end. As we know, however, from the analysis of all the sounds that occur in nature, there are innumerable possible envelopes, but they're not all very distinct, so we must make a choice of very simple ones and then vary them throughout the composition.

"THE SECRET OF TIMBRE COMPOSITION
LIES IN THE PRODUCTION OF
VERY SPECIFIC CYCLES OF RHYTHMIC CHANGES."

The composition of the dynamic envelope doesn't necessarily have to apply only to one sound; it may be a whole crowd of sounds which can't be individually analyzed in the listening process. Instead you get an average color as in a pointillistic painting by Seurat; the figure you see is the result of many differently colored dots. *Klangfarben* or timbre composition isn't just a matter of changing the overtones, as many people think, or working with filters and filtering out or adding overtones or noise bands of certain widths. The secret of timbre composition lies in the production of very specific cycles of rhythmic changes. At first it's not so important what these changes are because you speed them up to such an extent that the resulting timbre is a newly perceived unity. It has a certain timbre characteristic, and you don't consciously analyze how it's composed in its microstructure, you

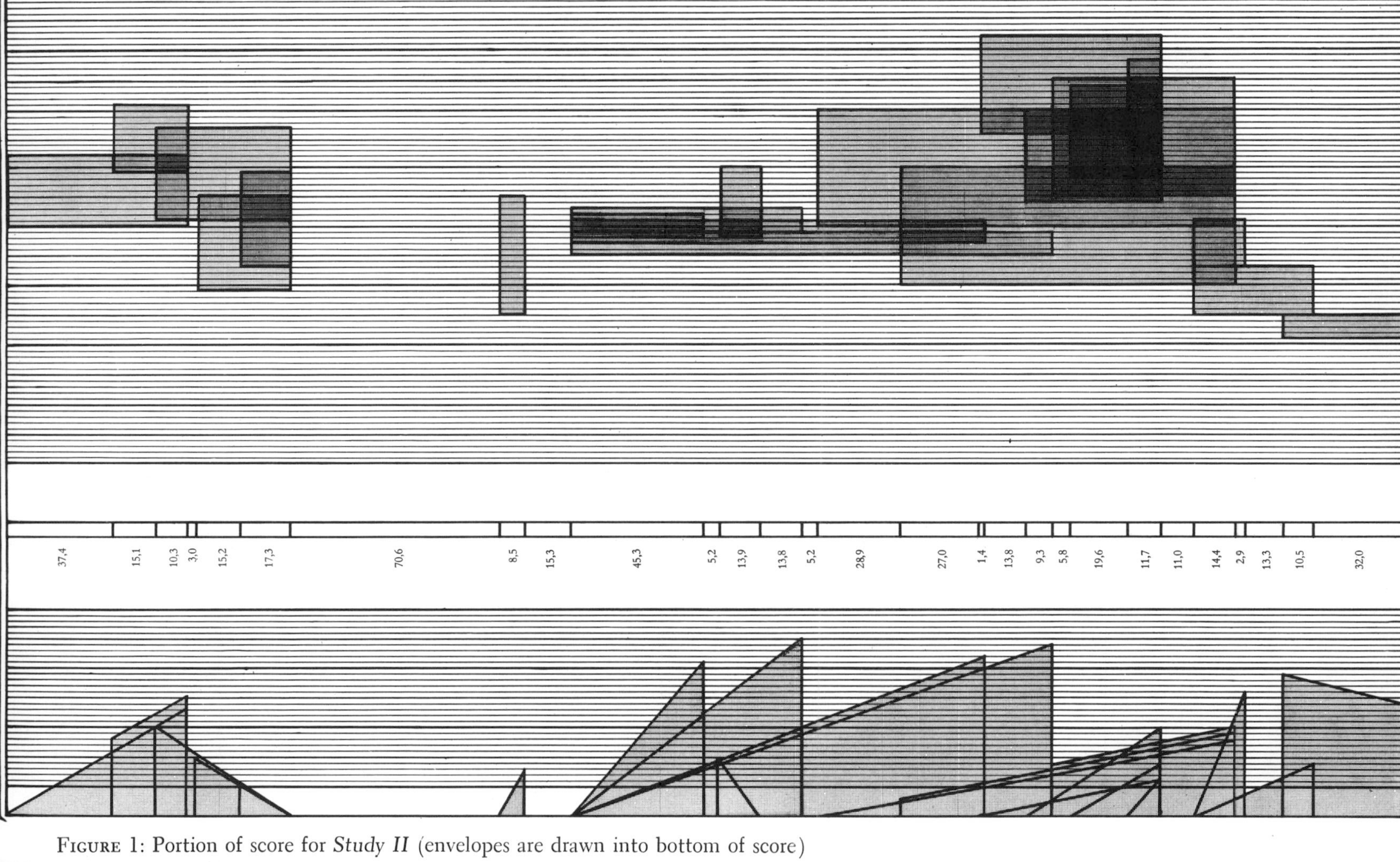

FIGURE 1: Portion of score for *Study II* (envelopes are drawn into bottom of score)

can no longer analyze the original components once such a sound is obtained, since the same timbre can be obtained in many different ways. So this process can't be reversed once certain timbres are produced. The timbre is thus basically the result of a rhythmic microstructure which is speeded up enormously so that all the parameters become interchangeable somehow because you can determine a whole group position only as a sequence of dynamic changes. And if these dynamic changes, no longer heard as individual changes in a dynamic curve, occur fast enough to take the shape of the envelope of an individual cycle in, let's say, a periodic wave of a thousand cycles per second, then these dynamic changes produce the impression of timbre.

STUDIO EXPERIMENTS: ENLARGEMENT OF THE MUSICAL PARAMETERS

Everything can be interpreted as being dynamics. Everything can also be interpreted as a change of rhythms. Very early on I made some experiments: let's say splicing electric pulses that were produced with a pulse generator in different rhythms and speeding up these rhythms in periodic sequences. What I first did was make different distances, measured in time—let's say in inches on the tape—from one pulse to the next, then from the second to the third; let's say this was a serial structure of different durations, or distances. I could also achieve the same result simply by taking a sustained tone and changing its dynamic curve—let's say very loud, third degree of loudness, sixth degree of loudness, second degree of loudness, fifth degree of loudness, seventh degree, etc., in a row. And I could do this periodically with a potentiometer and then make a loop of it, speed this up, too, and I'd obtain the same result as I obtained with the pulses in different rhythmic intervals. It became very clear to me that certain aspects of time composition or spatial composition—insofar as we mean the different energies of air pressure, which are dynamics—can lead us to the same results. It's just a matter of attaining something the quickest way; and it shows that these parameters are only theoretical parameters that make a certain method of sound production composition possible. But you could approach music entirely from any one of these aspects and achieve music that's varying in all parameters, I mean in all the parameters of perception—a changing of color, rhythm, dynamics, even a changing of the space position.

You know that space impression is just a question of time delay, of phasing. So I don't really need to put the original sound sources at different distances in the hall if I'm able to make the sound artificially with these particular phase proportions. The sound can move from the left to the right though nothing that produced the sound physically has moved in that direction. As I said, this is a question of a sound being more or less out of phase with itself, within microtime units, very small time units. . . . Again, let's take the example of a thousand-cycle tone which is approximately the C in the third octave of the piano above middle C. One single period of this sound is one thousandth of a second, and this period must be out of phase with itself in order to give the impression that it comes from different places.

HISTORICAL DEVELOPMENT OF MELODY, RHYTHM, DYNAMICS, TIMBRE COMPOSITION, MUSIC IN SPACE

I'm constantly occupied with the enlargement of the traditional parameters. It's sometimes worth looking at these things historically. The most developed characteristics of Western music —though not only Western music—are those of melody. But perhaps before there was pitch construction, before people sang melodies, we made sounds like animals. Even though one stays on the same pitch, a change of timbre gives certain information. When you hear a dog barking, the pitches are obviously less characteristic than the rhythmic sequence of these individual sounds, the accent on each sound, and then the timbre.

But what I mean is that melody is already something quite subtle. There was a long period in early Western music when you had the chironomics—the drawing of the movements of the melodic figures with the hand in the air—and people would sing according to the hand signs: you can still see the use of these signs in Indian music. The first Gregorian chant notation used neumes, which are nothing but these hand movements. There's the *torculus* which notates low-high-low; the *pes*—low-high; the *clevis*—high-low; and the *podatus*, the *porrectus*, etc. . . . You can investigate these things.

You also find this in Japanese No theater, where the people are all sitting reading a text, on top of which you see these signs, little lines going up or down, and little drawings showing the actors' costumes. And they can follow the melody perfectly and know how to sing the text just by following these lines which are relative, not absolute; the singer follows the tuning of the flute and the percussion instruments.

What I want to say is that melody is the first historically developed parameter. The St. Gall manuscripts show the first experiments in drawing lines. They had two colored lines—yellow and green—and only a hundred years later did they invent the five-line system to write the diatonic modes. Rhythm was still fairly flexible. Like the way we speak, it was important that the accents occurred on certain syllables and on the tones of these melodic fragments. But the moment they started to sing two voices together and wanted to control it a little bit better—the beginning of polyphony—once they became interested in the intervals that were produced, they then needed a common beat so that singers didn't enter too early or late. They needed to notate rhythm, so they started inventing signs for different lengths and subdivided each duration into multiples of units. Then you find binary and ternary forms; and you could sing the same music in either rhythm.

Historically, the differentiation of rhythm and the precise measuring of the durations developed much later than the pitches. And the third stage in this historical development is marked by the composition of the dynamics. During the baroque era we find terraced dynamics; the organs didn't have swells, and the harpsichord had fixed dynamics of piano, perhaps forte and mezzo forte, or just loud and soft, that was it. Many people say that Bach himself loved instruments that responded to the pressure of the finger on the keys like the clavichord. But he didn't compose crescendi and decrescendi, continuous changes of dynamics. The dynamics were practically neutral, having perhaps two levels. And we know that with the Mannheim composers a great revolution took place. People were standing up from their chairs and shouting and yelling when the first crescendo was performed.

Then the next revolution, which occurred at the end of the last and the beginning of this century, was that of timbre composition, the *Klangfarbenmelodie*, as Schönberg called it—making a melody just by changing different timbres and adding different timbres consecutively one after another without changing the pitch. And you can compose an entire piece by making the pitches neutral—the extreme case is *Stimmung*, for example—where you work out the whole musical structure through timbre changes.

So historically we have these four enormously important steps, which show a hierarchy right up to our present-day music.

Our instruments have perfect mechanical construction. The strings of a piano are logarithmically measured in order to produce an equal eighty-eight steps. In 1954–55 I wrote several articles in which I suggested the development of all parameters, so that they all would come to have an equal level of importance. This means that we need scales for dynamics, which would have at least eighty to ninety precisely measured degrees of dynamics, as on a piano; and I suggested even building a dynamics piano such that if you hit a higher or lower key you'd get a very precise degree of loudness. Or having a piano which has eighty-eight different degrees of timbre, a timbral scale, just as you have a color scale in the Oswald color catalog which shows about 360 colors.

Then naturally we enter the area of the whole psychology of perception. How many timbres can we really hear? How sharp can our perception be? This would apply to dynamics and to rhythm, because rhythm is always counted with bodily movements. Let's say that, as a conductor, I make movements with my hand in order to indicate time subdivisions or periodicities. Let's say a musician nods with his head or counts innerly. But without the counting process, we have very little experience in estimating the absolute duration of a sound. We always subdivide it as multiples or subdivisions of a certain unity which we count periodically.

And that's why the so-called irrational rhythms . . . it's unbelievable, that's a technical term in music . . . they're not irrational rhythms at all, just the rhythms of the numbers three, five, seven, nine, eleven, thirteen—subdivisions of a unity. In technical terms that's called "irrational." Imagine how primitive it is! It's not irrational at all, it's just *uneven*. The uneven numbers are called irrational. And when the first measures of fifths and sevenths came into music in the late nineteenth century, everybody thought the musicians were going crazy.

So what I mean is that the rhythmic system, in general, is far less developed than the pitch system; and timbre still much less than the rhythmic. The timbre parameter has only really been elaborated since 1950 through electronic music. With this new production of timbres, we now have a better system to describe precisely degrees between the dark and the bright, between the vowel and the noisy sound.

And the same is true now for music in a given space—let's say, in a hall or even outdoors. With *Gesang der Jünglinge* I had five speakers surrounding the audience. And the sound moved from one speaker to the next, sometimes in circles around the public, or made diagonal connections moving from speaker three to five, let's say. The speed of the sound, by which one sound jumps from one speaker to another, now became as important as pitch once was. And I began to think in intervals of space, just as I think in intervals of pitches or durations. I think in chords of space.

UNIFIED NOTATION

C: Do you think of all these levels at once?

S: Sometimes you have a kind of sound vision which is very global. Then you imagine certain sound events passing by, you hear this innerly. But in the practical work, you mainly start with one parameter and then relate the other parameters to the first one, the second one, the third one. You can't do everything at once because we no longer have a unified notation. For every sound characteristic we use a different symbol. I tried to find a unified notation so that with one sign I could indicate a sound which has a certain pitch, a certain duration, a certain timbre, a certain loudness, and a certain position in space. But imagine what a complex new notation you'd need. It would be like introducing into our Western analytical way of writing—also of writing music—which is always an additive one, something like ideograms.

C: The Chinese have something called *chien tzu* notation and also drawings of insects and flowers that aid in illustrating zither finger technique.

S: Yes, but that's mainly to describe a musical action. What I'm talking about now is an ideogram which, in one sign, describes all the characteristics of a sound, so that a musician doesn't need to read several instructions in order to make a single sound. Suppose that the position of a dot on the paper indicates the pitch—higher or lower. From left to right we'd indicate time. I've tried all sorts of different combinations—let's say that time would be from top to bottom and pitch from left to right. And loudness would just be represented by the thickness of the note (but this becomes complicated because the size of the dot also indicates time length, you see—if it's bigger, then it takes more space).

So the notation has many unsolved problems. Also, the instruments themselves don't help us, really, to play a piece which is very precisely scored in terms of dynamics. How can you ever produce eighty degrees of dynamics? And I'm not speaking now about the amplitude—I could use numbers from 1 to 80 and not care if anyone could realize it; that's not what I mean. I mean something more subtle—for instance an orchestra piece where you'd use the density of the instruments, a number of instruments playing the same sound in order to produce a certain energy. So that the *number of instruments* indicates the dynamics, and nothing else. If I take one instrument, two instruments, three instruments, etc., I'm following a scale of proportions. If I have twelve string players and I add a thirteenth, this doesn't change it at all. I must add at least another six in order to attain the same effect as I did by adding a second to the first one. We begin to see all sorts of problems which we just haven't studied.

C: Pierre Boulez writes: "Pitch and duration seem to me to form the basis of a compositional dialectic, while intensity and timbre belong to secondary categories."

S: As a matter of fact this is true if you simply analyze the situation as it is. But I think that perhaps the basic difference between Boulez and myself is that my interests have always somehow been more prospective, God knows why. Prospective in the sense that I've posed problems which couldn't be solved at the moment, which were futuristic, and which necessitated a complete change in the manner of teaching musicians, in constructing and using these instruments. Whereas Boulez is a more practical man, not moving too far away from what is available and where we are.

CHINESE MUSIC

C: On the other hand, the classical Chinese tradition emphasized pitch and timbre as the two main musical resources.

S: Yes, clearly, because their music was primarily heterophonic and linear. I said before that if rhythm has become so important to us it's because Western music has evolved toward polyphony. And in polyphony, the relationship between simultaneous elements is the most important in order to control what happens. Eastern music has quarter and sixth tones, much more subtle subdivisions of the semitone than we can afford in polyphonic music. Actually, nowadays we can switch in one and the same composition from parts which are more polyphonically composed to more linear ones. In *Kontakte,* for example, there are long sounds which are perfectly linear; there's no superimposition, no polyphony; and there I use intervals which are even smaller than the Pythagorean comma, let's say the interval from 800 to 810 cycles per second, which is normally not considered to be perceivable. That's not true at all, you can certainly perceive it. If it's a sound wave then you can hear very, very small intervals, but only if it's a single line and if there's nothing else that you have to listen to at the same time.

PYTHAGOREAN COMMA

Let me explain the Pythagorean comma. Let's say you have a frequency, and you build 2:3 frequential proportions on top of this frequency. Let's say Pythagoras has a string and subdivides it in the proportion of two to three; then he gets a fifth, the interval of the fifth in relationship to the fundamental. If you subdivide the fifth, then you get the fifth of the fifth, etc. You can do this twelve times, and then you reach the original tone again. But there's a small difference, which is the 80:81 proportion. It's not exactly the same frequency. If you superimpose fifths, if you start making a scale of fifths going upward from the bottom to the top of the piano—let's say you'd start with the low C, then after twelve fifths you'd again reach a C; this C on the piano is supposed to be the same C. But in mathematical relationships, it's not the same, there's a difference, and that difference is the Pythagorean comma.

The best scale for polyphonic and especially for homophonic—functional tonal—music is the chromatic scale, which, in fact, is made up of the superimposition of the twelve fifths I was talking about. This seems to me to be the optimum—if you make smaller intervals you get all mixed up.

MICROTONES

C: Are you interested in the elaboration of microtonal scales?

S: Certainly. What I've just said applies only to structures or to parts in music which are more linear, more melodic. We have to go into the microtones, and I've been concerned with this in electronic pieces (already in *Gesang der Jünglinge* I used several microtonal scales) as well as in *Mixtur*, where with the ring modulators I changed pitches within the semitones. But this can be heard best only in the more linear constructions. The denser the verticality—and I don't mean the band composition that we discussed before, band textures where you should probably *use* very small intervals in melodies, superimposed, in intermingling lines. If you want to *hear* the intervals and the chord constructions, however, then the semitone scale is best. The more linear the music, the smaller the intervals; the more harmonic the music, the larger the intervals. But not too large. You see, the semitone is ideal.

We can apply this in other ways: the noisier the music, the larger the intervals must be, which means the fewer the steps you should have in a scale. The purer a sound, the more steps you can have. That's why the chromatic scale is perfect for all of our traditional instruments which avoided noises. The moment you introduce noise you need scales which contain much larger intervals. And in *Kontakte* I've made a subtle relationship between the degree of a sound's noisiness and the scale that it's used in—there's a direct relationship. And the largest scale is only fifths, with the broadest noises which were in octave-wide noise bands. If I wanted to shift them in pitch, then I had to shift them a fifth in order to hear that difference.

C: But getting back to the Chinese tradition, the classical theoreticians emphasized the single tone as the embodiment of all intrinsic meaning, which implied an interest in the articulative aspects: inflections, trills, tremolos.

TRANSUBSTANTIATION OF RHYTHM INTO PITCH AND VICE VERSA

S: This was perfectly true for the time, but it shows the situation of their music and their way of thinking. Why, for instance, is the connection of two sounds as a figure, as an interval, less interesting than that of a single sound? Both are important. We don't want to have an exclusive system again. Let's embrace all the possibilities. So this is a special case, like the classical dynamics in physics or the classical laws of mechanics. They are not buried forever, but rather they're enlarged by relativity. And today we see that what applies to timbre can also apply to the movement of sound in space; they'd have never thought of it.

Now that we have speakers, why shouldn't we make the sounds fly? There's no reason to say that timbre and pitch are the most important aspects any longer. I can make a piece with only five sounds and never change the timbre and the pitch, but just change their position in space, which will automatically change the impression of both these parameters, too. Because if a sound passes at a certain speed you become aware of the Doppler effect—the pitch changes when a car passes by: the speed of the sound changes the pitch automatically. I could in fact compose pitches by only changing the speed of the sounds in space.

So what *is* the pitch? Is it the speed of the sound, or is it just a string that's tuned with a certain tension? Different impressions that we have in the pitch field can also be produced by dynamic differentiation. It all becomes relative.

C: So you'd believe in the relevance here of the law of complementarity.

S: Absolutely. It's all one truth, but it's the different aspects of perception, of which the system that we've lived with was always a function, that have given primordial importance to certain aspects.

C: When Boulez talks about a dialectic, he's mainly referring to pitch and duration, whereas you seem to be attempting to operate on all of these levels.

S: Well, one can be the other. Dynamic structuring can be created by differentiating durations. A rhythmic composition can be achieved by changing the position of sound in space: coming from the left, coming from the right—that's a change in time which automatically produces rhythm. Each parameter can take care of all the others.

I've written an article about the unity of musical time, describing what I'm doing in the studio. Let's say I have a rhythm, what I understand as rhythm, which means there must be a sequence of changes, any changes, which are between one-sixteenth of a second and eight seconds. Any longer than that and memory can't remember the durations precisely; and any longer than sixteen seconds and you begin completely to confound twenty-eight with thirty-two, for example; memory no longer works precisely. If *faster* than one-sixteenth of a second, then you also can't perceive it any more as individual changes, because fractions of time, of changes that are smaller than one-sixteenth of a second increasingly become what we call a pitch—if they're periodic—or a noise—if aperiodic. If you have a sequence of time variations of one-thirtieth of a second, then what you hear is a tone which has thirty cycles per second, it's a low organ sound. You see, the rhythm has become pitch. Or if I take any sound that has a certain pitch and spread it out in time, enlarge it, blow it up, so to speak, in duration, then I get a rhythm.

Let's say I produce something in the low registers—generally it must be low because up to now we haven't had the devices to transpose in time without transposing in pitch. We have only now a special machine, called the Springer machine, where you can stretch or condense time without changing the pitches; or you can transpose the pitches without changing the duration. (But this machine isn't really that good—it makes too many mistakes.) It's a semimechanical, semielectronic device. Sometimes I make a musical structure which, let's say in one piece of music, lasts three minutes, in the low registers. Using this machine, it's just three minutes long in any register. Then I speed it up to such an extent that it only lasts two seconds. Well, what was form before—the formal sections and the rhythm—is now perceived as the *timbre*. It's one sound which goes by in one or two seconds. It has a certain envelope—dynamic curve—a certain timbre, and it's perceived as a unity. But the characteristics of this sound are the result of all the structuring which, in another perspective—if it's stretched out in time—is perceived as rhythm or as formal characteristics.

We think or feel basically in one parameter, though our mental process, naturally, then subdivides these different times. If I sped sound vibrations up, then they'd go beyond the aural range of vibrations and you'd enter the next range; they would become warm. And if you sped them up still faster, you'd see them as light.

C: I wanted to ask you a bit more about the transubstantiation, so to speak, of dynamics into pitch or vice versa.

ROTATION TABLE EXPERIMENT: "YOU CHANGE THE PITCH BY ALTERING YOUR POSITION IN THE ROOM."

S: If revolutions of sound in space go beyond a certain barrier of revolutions per second, they become something else. With the Doppler effect, as I mentioned before, the speed of a sound determines its pitch. But let me tell you about a wonderful experiment I made which illustrates what I'm talking about.

I set up four speakers in four corners of a small studio of the Cologne radio—a very dry room with almost no echo. I had just received a rotation table, which I designed, that turned by hand. It's difficult building such a table because when it reaches about seven revolutions per second it has enormous centrifugal energy, and you have to have an enormous weight for it. . . . Anyway, I can attach a speaker to the center of the table and rotate it with the table. I can put any sound on the speaker, with four microphones around the table, and then record on four channels and reproduce this four-channel tape on four speakers in any fairly dry room. Let's say the movement of the sound goes in circular revolutions—though they could be slopes or spiral movements—around your head: you stand at the center of the room while I now speed up the revolutions per second. During the playback of the recording I speed up the four-channel machine. With fourteen or fifteen revolutions per second you still hear the movement circling around you. But suddenly you get an effect like that which you sometimes see in movies—where a chariot wheel, which isn't exactly aligned with the number of frames per second, appears to go backward.

C: It's also like the effect you get when you're in a moving train, looking out at the tracks and they start moving backward.

S: Exactly. And the same thing happens with sound; it starts dancing completely irregularly in the room—at the left, in front, it's everywhere. It's no longer periodic though the sound produced is revolving around your head. And if you go still faster something extraordinary happens: the sound stands still: it's no longer heard outside of you, you hear completely within your body. You *are* the sound physically. When you move your head slightly to the left, all of a sudden you're hearing an octave lower because you're subdividing the number of speakers by two: you come closer dynamically to the two speakers on your left side. If you take a step forward toward the corner, you're hearing only one fourth, two octaves lower. Though there's no change of pitch whatsoever, *you* change the pitch by altering your position: you make your own melodies by walking in the space.

C: You've said that everything that applies to the microcharacteristics of a single sound also applies to an entire composition. When you start working on a piece, do you first think in terms of the smaller or larger aspects?

S: The method changes during the course of composition. Sometimes I start with the small and go to the large; other times I subdivide or derive the small from the large. It depends on what comes first in my imagination. If I don't relate to imagination at all, if the music I compose is just the result of certain combinatoric activities, then I'm amazed myself by what's coming out of it.

C: Boulez has written that there's sometimes "a deep-rooted antinomy between global and partial structures; even though the latter may have been 'foreseen' as subordinates of the former, they acquire, through their own particular lay-out, an autonomy of existence, a true centrifugal force."

RHYTHMIC CADENCES IN MOZART'S MUSIC

S: It's always true, and different systems of music in diverse cultures demonstrate clearly what he's saying. In particular, our own traditional music's harmonic system reveals precisely the relationship of harmonic and rhythmic values. I once analyzed the rhythmic cadences in Mozart's music. And what I meant to show was that there are very precise cadences which are based on different types of syncopation and regular resolutions, just as pitch cadences or chords are based on dissonances and consonances. I primarily described sixteen different forms: anticipation of syncopation, delayed syncopation, etc. Just as the seventh, in classical harmony, has to be resolved into the octave or the sixth, so must a certain syncope. I've given all the models for measures based on two or three periods per measure, all the different forms of possible cadences. I showed that in Mozart's music—and it's the real secret of its perfection—there's a real counterpoint going on all the time between harmonic and rhythmic cadences. For example, you'll have an opening harmonic cadence—let's say the fundamental triad and then the dominant. At the same time Mozart might use a rhythmic dominant and tonal triad [demonstrates on piano]. Thus the rhythmic syncopation dum da-*dum* must be resolved into the simpler da-da-da—from the rhythmic dominant into the rhythmic tonic: a closure. Harmonically, however, Mozart presents the opposite—the opening of a cadence—allowing a counterpoint between rhythmic and melodic cadences.

There's a fantastic interplay. Let's say you have a period which lasts eight measures, during which you make a rhythmic opening and a harmonic opening and closing. This music is still open to continue, whereas at the very end of an entire movement everything's closed. . . . The same thing applies then to dynamics: rather than doing them all equally, without changing any duration, I can form cadences just by changing the degrees of the dynamics and work with them in such a way that they're parallel with the harmony and pitch relationships, or against them. Imagine the interplay among rhythmic, dynamic, and pitch cadences! If you want to include the timbre cadences, you can go from a certain degree of noisy sound to pure sound, which is always perceived as a resolution, as something purifying, while at the same time the other parameters take other cadential directions.

C: Was Mozart doing this consciously?

S: Well, by Mozart's time the rhythmic and pitch proportions were completely prepared by previous composers and the evolution of music. I don't think he needed to think about it. It's like when you learn how to write in school; the syntax, the grammar is clear, so when you write a sentence you don't reflect why you're writing like that. Mozart didn't *need* to think about it, but I think he knew what he was doing.

C: In an influential essay you published in *Melos* magazine in the fifties, you discovered and analyzed the important parametric aspects of Webern's *Concerto*. It seems your elaboration of the hidden unity in Webern's music is similar to your analysis of Mozart.

S: Certainly since Webern the four major parameters are actively taking part, not with equal differentiation and importance, but they *are* consciously taking part. You see it in his sketches—rows of the time values and of the timbres which, at this time, were represented only by the instruments. Today we don't need to say that we've only as many timbres as the number of our instrumental sounds. We can make any number of timbres with the electronic media or by transforming the sounds that we find, recording and transforming them into any other sounds.

SERIALISM

C: A number of musicians, thinking that you've gone on to other pastures, have wondered what your ideas are now concerning serialism.

S: Most American composers identify serialism with historical time. And this is really childish. Because serialism means nothing but the following: rather than having everything based on periodic values in any parameter, what we do is use a set, a limited number of different values—let's say 1, 2, 3, 4, 5, 6. And a series which is based on a scale of different values is simply the permutation of these individual steps in a given scale. We have two conditions to follow. In order to have a serial sequence of individual values—whether it's pitch, timbre, duration, the size of objects, the color of eyes, whatever—we need at the base to have a scale with equal steps. If we leave out certain steps of a scale we get a modal construction, as in old folk music. Chromatic music is the most neutral kind because it doesn't seem to belong to any particular style, it incorporates all the other scales within itself—you use all the steps with equal importance. In serial composition, we use all the notes within a given scale of equidistant steps. It could be 5, 13, 15, or 32 to an octave—32 is an important scale. But we have to use them, statistically speaking, with an equal number of appearances so that there's no predominance, no one tone becomes more important that the other. And we don't leave out notes. I make a series, a particular order of these scalar steps, and use this as a constructive basic principle for certain sections of a composition.

LE CORBUSIER

As I've said, you can apply this to anything—Le Corbusier's modular system, with its red and blue scale of proportions, for example. He designated the subdivisions of the human body in order to find the golden section. For the Mediterranean man he made a special scale, and another foı the northern man who was on the average a bit taller. He stated that you could use all the measures of this scale, permutate them, and make series—then create, for example, a facade of a building with the permutations of these basic measures. Or prefabricate all the elements for a large skyscraper or a whole city.

So serial thinking is something that's come into our consciousness and will be there forever: it's relativity and nothing else. It just says: Use all the components of any given number of elements, don't leave out individual elements, use them all with equal importance and try to find an equidistant scale so that certain steps are no larger than others. It's a spiritual and democratic attitude toward the world. The stars are organized in a serial way. Whenever you look at a certain star sign you find a limited number of elements with different intervals. If we more thoroughly studied the distances and proportions of the stars we'd probably find certain relationships of multiples based on some logarithmic scale or whatever the scale may be.

C: But you're not using the serialization of music parameters in your recent compositions, are you?

S: Certainly. Only *more* than previously. Which means that since the end of the 1950s, I've no longer applied the serial technique to the *quantitative* differences of things—of inches in duration or of decibels in dynamics—but to the *qualitative*. I give a value to what I perceive as a unified impression of a certain sound event. Naturally this can't be analyzed as easily, because it's qualitatively defined. It's not like a soup made with many spices, additionally; it's one unified event. And next to it I put another unified event which has certain things in common with it. There's nothing in the world that doesn't have something in common with any other thing. How much things have in common determines the scalar relationships. If the differences between the things are more or less equal and are qualitatively perceived as being equal, then again we have a scale. I can perceive entire complexes or sound events as one unity, put another next to it, and treat them as serial unities.

"NATURE CREATES DIVERGENT SPECIES BY EXPANDING CERTAIN PARAMETERS."

C: I was looking through a book that's on your shelf—*Organisms, Structures, and Machines* by Wolfgang Wieser—and all those extraordinary illustrations suggest what you're saying about serialism.

S: It's amazing to see how one type of fish is transformed into another just by the blowing up of one parameter. Let's say you have a fish that's a certain size, length, and form: if you place it in water that has a higher electrical charge or more warmth for a longer time or put certain chemicals into it, you'll then see the fish blow up vertically and become a completely different species. You can observe how nature creates divergent species by expanding certain parameters—blowing them up or shrinking them. Parametric transformations—that's what serial music is all about.

C: Why all these musical "schools" then that claim to represent the correct approach?

S: It's a kind of self-defense. One system wants to define itself by denying others. What we call serial music is based on a serial way of thinking. Every element that participates in a form at a given moment must have its own time and space to develop. You don't suppress or make hierarchic forms in which certain elements are automatically subdued forever, as in the tonal system.

BOULEZ ON MUSICAL "SPECIALISTS"

C: In terms of the fragmentation of the musical community, Boulez has criticized what he calls musical epigones and persons who establish certain provinces for themselves; and he disparages what he terms "epidemics": "There was the year of numbered series, that of novel tone colours, that of co-ordinated tempi; there was the stereophonic year, the 'action' year, the 'chance' year; the 'formless' year is already in sight, the word will spread like wildfire. Let no one suspect me of over-facile polemics, for proofs abound, as do slavish and minor talents; for this reason I will go no further but will simply state that all collectivity, especially when it is restricted, as with a collectivity of composers, generates changing fetishes: numbers, large numbers, space, paper, graphics . . . information theory . . ." According to Boulez, "choosing the basic ideas in terms of their own specifications and logical relationships seems to be the first reform urgently needed in the present disorder."

S: Yes and no. That's the attitude of the man who wants his garden in order. There's always the danger, if you go too far in this direction, of eliminating the game of life. All these people he mentioned are also useful somehow. He forgets that in all fields of science or applied science there exists increasingly a society of specialists. So if Mr. Ligeti concentrates mainly on one problem—Mr. Xenakis even more so—then it's like a doctor who specializes in a certain part of the body. But if he does a little research, he knows more than Mr. Boulez does because he's dealt with the problem for several years. And why not? It comes back to the collectivity, and we can use it. Specialists exist in the field of music as they do everywhere.

We always think that the great artist should be a person who embraces the whole world as much as possible and integrates rather than chops things up. But there are people who have written practically only songs or only a certain kind of piece in one style and have done beautiful work. We think of Goethe as a greater artist than . . . Mörike, for example. But Mörike had his own qualities. So going very deep and specializing on one point is also necessary in the total situation. It's like in science where every year there's a Nobel Prize for important work. Why not in music? I don't see why we should be against this.

I understand what Boulez is saying, though, and it's true, too. Albers, for example, always paints the same kind of squares within squares with all the combinations of colors possible. Still there's something in it. He's become a unique thing in the world. But this uniqueness by exclusion is a very special kind of quality. You can always immediately identify this "style." A vaster mind, however, tries to compose a polyphony of styles: one style for him is what a single *sound* is for another person.

History tells us that only at certain periods of time are such beings possible. They need four eyes—two looking into the future and two into the past—and also a very lucky constellation of life events. They need so many skills at once and a long time to develop them. Certainly Bach was such a person, though his followers accused him of being too conservative. Which seems strange to us now because he was really an embracing, great mind. But also history helped him to be in this position. And for Goethe it was the same.

SPACE-AGE CONSCIOUSNESS

Today we're in the opening period of a completely new era. But consider what babies we are when we think of the speed of the cosmos. In 1980 they want to go to Mars or Venus. Compared to all the stars that exist, what an embryonic state this is in the space age! Yet it revolutionizes everything: our time concept, the concept of how long our bodies will have to last in order to travel several thousand light-years. We must transform our bodies, which are completely relative nowadays: the human being has been made relative by its consciousness.

C: It would be interesting if human consciousness could be expressed in all its possibilities on some kind of computerized X-ray paper.

S: Invent one, and then you're a genius. The space travelers would be grateful if you could modulate a wave with a human being who has been transformed into purely electric information and let it reappear on a distant star. . . . I'm really not interested in staying in this body for an unlimited time because certainly I want to fly without airplanes and go much further and faster. I want to see much more than my eyes can see and hear much more than my ears can hear. I expect as much as possible since I think that at every moment you prepare the next state. And I don't think this happens just for nothing. You can speed it up. You can achieve in one lifetime what another being can achieve only in a hundred.

Kataragama,
Ceylon, 1970

Left: With Edgard Varèse, Hamburg, 1954

Opposite: Stockhausen concert in the caves of Jeita, Lebanon, November 1969
MANOUG/NATIONAL TOURIST COUNCIL OF LEBANON

Below: With Igor Stravinsky, Donaueschingen, 1958

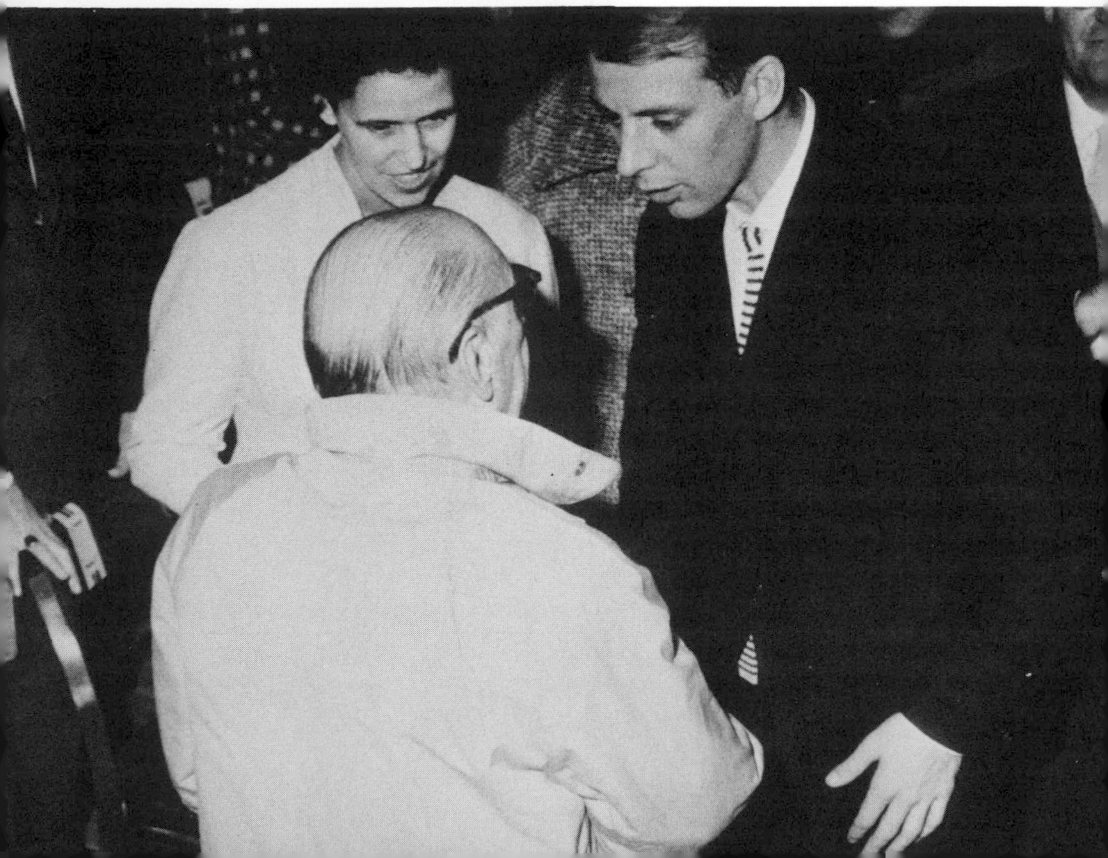

Zum

1958

Stockhausen with his children. Back, left to right: Markus, Majella, Christel, Suja; front: Simon and Julika.

Opposite above: Konigswinter, Summer 1964. Top, left to right: Carolyn Brown, Merce Cunningham, John Cage, Doris Stockhausen, David Tudor, Michael von Biel. Below, left to right: Steve Paxton, Karlheinz Stockhausen, Robert Rauschenberg.

Opposite below: At the Brussels World Fair, 1958. Left to right: John Cage, Henk Badings, Mauricio Kagel, Earle Brown, Henri Pousseur, Luciano Berio, Marina Scriabine, Luc Ferrari, Pierre Schaeffer. Seated: Karlheinz Stockhausen.

Opposite: Karlheinz Stockhausen, London, 1972
ALEX AGOR

Aus den Sieben Tagen (From the Seven Days): Stockhausen with potentiometers and filters; seminars at Böllenfalltor, Germany: September 1969.
WERNER SCHOLZ

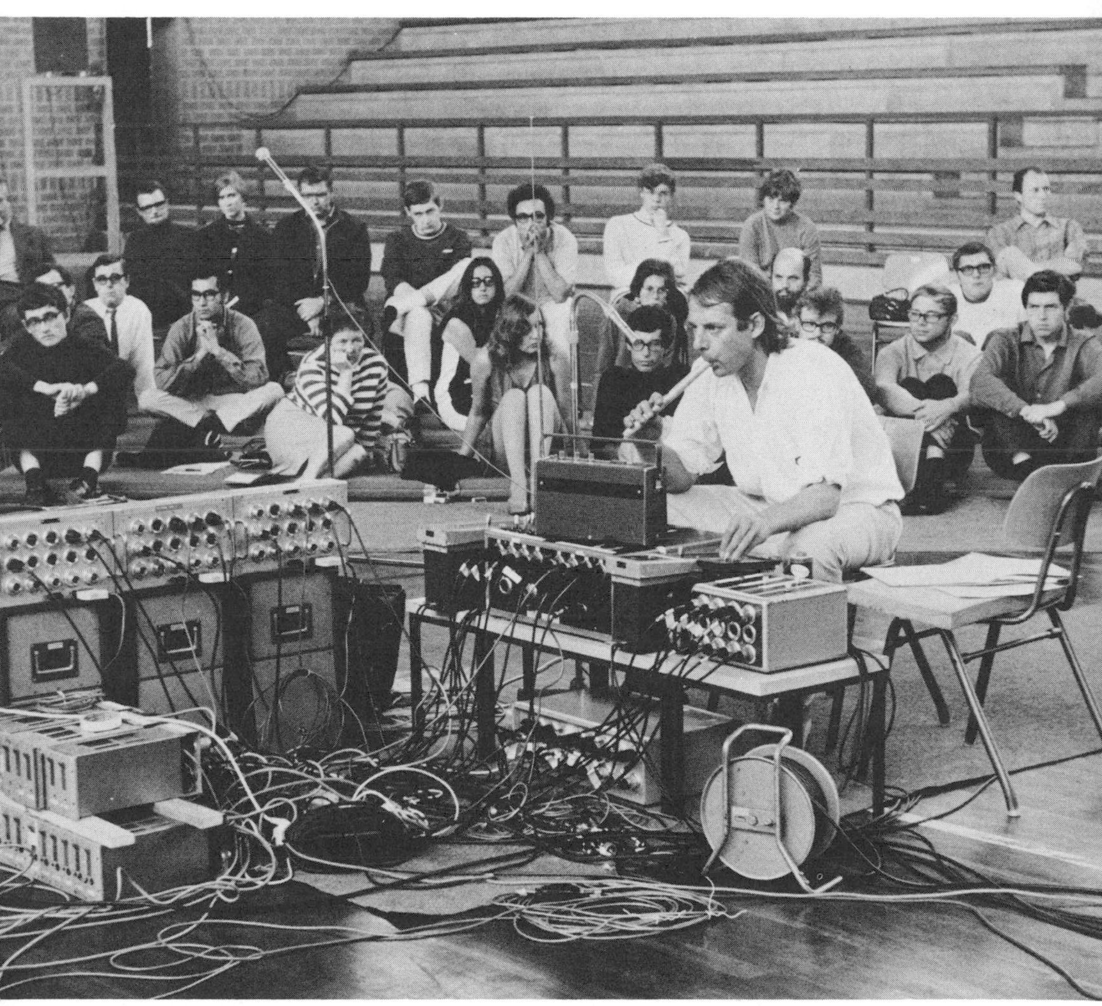

"The value of the dwelling is in the dweller."

ON BEING CALLED "AUTHORITARIAN" OR "RADICAL"

C: Persons have criticized you for being either too authoritarian or too radical.

S: If you achieve a certain independence in your work, you're automatically attacked by all sides, last but not least by your own colleagues in the different countries. It's fairly difficult nowadays for composers in general, and in particular for younger composers, to get performances or teaching jobs. And if someone like me has all his works regularly performed—very complicated works like *Gruppen* for three orchestras; *Carré* for four orchestras and choirs; or *Mixtur*, which requires a lot of electronic equipment, four sound engineers, another four persons playing the sine-wave generators, a lot of rehearsals—then there's automatically a lot of jealousy. And I can understand this feeling. Then, there's also another reaction coming from people who have a traditional musical education and are very much disturbed by what I do.

When I first went to America in 1958, I gave thirty public lectures in six weeks; all were in different cities, mainly on university campuses. I remember I was openly attacked several times while I was speaking by people who were shouting that I was a Communist. It was during the McCarthy period, and that was the greatest insult. Some people even called me anti-Semitic, I don't know why. I had said in my lecture that the opera is a remnant of bourgeois society, which in this context just meant the people of the so-called cultural "middle class" who wanted their entertainment—something which is still continuing in European cities. I said that this institution lives on an old-age pension and is certainly no longer vital. Very few important operas have been composed during this century. But people took it as a personal insult that I formulated it in this way.

I've also had protests from so-called left-wing students. You can nowadays harm a person in Germany—even more than in France or Italy—by calling him authoritarian. In Eastern European countries I was accused for several years of being a capitalist. At the Brussels World's Fair the official Russian speaker said that I was the incarnation of the Western capitalistic system and of Western decadence. These were also the words used during the Third Reich, with slight differences, against Schönberg, Berg, Webern, and Stravinsky. The method is always the one which is conditioned by the political fashion.

STUDENT DISRUPTION OF AMSTERDAM STIMMUNG PERFORMANCE

C: I gather that hecklers disrupted a performance of *Stimmung* at the 1969 Holland Festival.

S: The newspapers wrote that there were about a dozen so-called provos, several of whom were composers. We started performing—it started off unusually well—and after twenty minutes some people in the hall started a comic imitation, making somewhat similar sounds to those of the singers, then meowing or barking like cats and dogs. I saw that the singers were very worried, it was the first time they were so openly disturbed. They were beginning to become imprecise, concentration became quite impossible. So I stood up and asked the man sitting near to me to switch on the lights. I then said: "Let's at least finish this music before you react. It's impossible to perform this music with these noises. For those who are making these noises I recommend that you leave the hall because the piece will continue in the same way as it began, it won't change." We switched off the lights again, and for the first two minutes everything was quiet, but it started up again even more loudly. I stood up and went to the musicians and said, "We're going home now. It doesn't make sense to perform under these circumstances." They switched on the lights, and I began packing the cables. All of a sudden a crowd of young people rushed on the stage, got hold of the six microphones, and took advantage of the fact that this performance was a direct radio broadcast. They made a kind of a manifesto for themselves and their own interests and then started a discussion among themselves. One said, "Why did you do this?" to one of his friends, who responded, "Well, you see I felt I should participate." Peter Schat, the composer, said to another, "This piece isn't made for it. You can do it for another piece, but not here." He got the answer, "What does it mean if in music performed today I can't react the way I want. I felt that I should make these sounds, and if the music doesn't accept it, then it shouldn't be performed. The music is authoritarian."

I was backstage and was asked if I would come up to defend myself, and I said, "Defend myself from what?" The man—it was the composer Andriessen—said, "Well, you were criticized. Make a stand and come up." I said, "If you don't let me finish my musical phrase, I don't think I should have a discussion with you." He was very furious and went on the stage and announced that I wouldn't talk to them. That was the end of it. The German radio stations all said it was a political action against my "too authoritarian music."

The right-wing papers, on the other hand, say that my music supports what they call the vandalistic, anarchistic spirit that manifests itself in young people today and that my music is just the right drug to excite them. I don't think we should give all these things too much importance. When Frankfurt radio reported on the reaction in Amsterdam—which was the only one of that kind out of more than 120 performances—they said that the music lacked social necessity. This is the sentence that has become a kind of a tag: "lacking social necessity." This is what some Russians say about music that they think is abstract and not "for the workers." They said it in Gerimany during the war, and they might say it in China, too. They don't realize that I might be one of the workers who works the hardest.

MUSIC AND SOCIAL "REALITIES"

C: I'd like to believe that the kind of unity one experiences in your music might be able to manifest itself on a social level as well.

S: Then the music functions as a wonderful experience of nature. You can bring the most unconscious being who's just committed the worst crime to a place where a natural miracle takes place. In every being there is still something that vibrates and shows it's a human being. Nobody has made himself.

C: I still can't understand how someone can listen to a Bach cantata or your music and then go out and actively support situations that are destructive of human dignity.

S: Well, it would be more interesting to try and understand it, rather than stopping the question and just making some kind of judgment.

C: In *Mikrophonie I*, you talk about the idea of interaction and autonomy. Concerning *Telemusik*, you've referred to a vision of sounds, new technological processes, formal relationships, pictures of notation, human relationships. If we take the ideas of autonomy, interaction, and human relationships, and also the ways in which you've talked about how you go about giving time and space for individual sounds to exist, there seems to me to be a relationship you're making. . . .

S: It's an identity when I say that if people really listen to music they become the music. The music "forms" them because, first, there are acoustical waves which, on a physiological level, touch human beings, and then they're transformed into electric waves—they modulate the person. And that's why I say a person will never be the same after having listened to a piece, no matter what the brain records as the reactions of the body. Even if the reactions are violently against it, that shows that the system has been shaken up very much.

C: Do you think they'd be able to change social realities as well?

S: Little by little, very slowly, people would start behaving a little bit differently. First of all there are, theoretically, two possibilities. You become what you eat—and I mean by eating also what you hear. But you can also attain a certain level so that what you eat becomes what you are. Between these two extremes, people vary. Some are very strong and integrate and filter out and take what's good for them; and others eat anything and, naturally, become completely mixed up. Their stomach is never well equilibrated. And I think the more an individual develops a consciousness of what he is, of himself, the more he's able to transform what comes into him and integrate it into some substance or energy, which is also creative, creative for constructing and building things.

So the people become what they take in, but they also transform what they take in. The more highly developed a person is, the more he can digest; the digestive system, on a spiritual level, is very refined. When a certain kind of music is played somewhere, I must go away, because I know it will affect and transform me: it will pull me downward. And I quit.

C: Why not apply everything you've said about music to society—an ideal vision of what society could become. Wouldn't it be like your music?

S: No, that would be terrible, that would make everything uniform. That would cut out all the other possibilities. My music is only one possibility, and I myself still want to discover new music as long as I compose. That would be horrible because then the society would be just the way my music is; it would be very poor compared to a society that's influenced by many other things.

C: You do believe that people are in part defined by their surroundings.

S: Certainly, that's also true, that's part of it. On a general level, most people are the product of what comes into them. But then other people add a lot, because they live on an intuitive level, and they've learned how to take in influences that make them richer. They're always more than what they've been an instant before because they know how to take in cosmic influences and use them. It's very hard to define a person who has learned, through certain techniques, to open himself to cosmic influences.

C: Let's compare a fascistic society to the Horst Wessel song, and a truly democratic society to *Momente*. The former embodies the spirit of a certain kind of rigid, suppressing system; whereas the latter is open and free on the aesthetic level.

S: Let's say that you were theoretically able to wipe out all the music that you identified with the former, then the relativity would be taken away with regard to *Momente* and the Horst Wessel music, and it wouldn't be what it really is.

C: There are a number of young persons who love your music, but who are involved in what they consider to be a social struggle and would find some of your ideas irrelevant to their struggle. And some of them might then reject the music.

S: Well, then they can go away. There are certain seeds which only bring fruit a hundred years later. You can't even see them on the surface, but they've had a very important role. I think in the field of spirit there's nothing done in vain. And if these people think that they'd stop loving my music, then they're unmusical, really, they should stick to their experience, rather than being influenced by my words. They think I'm a guru? Well, they shouldn't identify me with anything, and they should make up their minds about the music itself.

HENZE'S NEW MUSIC

C: I notice that Henze has adopted radical political ideas, and yet his musical palette is from the twenties.

S: Because now very banal effects are symbolically identified with certain political slogans. He says, for example, that hitting a metal chain against a tam-tam will remind the people that there are people in chains. It just sounds *blang,* musically speaking. So everything becomes symbolic on a very primitive level.

C: In Henze's case, I might feel that his recent music is negligible, but that his politics are OK, his heart's in the right place, which creates a split.

S: You can say that the music is the brainwork of an individual who has made up his mind and is following a certain ideology, which means excluding a lot of other people who think and behave differently; even if you think they're bastards, you exclude them, and you think you're superior. Now, for an artist to make, under these circumstances, this kind of brain product . . . I'm not interested in this, neither in the producers, nor in the consumers.

THE FUNCTION AND MEANING FOR A TRUE ARTIST

I think the only function and meaning for a true artist is that of receiving something in terms of sound visions and then creating something which hasn't existed before and cannot simply be justified or explained by what's happened before—by what others have composed, by what history has provided. In that moment, as I have said, it doesn't belong to you. You're surprised as much as everybody else is by what you're doing. You function like a very—if possible—like a very good radio set which doesn't distort too much. And in that moment I shouldn't say that this is only meant for certain people or that it should be restricted only for people who believe in certain things I believe in. I can have a political opinion as a composer, but I shouldn't try to limit the music that comes about through me to what I think politically. That would be the worst thing in the world, because it immediately cuts out all the people who have intellectually different opinions. No, music is like the air. You inhale it and use it in order to live. Everybody has a different system, and it shouldn't be verbalized, what the sound and sound combinations mean; the more you verbalize the more you kill the music.

C: Here we are talking for days and days.

S: Yes, well why do we do that? I think that this book has more of negative function, which means "to clean," to take away, rather than to suggest things. To make the minds and the souls of the people who listen to this music free from preoccupations and meanings and particular interpretations of the significance of the music; then we've done a beautiful job. And not only for my own music. It's of no interest if you a write a book about me and it serves only my interests. If it serves music in general, the appreciation not only of music, but of all the materializations of the spirit and the different forms of the spirit—whether it's in sound or light waves: in any kind of materialized form, it may be in dance, in talk, in a gesture; in any sort of action that you can see, hear, feel, or smell—then the book should help everybody who reads it to have a new approach, to realize for the first time that he should start anew, as the music has been composed—fresh.

They shouldn't behave like tourists who want every object explained to them, every old temple, every ruin. They should just listen and then discover or feel what it does to them. And then, little by little, try to remember what it did last time and then approach it in a different way; and not start too early to put it into words, but listen innerly to the vibrations inside the body, what it does to them. That's the best thing. And that's why literature about or accompanying music should eliminate more rather than add—it should make the people fresh and empty.

THE ERASER AND THE FIRE: A COMPOSER'S BEST FRIENDS

C: Schönberg said that the composer's greatest friend is an eraser.

S: There's a beautiful event that comes to mind. I was in Finland, and one evening . . . who was it? . . . there was a composer. Finnish people never talk, or hardly talk; they drink and sit and stare in a corner, two or three minutes, no sound, and if there are six or seven people, it's quite strange. And I always felt I should say something, but I thought, What am I going to talk about? Well, I asked a question, after a time of silence. They would say, "Hmm, nice day," and then nothing for a long time. "A little cold; would you like to have another drink?" almost nothing. Then I said, "Do you also use the eraser very much? I use the eraser quite a lot; I erase more than what's left on the paper." This composer was staring at me, and then all of a sudden a big smile came over his face and he said, "No. Fire!" He burns all his scores because he's never satisfied with what he does.

C: You told me about encounters you've had: one, after the New York performance of *Hymnen,* with a bearded man in goat's cape, carrying a shepherd's stick, who showed you a copy of *Urantia* and asked you to be minister of sound transmission—he wanted you to decide on which sounds from the earth were worth preserving so as to project them into outer space by means of electromagnetic radiation, just before the coming destruction of the world. And you also told me about the group of young persons in Boston whose speaker walked up to you after a concert, staring as if in a trance, and asked you to be their leader.

MASTER-DISCIPLE RELATIONSHIP

S: I told them to use the music for discovering themselves and their divine destinies. Be your own leader. Consider that my music is your property. I mean if you rip it apart, if you step on it, you do it. . . . I tell them that I too am only the child of a higher being, so I transcend their attraction to me. It would be wonderful if everyone found his own connection with the divine. As we know from group psychology, however, people need a nucleus, and that's wonderful. But I say, I'm not the source. Look through me further on.

C: This reminds me of the principle of magnetism.

S: Many scientists are trying to find out how to electrify a piece of wood in such a manner that, without screws, you can attach it to a piece of metal. Our conceptions of magnetism are changing. And one of the biggest revolutions of the twentieth century is glue.

C: "Far out," they'd say in California.

S: They call it Love in California—that's the interpersonal glue. But I'm talking about it on a larger scale. The other day two men brought a large mirror—4 yards high and 2 yards wide—to my house. They tried to attach it to the wall with two screws, but since the mirror was too heavy it began to bend. So they took a new kind of tape glue, cut a one-inch strip, placed it behind the mirror, and pressed it against the wall. I asked them to add another strip, but when they tried to get behind the mirror, part of the wall came off. You just can't remove this glue. And this is the revolution: the "glue" that connects people and materials which up to now couldn't be attached. We're just beginning to discover the secrets of electromagnetism on a larger scale.

No matter where you are there's always a particle that has an atomic structure that attracts other particles. And when people say that I'm being authoritarian when I instruct musicians, I say: Go your own way, be your own sun. And if you're a planet, there's nothing wrong about that. I'm a planet, too, in relation to people like Aurobindo or, when I was younger, to Anton Webern. Or to a woman—sometimes I'm nothing but a little piece of metal with regard to that magnet. There are always magnetic forces, and if I have a magnetic force as well, then I should do something good with it.

C: Do you believe in a historical continuity that can only be revealed by an extraordinary individual consciousness?

S: There is a spiral once and forever in the cosmos everywhere, which means that you come back, but never exactly to the same place. The spiral is in itself bent; it's not going in one direction. You reach the same point of time and space many different times, but you're never the same because you're conscious of having been there before, which changes everything. And that is the spiral, ultimately, but this isn't the spiral that's usually drawn. Let's say you put fifty points on a piece of paper in random distribution—the number isn't important at this moment. Now you start from one point and go to any other, sometimes returning to one you've been to before. You're always moving. But it's not the same as reaching the point for the first time. You're always one *winding* higher in consciousness.

EAGLES

C: You once mentioned to me dreams you've had about being an eagle, and I gather you accepted this as reality rather than as some kind of symbolic idea.

S: Yes, I've had recurring dreams, and this is a very solid and concrete experience that has come many times. I am it. I fly, I have a feeling of pushing the air and I see everything from the perspective of where I'm sitting or flying. . . . But there's no point talking about it. If someone's had similar experiences, then it's completely clear to him—it's like talking about music—and if not, he'll just laugh because he doesn't understand.

C: Nietzsche wrote: "On the tree, Future, we build our nest; and in our solitude eagles shall bring us nourishment in their beaks. . . . And we want to live over them like strong winds, neighbors of the eagles, neighbors of the snow, neighbors of the sun: thus live strong winds. And like a wind I yet want to blow among them one day, and with my spirit take the breath of their spirit: thus my future wills it."

FLYING SOUNDS IN HYMNEN

S: In many works I've been able to realize, practically speaking in terms of sound, these experiences of flying. The sounds really make the movements of long waves, like pushing the air with one motion of the wings, then waiting and gliding. The long sounds which have these accents lose dynamics, regain them . . . and then the next push. I've felt it here in the throat for years and I didn't know how to realize it in sound—flying very silently without any movement.

There's a long section at the beginning of the second Region of *Hymnen* like this—a wandering sound. As a boy I watched over my grandfather's and uncle's cows for weeks and weeks in the meadows. We had nothing to do, so we made flutes while lying in the meadows. Or we'd fish. I remember very particular places I haven't been to for thirty-eight years—I was four years old, but I could show them to you now, it was so important to me. I'd just lie on my back for an hour or more, watch the clouds, and a small propeller plane would appear circling with a soft sound in the sky. This sound was drawing its lines in circles, it's been following me my whole life. And you find it again in *Hymnen*—these slowly wandering sounds in the sky.

I get very excited when I see big birds gliding. I was in Sausalito for half a year and spent some time at a nearby beach which is visited by very few persons. There's an enormous rock there with thousands of big black birds just standing and chatting.

And sometimes a few of them go for a flight. There's an upwind at this high rock, so most of the time they don't have to make any initiatory movement in order to rise. It's fabulous watching them for hours. The rhythms they make have hardly ever been expressed in music. Almost all the rhythms in Western music are those of the human body—when we march or run or walk or move slowly—the rhythms of our limbs and their subdivisions and multiplications. A work like *Hymnen* incorporates rhythms and durations that are no longer bound to the body.

C: Plotinus once wrote that he who loves music too much will be reborn as a bird.

S: I always say to my colleagues that musicians are the birds of the animals. That's very clear.

C: Insects, too [buzzes like a mosquito]. But that's something else.

S: It's interesting, though. The glissandos are very subtle.

RETURN TO THE APOCALYPSE

C: In our first discussions you talked about the possibility of the apocalypse . . .

S: I think it will be the most horrible story in mankind's history, it has never happened before on such a scale . . . though we know from descriptions of certain epidemics during the Middle Ages that these plagues seemed to have universal proportions for the people at that time. They gathered in the cities, which were built as fortresses, and when the plague broke out it was as if the whole world were on fire; psychologically it was as if the world were blowing up. Today I feel as close to someone living in Tokyo as a person then living in Cologne would have felt with respect to someone living in Hamburg.

C: In a sense the bubonic plague which occurred in most of the countries in Europe was the first example of international communications: disease was a kind of medium which connected all kinds of people.

S: That's an incredible idea. . . . But let's think now about the numbers of persons who will inhabit the world in the year 2000. The spirit can't rise if we continue to multiply bodies. I once wanted to raise the level of the soil behind my house. And I discovered that if you started piling up an enormous amount of soil, you had to build two concrete walls at both sides of this pile in order to make an artificial restriction; if the base kept on getting broader you couldn't easily bring the soil to the desired height.

If you multiply logarithmically the base of humanity by billions, you'll naturally have people who are only concerned with survival. We're being told that in ten years the average age will be 90 years old, and then later on perhaps 100 or 120 years. Eventually someone will be able consciously to leave his body when he wants to take on another form. I mean our bodies are very clumsy, really, compared to what we can imagine. So we could theoretically replace only those persons who wished to get out of their bodies or who died automatically.

THE SPIRIT AND THE BODY

C: They're talking about freezing people's bodies and thawing them out in the future.

S: All that's important is who inhabits the body, what kind of spirit it is, and that the spirit can choose the body that suits it. Any spirit wanting to remain deep-frozen is really a stupid spirit! It would be scientifically important, however, to know—let's say in a thousand years—how a body of today functioned. They'd look at it as we look at an old car, saying: Isn't that interesting?

C: Let's say someone died and another person was frozen. Could the latter's spirit enter the first person's body?

S: This happens all the time. I do it, and you do it with me. In dreams thousands of persons enter my body without being asked—we've talked about this earlier. But there's a certain idea in the East which posits a divine mission for the spirit such that it *has* to enter certain bodies—I don't believe that.

C: "Foul rag-and-bone shop . . ."

S: Have you ever been to the catacombs in Palermo? In one of them you can see six thousand mummies—their real hair, eyes, hands, and feet. The corpses are dried out, with leathery skins and long fingernails and the expression of the moment of dying on their faces. But there's one that is perfectly preserved in a glass box—a beautiful child, perhaps two years old, who looks asleep, though it died in 1923. . . . If someone remained there for several hours, he'd begin to talk differently about the body and the spirit.

C: It's like when you're on a boat moving away from shore and you're watching the lights disappear. When the soul departs the body feels sad.

S: It's just the feeling of something going away. And it's obvious that the feeling of sadness announces the new beginning. Ultimately I think that a person who wants to get out of his body will just do it without pistols or poison: you'd choose a place to lie down . . . and then you'd leave.

diary entries

THE BODY OF BLACK LIGHT

Tuesday evening: Stockhausen and I are reminiscing about mutual friends in Berkeley, California, where I and composer Charles Shere first met Stockhausen in 1966. For some reason, Stockhausen begins talking about the great Colmar altar painting by Grünewald. While searching for the reproduction of this work, he comes across a copy of the San Francisco poet Daniel Moore's hand-engraved and illustrated visionary poem entitled *The Body of Black Light*. "I haven't seen this for a long time," Stockhausen says. And hidden in between the pages is the Grünewald reproduction. I point to one spot in the second of the three triptychs which shows several luminous and transparent angels. "Yes," Stockhausen says, "this is my world!"

GENIUS AND WEALTH

Wednesday morning: Stockhausen's tax accountant pays a visit and gives the composer a present—a book by a Mr. Heuer entitled *Genius and Wealth*, in which the accountant has inscribed: "To add wealth to genius." "Quite a gift!" Stockhausen says, showing me the cover on which a bust of Wagner is blending into a gold sovereign. The table of contents promises the following portentous chapters: "Caesar: Kaiser on Credit"; "How Columbus Was Financially Betrayed"; "Banking House Voltaire"; and "No Capital: Karl Marx."

Lunchtime: Looking over the galleys of the third volume of his essays, texts, lectures, and poems soon to be brought out by DuMont Schauberg, Stockhausen remarks how on receiving a copy of his first published score *Kontra-Punkte*, he was so excited that he took it to bed. Now, checking these new galleys, he seems more the proud parent and less the romantic lover.

Afternoon: Stockhausen comes in to show me an interview he recently gave to a London newspaper, which he has just received and read. He points to one paragraph in particular: "Liking is remembering. When you like something, you're not aware of the fact that you've been that thing already before." "Yes," Stockhausen says, "I remember waking up in London and thinking, 'Liking is remembering.' I'd forgotten about this, but I still think it's true."

THE GOLDEN EGG: MUSIC THERAPY FOR CHICKENS (WITH A WORD FROM *THE SECRET OF THE GOLDEN FLOWER*)

The Golden Egg: At dinner, Stockhausen tells of an amazing experience he had at Arizona State University. In 1966, he was delivering a fairly technical lecture about electronic musical processes to an audience of what he assumed were graduate music students. Looking around at the students every once in a while, he began to notice that most of them were only half listening or daydreaming, obviously thinking about things other than sine tones.

"What kind of work are these students doing at the University?" a slightly nonplussed Stockhausen asked the music chairman at one point.

"Well," he replied, "they're doing special research . . . in the field of music therapy . . . with animals . . . chickens."

"Chickens?"

"Actually, yes. Would you like to see firsthand what they're doing?"

"Absolutely!" Stockhausen said.

They immediately drove out to a farm where, as Stockhausen entered a special barn, he saw hundreds of chickens perched on railings. He entered a small studio at one end of the barn, and, through its windows, watched the lights go off. Suddenly, a planetarium-type sun rose up along the walls, and, through speakers, strains of the Blue Danube waltz filled the barn. Corn started dropping out of little chutes in the ceiling, the music got louder, and the chickens, suddenly awake, began clucking along with Johann Strauss and laying eggs furiously.

"They turned the lights off, made the sun rise two or three times a day, and played more unbelievable waltz music!" Stockhausen told me.

"What would happen if the chickens listened to your music?" I wondered.

"They'd have diarrhea!"

"Not if they heard *Stimmung*."

"No," said Stockhausen, "with *Stimmung* they'd lay the Golden Egg."

Later that evening, I was reading *The Secret of the Golden Flower*—Richard Wilhelm's translation of a Chinese Book of Life—and came across the following beautiful passage which I immediately read to Stockhausen:

> In the Book of the Elixir it is said: "The hen can hatch her eggs because her heart is always listening." That is an important magic spell. The hen can hatch the eggs because of the energy of heat. But the energy of the heat can only warm the shells; it cannot penetrate into the interior. Therefore she conducts this energy inward with her heart. This she does with her hearing. In this way she concentrates her whole heart. When the heart penetrates, the energy penetrates, and the chick receives the energy of the heat and begins to live. Therefore a hen, even when at times she leaves her eggs, always has the attitude of listening with bent ear. Thus the concentration of the spirit is not interrupted. Because the concentration of the spirit suffers no interruption, neither does the energy of heat suffer interruption day or night, and the *spirit* awakens to life. The awakening of the spirit is accomplished because the heart has first died. When a man can let his heart die, then the primal spirit wakes to life. To kill the heart does not mean to let it dry and wither away, but it means that it has become undivided and gathered into one.

CRAFT AND STRAVINSKY

Thursday lunch: I express my amazement when I hear about the small amount of money composers receive for the commissioning of their works. "I've heard that Stravinsky has complained about the fees he received for his *performances,* compared to those of Artur Rubinstein and others," Stockhausen says.

"I'd give twenty thousand dollars if Stravinsky were just sitting here now," I say jokingly.

"I hope you have the money!" says Stockhausen seriously (as the spirits in the room whir by).

"I take it back!"

"Ah ha!" Stockhausen exclaims.

"But what would Stravinsky do with the money now?" I wonder.

"I don't know—perhaps buy a plot of land to bury Robert Craft in."

There have been rumors to the effect that Stravinsky wasn't too directly involved in his recent conversation books. (But if Craft has really been responsible for all the writing, then he has accomplished an amazing shamanistic act, since "his" Stravinsky is so much warmer and wittier than "his" Craft.) And ever since Stockhausen once questioned Craft's conducting abilities, Stravinsky's recent comments about Stockhausen have become nastier and increasingly critical.

"I've never believed that these texts came from Stravinsky," Stockhausen says. "I met him several times in person, and it's unthinkable that this man who was preparing himself for death—and as religious as he was—would become so petty and aggressively mean. He was basically generous as a person, and I don't think he would have put some of my colleagues and someone like me down after having praised my work previously. He would have simply remained silent."

STRAVINSKY AS ENGINEER AND WAGNER AS GAGAKU COMPOSER

Thursday evening: I ask Stockhausen if he has read the comment about *Stimmung* which appears in Stravinsky's and Robert Craft's *Retrospectives and Conclusions*: "Stockhausen's time scale is that of *Die Götterdämmerung*." And I wonder how Stockhausen now feels about both Stravinsky and Wagner.

"I share a certain attitude," Stockhausen says, "which dates back to the time when Stravinsky was very famous after the war—an attitude that reflected his so-called neo-objectivism and neoclassicism. You know, Stravinsky liked to be photographed with all the stopwatches and metronomes in his room. He wanted to give the impression of being a musical *engineer*, and this was necessary in order to get rid of all that emotional *cream*, those romanticisms which had given rise to a lot of self-expressionistic overstatements. And I can understand this dislike of Wagner.

"But Stravinsky should have understood that Wagner, more than any other Western composer, expanded the timing of European music: he would have been the best gagaku composer—if gagaku had been composed—or the best No drama listener in the world. Because he really brought forth this incredible *breath*, this duration which no longer depended solely on what the human lungs or limbs could produce.

"In his comments (via Robert Craft) concerning *Stimmung*, Stravinsky is probably referring to that one chord in *Die Götterdämmerung* which lasts several minutes. But Stravinsky never really understood what timbre composition was all about. He thought it was 'instrumentation,' which is only a small aspect of timbre composition. It's like painters always mixing colors in order to find a particular color for a specific painting. But it's no longer just a question of mixing pre-existing colors in order to discover their technical possibilities; it's rather that of going into the microstructure and leaving enough time so that the interferences between the vibrations can occur. The faster you change the pitch, the fewer the possibilities of timbre composition; the slower the pitch change, the better you can listen into the spectrum of the sound."

"It would be as if in *Petrushka* or *Agon* Stravinsky had made fermatas . . ."

". . . and you'd be able to meditate on and listen into the sound," Stockhausen replies; "—rhythm and melody would stop. Stravinsky is a language composer: he uses musical rhythm which is derived from talking, and practically all Western composers do this more or less unconsciously. And I think we should get away from this talking rhythm once in a while.

"I wouldn't give up the chance of allowing the listener the possibility of finding himself rather than always being attacked by changes. The faster the changes, the less you come to yourself. The more static and quiet the music, the more meditative it becomes. But, of course, that's not all of Wagner: he uses the sustained chords as a dramatic force. You can't do everything at once; you must pass from one state to another."

THE POPE AND THE CATS—A STORY FROM ROME

Friday: Late morning, Stockhausen receives a call from Italian Radio in Rome. It seems that a concert of his music, scheduled for October, has to be canceled. The reason, given after some embarrassed hedging by the RAI caller, is that two nights previously the Teatro Argentina was invaded by hundreds of cats who usually hang out in the ruins near the Piazza Argentina. A little after midnight they sneaked in and, according to the official, "shit all over the floors, the carpets, the seats, the red velvet fauteuils—everywhere!" It's going to take weeks to clean up the mess. And a concert which was supposed to have been presented for the Pope must now be postponed and given on the date originally set for Stockhausen.

After he hangs up, Stockhausen shows me the contract for the concert, which concludes: "This engagement is subject to cancellation by either party in the event of war, labor dispute, fire, epidemic, force majeure, or act of God." "This must be considered an act of God," Stockhausen laughs. "No, better still, force majeure. . . . Imagine the headlines: *Pope Reconsecrates Hall After Cat Catastrophe!*"

AN AMERICAN INDIAN FOLKTALE

Friday afternoon: Stockhausen's two youngest children, Julika and Simon, have come to visit, and late in the afternoon they walk over to a little wooden hut which rests about 150 yards from the main house at the edge of a steep hill, down and across which you can see several chopped-down trees, masses of autumn leaves, and fields surrounded by the seemingly endless woods. The hut contains nothing but an enormous haystack (and a couple of friendly field mice), where Stockhausen's oldest son Markus and friends often camp out when they visit. Today, lying back in the hay, Stockhausen reads his children a version of an American Indian fairy tale entitled "Star Maker," which he translates from English to German, embellishing and emphasizing certain details and episodes:

A young Indian named Algon, while hunting for deer, comes across tiny footprints in the woods. Suddenly a basket of silver reeds floats down near him, out of which step twelve beautiful maidens, stars glimmering in their long black hair, and all singing: "Their voices were low and clear and oh, so sweet—like the warbling of birds a long way off, or like birds singing in their sleep." Algon tries to catch the most beautiful maiden, but she and her friends jump in the basket which begins to rise and disappears.

Having fallen in love, Algon visits the medicine man, who gives him a sunflower seed wrapped in a tobacco leaf. "Place the seed on your tongue when the maiden appears," he advises Algon, "then make the most of your opportunity." The next time Algon sees the maiden dancing in the fairy circle in the woods, he follows the instructions and turns into a mouse. Wanting to play with him, the maiden catches him. Algon spits out the seed, becomes a man, and carries her to his village, where they soon get married and later have a child.

The maiden is always asking her husband where her home is. "It's much better," she tells him sadly. Soon Algon goes off to war. One starry night, she takes her child to the fairy circle where, as she begins to sing, she grows smaller. Constructing a basket out of star beams, she strews it with prairie flowers, after which she and her child climb in and float up to her home. Her son asks her repeatedly about his father, but she doesn't remember him. Then one night she dreams she sees him weeping and agrees to try to find her husband. They descend to earth where they are reunited, but the star maiden wants to go away again. Algon tells her that if she goes, he will, too. They return to the fairy circle, and, as the story goes, "either the basket grew bigger or Algon grew smaller," and they all rise to their home. Every once in a while, though, Algon returns to visit his tribe in the guise of a beautiful white falcon.

THE INTERPRETATION OF DREAMS

Saturday evening: Talking about dreams, Stockhausen says that some are announcements: "They're like master keys, and I immediately follow and act on what I've learned from them. But others simply clarify situations; they show several possibilities from which I make a choice in 'waking life.' "

I mention a dream I had a week before in Amsterdam, where I was visiting friends before coming to Cologne. In the dream I saw myself sleeping in a bed where I had become Stockhausen's music. And in order to protect it from a swarm of mosquitoes, I pulled sheets and blankets around myself. At that moment I woke up with the sound of mosquitoes all around my head.

"This dream," Stockhausen comments, "is a way of showing you that the book you're doing with me isn't a waste of your time and energy. I mean, why write a book about me? Why not just do your thing? So the dream justifies your interest as it also suggests that the book will help to protect my music. There are parts of us that want to question things in order to destroy them, they want to make everything relative; these are the uninvited guests, and they like to stay around as long as they can. But the dream is you as well, and here are the good spirits that protect that which is young and vulnerable."

"But your music . . ."

"Oh yes it is. My music needs protection."

"What do you think about psychology as practiced today?"

"Sri Aurobindo felt that psychology was in the state of childhood, and I agree. In itself it's very unconscious. And diving with unconsciousness into the unconscious of other people is misguided if not dangerous. Only if you've gained supraconsciousness can you bring light into the caverns of our subconscious. Most psychologists attempt to bring subconscious elements up into our so-called consciousness—but this is only a limited and transitional consciousness."

THE PIANO OF PAIN

Sunday dinner: Stockhausen recalls his first public lecture at the University of Pennsylvania where he was visiting professor for one semester in 1965. A few minutes into his lecture, he heard a high-pitched yelling sound. "What's that?" Stockhausen asked. The sound reoccurred. "My mouth was getting dry, and I was having trouble concentrating, so I walked over to the chairman of the music department, who was sitting onstage. 'Don't worry,' he whispered to me, 'I'll explain later.' " Stockhausen finished his talk, but before the question period, as the sounds of excruciation persisted, he said he wouldn't continue until he found out what was going on.

"Listen," the chairman told him at the side of the stage, "we're in the same building as the biology department, and they've built a new piano up there."

"What?"

"They play a keyboard that tests rats' threshold of pain—each note has a certain voltage, and there are differently colored lights ascending the keyboard—green, blue, then red [the killing threshold]. You know, some rats even go beyond the red."

"That's what he told me," Stockhausen tells me incredulously, "*some rats even go beyond the red!*"

"Imagine an electric chair like that," I remark, "where you could die to any piano piece on request!"

"What would you choose?" Stockhausen asks with curiosity.

"Maybe a piece by Morton Feldman."

"That would be the *most* torturous: with all those instructions to play as *slowly and quietly as possible,* death would take three days. No, I'd prefer Boulez's *First Piano Sonata* [hands slamming the table]—*bang!*"

TELEPATHIC MUSIC AND NERVOUS MUSIC PUBLISHERS

Sunday evening: After dinner, Stockhausen tells of a lecture he gave in Vienna in 1968 to a congress of publishing directors who protect "spiritual property" with regard to broadcast, recording, and performance rights. Stockhausen talked about the present state of music, about many composers' interest in moving away from written music. The directors sat with earphones, listening to the translation of the talk and to the number of musical examples Stockhausen presented. As he mentioned the difficulties involved in publishing the scores of electronic music or of a work like his *From the Seven Days,* for example—and when he suggested the possibilities of a kind of psychic music in which a "composer" would instruct performers telepathically—the directors, imagining they'd soon have to look for other work, began to cough, shuffle, fidget, and nervously took their leave as soon as the lecture was over.

"That was wonderful," one insouciant and smiling director named Mr. Schultz said to Stockhausen outside. As if having decided on a new calling, Schultz fell to the street on his knees, amazing the onlookers. "Master, bless me, I want to play."

"Bless you, child," Stockhausen gestured, "you will play well."

AN ANGRY POSTCARD

Monday lunch: Stockhausen shows me a postcard he's just received in the mail. And it's amazing that it has arrived at all since it's addressed, in an almost unreadable scrawl, simply to: STOCKHAUSEN, WEST GERMANY. It turns out that the card—with each letter overlapping the previous one—has been written by a blind woman who apparently lives in a south German nursing home in response to her having heard a radio broadcast of Stockhausen's Charter for Youth statement—a broadcast the composer knew nothing about. "They must have read it," Stockhausen surmises, "then played some of my music afterward."

"Though I am blind," Stockhausen deciphers the card and translates it for me, "I protest your statements I heard on the radio talk concerning young people's development of a higher state of consciousness. Our youth are completely miseducated, and through excesses of sex, alcohol, and drugs they have become mentally ill and degenerate. Your attempt to support them only guarantees this disintegration. You want a more beautiful world, but the great initiates of this world know that the only way is that of renunciation—not wanting anything. Your music does not mirror the harmony."

"I didn't want to be on the side of conservative people's eternal criticism of the young," Stockhausen says sadly. "I find it ugly. These are my children or their children. At any given moment, I'm eighteen or twenty-three, too. I can switch immediately into my eighteenth year, and I remember not having had anything, not knowing what I wanted, feeling no admiration for older persons. When young people ask me for advice, I think: what did I do? . . . How can you advise people what to do unless you're *in* the person?"

SEMINARS FOR ORCHESTRAL MUSICIANS

Tuesday lunch: Stockhausen talks about some ideas which he's going to present at a nationally televised Donaueschingen seminar in three weeks concerning the future of orchestras. All orchestral musicians, he suggests, should, as part of their work, participate in special three- or four-week training seminars each year, performing new music in small groups. Musicians who play new instruments could demonstrate unaccustomed instrumental possibilities and also novel uses of mikes and contact mikes and of transformation devices which modulate and change instrumental timbres. Orchestral players would additionally have the opportunity of learning a second, perhaps electronic, instrument.

In addition to the training seminars, Stockhausen also has envisioned a new procedure in which all members of the orchestra would split up into small chamber groups for about a month during what would be one of two six-month orchestral seasons in order to perform compositions of their own choosing, then record and tour for a second month before taking a vacation. The orchestra would then reunite to perform "collective" works (Bach, Beethoven, Debussy), record, and go on tour for two to three weeks together. And after another month's vacation, the musicians would participate in the training seminars. This six-month cycle—chamber work, tour, vacation, ensemble, tour, vacation, training—would then be repeated.

"The West German radio stations," Stockhausen says, "have more than enough music on tape to let their orchestra members spend at least twenty percent of their time in these retraining seminars. Business people do this, and so should musicians. Specializing and just playing one instrument your whole life is obsolete. And I think the musicians would prefer and enjoy doing this."

(It's interesting to point out that after Stockhausen presented these ideas at Donaueschingen, a number of musicians' unions and radio orchestra managements—far from being complacent and skeptical—immediately asked the composer to help them get such a program under way.)

THE LOSS OF MELODIC FEELING IN CONTEMPORARY MUSIC

Later, Stockhausen mentions his disappointment over the fact that many musicians specializing in "contemporary" music seem to have lost any feeling for an organic melodic line and that their playing is suffering because of this. He tells me that he's thinking of writing a piece that would feature a new kind of composition with "real melodies." And he's reminded that when Aloys and Alfons Kontarsky were preparing the first performance of *Mantra* he and the musicians were always whistling after the rehearsals. "We were whistling the mantra and its different forms—on the train, in the airport, wherever it was, very often unconsciously. I was delighted that here was a new way of writing melodic sections; here was a way of making melodies that were seemingly simple, yet exceedingly differentiated and rich. Every note in *Mantra* is really a world in itself. And here were the musicians always singing and whistling! I wish I could compose more of this."

FELDMAN AND BERNSTEIN

Tuesday afternoon: I come across an interview in a French music magazine between Françoise Essellier and the composer Morton Feldman. "For my colleagues in the avant-garde [Stockhausen]," Feldman says, "it is extremely à la mode to be antibourgeois. Quite frankly they are Marxists." "Not Stockhausen," Essellier replies; "he attacks everyone who wants to give a political intention to his music." "That's what I said," Feldman replies. "I've always thought that . . . I've lost my thought . . . Help me recover my thought."

Feldman must be putting him on! I'm thinking. But no, Feldman goes on to compare Stockhausen not only with Till Eulenspiegel (saying that he should be put in a house of correction) but also with Lucifer. "Stockhausen is the devil," says Feldman, "he gives the most convincing argument for how to sin in music." And the composer modestly concludes: "The choice is not between Karlheinz and John Cage. It's between Karlheinz and myself."

Later, I laughingly ask Stockhausen about this interview. "I once told Feldman that one of his pieces could be a moment in my music, but never the other way around. Yes, he's always talking about me. But I must tell you of a wonderful event that occurred in New York.

"Feldman and I were sitting in the front of the balcony in Philharmonic Hall when one of his works was performed by Leonard Bernstein and the New York Philharmonic. After the piece ended, Bernstein turned around to bow to the applauding audience.

"Now before the performance of his piece Feldman agreed that I would take his bow. So I stood up . . . the spotlight was on me . . . and I smiled and waved to the crowd. Lennie's hand was raised to the balcony, but when he saw me his smile just froze, and he looked away angrily, muttering: 'That fool Stockhausen.' I sat down, the applause continued, so I got up again, and graciously received the ovation and gratefully gestured my thanks. Now Bernstein came out a third time, told the orchestra to rise, and as I stood up again, he grumbled: 'Sit down, Karlheinz.' It was the fourth time that Bernstein was returning to the stage. 'I'm making a great success for you, Mortie,' I said as I started to get up again. But this time Morton had had enough and I felt his hand pulling down on my shoulders. 'Listen, Karl,' he said, 'you can't do that to me. My mother's in the audience and I'M STANDING UP!' "

REPETITIONS

Tuesday evening: "Have you been getting enough material?" Stockhausen asks me after dinner. "It's going everywhere."

"Yes, it has to be corralled."

"No, it would be marvelous if the book communicated this multiple quality."

"Every once in a while," I say, "you return to things you've discussed before, and sometimes I think you're repeating certain things, but actually I realize later that you've been speaking from a different perspective and therefore what you're saying is new."

Later in the evening Stockhausen asks me for a copy of the interview we did in New York. The next morning he says: "You know, Jonathan, I must apologize. I haven't read the interview in three months, and I've been repeating a lot of the things I said then. It really is remarkable, I don't usually like hearing people repeat themselves. But in a way I was happy that I've been saying the same things again. I was overexcited and tired in New York, rehearsing at night, and I'm happy hearing myself say these things again when I'm more relaxed. I'm saying them as if you were a different person, and I had to tell you this. There's something positive here—I always want to get these things clear and communicate them."

"What happens when you repeat things in one of your works?" I ask.

"In composition, whenever you come back to the same thing, it's no longer the same—other things have occurred in the meantime. And this return is really a confirmation of having gone through completely new insights and experiences. The same isn't the same, it's a matter of context, whether it comes before or later."

STOMACH OF GOD

Wednesday dinner: Before starting our meal, Stockhausen tells me of an image he sometimes has of himself as a piece of food in the stomach of God, a god who is continually devouring and digesting himself, "turning pies and peas and pigs into light and music," as the composer puts it. "I try to take care what I eat," Stockhausen continues, "because I want the food to become me and not me to become the food."

I mention Rabelais's giants who, like alchemists, transform food into energy.

"Look at what the plants do," Stockhausen says, "taking the sun's light in order to be what they are. Meanwhile, man has just about finished off the crust of the earth, transforming everything into human bones and flesh."

THE THIRTEEN TEARS

After dinner I mention a dream I had the night before—about a young woman named Carré—and we talk about other dreams that other guests in Stockhausen's home have had. The composer remembers a very special one dreamed by the electronic composer G. M. Koenig.

In his dream, he, Stockhausen, Boulez, Michael Gielen, and other musician friends who were closely associated in the early fifties had become old and found themselves at a meeting on a Rhine boat restaurant—as if at some fiftieth high-school reunion. They had a good meal, drank, and talked a lot. And then at a certain moment, Stockhausen went over to an upright piano, opened the lid, and began to play some of the old thirties tunes he used to perform for years in Cologne bars after the war in order to make a living. In Koenig's dream, all the friends tried to hide their sentimental feelings as they listened to these twilight songs. Then all of a sudden the composer stood up with a slightly far-away look on his face, tears running down from his right eye. He placed the tip of his right little finger on his eye and made a half-circling motion under it; then staring at his finger he began to count, saying quietly: "There are exactly thirteen tears, my friends."

Suddenly Stockhausen says to me: "Let's go inside." And when we enter the study, he begins playing—with wonderful feeling, phrasing, and rhythmic delicacy—some of these old songs on the piano—"Honeysuckle Rose," "Tea for Two," and, most beautiful of all, "I Know Why." Stockhausen shapes this last lonely piece as if it were one of his own compositions, with rapidly changing dynamic, rhythmic, and timbral levels, thereby expanding its dimensions and making it sound as if it were the last song in the world.

"You see," Stockhausen says, as if to explain his unexpectedly haunting and nostalgic performance, "it's because of the thirteen tears."

LISTENING IN THE DARK

This afternoon, with rain falling against the glass—the lights off and the house empty—I play Stockhausen's *Telemusik* on the phonograph, and during this extraordinary work I feel as if inside a grain of sand, or air inside a veil, rising and then bursting at the end into silence.

Later, after hearing a recording of *Kontakte*, I remember wondering where you go when you become the music, as music enters certain spaces. I remember passing through—like hands falling away in icy flakes, or pigeon wings waving good-bye, reaching through the moon, now with gaseous nails, circling shadows of colored noise.

Another time, sitting on the slope of the hill and listening to a recording of Beethoven's *An die ferne Geliebte* through the half-open glass doors, I jot down a poem about looking into and out through the ceiling-length windows of this slowly shifting listening room:

This room turns away
Phosphenes on the eyes
make shadows against the house
passing through a face
too deeply in
The insides sink
and rise with light in water
the way you sit in glass
reflections falling
a swarming on your mouth

"Es atmet mich" (It breathes me).

THE BREATH OF THE WORLD

C: Goethe wrote: "I imagine the earth with its circle of vapors like a great living being which inhales and exhales eternally. If the earth inhales, it draws to it the circle of vapors which approaches its surface and thickens into clouds and rain. I call this state the *aqueous affirmation;* if it lasted beyond the prescribed time, it would drown the earth. But the earth does not permit that; it exhales again and sends back up the vapors of water which spread into all the spaces of the high atmosphere and thin out to such an extent that not only does the brilliance of the sun cross through them, but the eternal night of infinite space, seen through them, is colored with a brilliant blue tint. I call this second state of the atmosphere the *aqueous negation.*"

I'm quoting this because this sense of the breath of the world reminds me of the sounds of breathing that occur at the end of both *Hymnen* and *Stimmung*. How do you relate this breathing formation to the whole process of your work?

HYMNEN: A PERSONAL AND ANALYTIC DISCUSSION

S: At the end of the Fourth Region of *Hymnen* I decided to take the last chord of the Swiss anthem as sung by a male choir and repeat it a few times with an accent on each repetition. I made a tape loop of this single chord. And when this tape loop was running, I was so strongly taken by it that I went on listening to it—I didn't know at that time that I'd use it with as many repetitions as I finally did. The loop was on the transposition machine, and I changed the periodicity slightly—a little bit faster, a little bit slower—so that individual chords occurred at different distances. The longer I listened, the more fascinated I was because in my previous work I'd always excluded periodic repetitions. There are a few exceptions, which we've discussed earlier, where the repetitions occurred so fast that they resulted in a continuous sound. But periodicity as such, like ostinato pulses, I'd never used before.

And I decided during this experiment to use this periodic, slightly varied chord for several minutes. I felt the more often it recurred the more involved I became with the inner characteristics and with these slight changes of the periodicity. And then on top of this I made these walls of glissandos. They're a unifying element, sliding glissandos which begin as high and end as low as possible. There are many, many layers superimposed, each glissando beginning a little bit later, and when the sound arrives at the bottom, starting again at the top. Now in parenthesis, I'd like to add something about these sliding glissandos before I talk about the breathing.

I once was in Yosemite Valley for a couple of days and watched the waterfalls. As you may know, the walls of the mountains are very steep and high, several hundred yards high. There are two places where you can go very close to the waterfall. The water comes through a little cranny at the top of the mountain, and when you follow it with your eyes from the top to the bottom, from the point at which it hits the rocks, then the water's no longer a stream, it has already vaporized, it's a fog. I was fascinated just watching one waterfall for several minutes. The rocks themselves have slightly mounting broken horizontal lines—there's a horizontal line pattern, what I call the veins or nerves of the rock. And I followed one of the more condensed white points of falling water until it reached the bottom, then I started again at the top. The speed of the falling water seemed to be fairly slow—the fall is so high that it takes several seconds before such a water concentration reaches the bottom.

And then something very interesting happened. At one point I wasn't precisely watching any particular spot in the water and my eyes weren't moving. I was just staring—the way children do until an adult comes and says: Don't stare like that!—not looking at anything in particular. This always happens when I've looked at something for a long time and suddenly see the totality. The whole pattern of the veins in the mountain was moving slightly upward. And I thought at length about this event where the whole mountain was rising because I'd looked for such a long time through the falling water. Later on in the studio I wondered how I could make something like this. And I experimented for several days until I found the way to do it.

In *Hymnen,* these slow glissandos on top of the periodic pulse start softly, then increase in dynamics until they're all very loud. And at the bottom they become softer again so that they're, so to speak, dynamically round at the edges. You have the impression, literally, when you listen to this—it lasts at least three minutes—that it's always going down, never arriving anywhere. And you also don't notice the new sounds re-entering at the top. Already at the end of this event, there are lines of continuous sine waves which are very long, just straight long sounds. Everybody tells me that they go slightly up in glissando, but they don't. And this results from the fact that you've listened to this long section of slowly downward gliding glissandos. There's a pulse underneath which is always noticeable and slightly irregular. This effect increases so that you have something periodic occurring simultaneously with something which has no rhythmic subdivision whatsoever. Finally the whole glissando blocks begin to have a pulsation, through they physically don't have a pulsation—I haven't made any dynamic curves. This also results from the periodic ostinato underneath.

When this section ends, the sine waves remain alone. You get the impression that they're going up slightly. In fact, there are two sine waves which I made come closer to each other. The upper one, however, is straight, while the lower one's slightly going up in glissando; but the upper one, too, seems to be going up in glissando. And I think I managed to realize this pretty well.

C: Have you attempted to recreate musically any other visual experiences?

S: We can talk about this later. But briefly . . . in *Gruppen,* for example, whole envelopes of rhythmic blocks are exact lines of mountains that I saw in Paspels in Switzerland right in front of my little window. Many of the time spectra, which are represented by superimpositions of different rhythmic layers—of different speeds in each layer—their envelope which describes the increase and decrease of the number of layers, their shape, so to speak, the shape of the time field, are the curves of the mountain's contour which I saw when I looked out the window. . . . And there are others. Yes, oh yes, naturally, we spoke of this last night when we said that any shape, any linear event, or any natural event of forces moving against each other or away from each other or crossing each other can immediately be transposed into the sound composition.

Let's continue. At the end of this section I came to a spot where I wondered what to do next. At the very beginning of *Hymnen* I used single words or sentences from a roulette session, numbers like six and nine: *Faites vos jeux, messieurs et mesdames, s'il vous plaît; rouge*—but then *rouge* undergoes a whole development. I used an English watercolor catalog, mentioning all the different reds that exist and also putting in some jokes, like the Vatican *rouge* and the fire-engine *rouge* and the Chinese *rouge*. Everything that you can imagine relating to *rouge* I placed, like satellites, around this word; and later, in the final region, I used *Rien ne va plus, messieurs-dames, s'il vous plaît*—and a very long silence follows.

Many people speak about thousands of airplanes passing over their heads in the Fourth Region—once for two minutes rather soft, and then very loud for almost four minutes. And there's something to this. After this forceful, seemingly dissolving event, I felt it was good to reinsert the voice of a real croupier: "Place your bets, please, ladies and gentlemen." And then this is repeated once more, with a slightly higher, very calm tone: "Place your bets . . ." Then the pulse of this male choir chord, which was always present, disappears. You're in a state of complete loneliness, you've given up everything. It's like in wartime when after a battle or an airplane attack everything's suddenly calm. It's then you hear the blood in your ears, you hear someone breathing or moaning. . . . And these, then, are the direct references to experiences in life.

I didn't know how to continue. I faded out, and my first thought was that I'd stop. But the night afterward I had a strong re-experience of the whole section—I'd heard it entirely during the day—and I heard my own breathing in the bed. Next morning, I got a microphone, took my jacket off, put it over my head, placed the microphone under the jacket and started listening once more to the rhythm of the slow four-minute section. And, continuing with exactly the same rhythm, I started breathing. In all, I think I recorded twelve minutes of breathing. I listened to it and said OK, I'll take this.

Then I had the last idea of *Hymnen*. I cut out a few of my

breathings and counted them. They were somewhat irregular, differing from three to eight seconds for one breath. The inhalation is always shorter. [breathes in and out.] I was listening to the pitches, this melody of the wind. And I thought: I can't finish like this.

APPLAUSE FEEDBACK IN MOMENTE

I felt this enormous impact of breathing, just as I felt something similar in *Momente*. I remember one night in Sicily . . . You see, when I compose a new piece, I always pre-experience the first performance. I already know the hall in which it will take place, I see the public coming in and hear what they're saying, what they're talking about afterward, etc. So I saw myself going on stage to conduct and heard the usual applause. All of a sudden, after bowing to the public, I saw myself quickly turning around to the choir and orchestra and giving the cue to applaud to the public. In other moments of *Momente*, I'd previously used shouts that I'd heard during other performances of my pieces—acclaiming ones ("Bravo," "Wow") or protesting ones like "Oh, no!" or "Stop it!" So I used the applause as material and composed a whole movement in which the applause becomes more and more precise. In the "applause moment," I give the entrance to one group and then to another; stop one applauding, then the other. The same movement can occur before or after the intermission or at the very beginning. When this moment occurs before the intermission, it's the reverse of what happens at the beginning. Then it starts with the more structured music, and afterward we hear more and more natural noise—shuffling of feet, breathing, coughing—and ending with the applause of the choir and then of the public. Because I turn around, make a sign to the public that we're finished, and at that point we'd both be applauding, you see. During the first performance in Cologne, we started applauding and the audience laughed and continued applauding. So there was a dialogue of applause before the public gave up, and then we structured the applause. With the breathing, now, it's the same. I was aware of all the connotations—of the breath of the world—at this moment at the end of the Fourth Region of *Hymnen*, after almost two hours of music. All the figurative elements are washed out, and there's just these blocks of sound, with a few shouts and echoes that repeat—seven, eight, nine times—names of women that

I've loved. You hear "*Iri!*" in these enormous blocks of sound, and the echoes disappear. *Nacar* was another name. Or *Maka*, my wife Mary—*Maka* combines Mary and Karlheinz. So that's the end, the last name. I was feeling desperate. Because when I composed this whole last Region, I'd just come home from a tour. I'd had an affair with a girl I called Iri and felt somewhat strange toward Mary because she was the only person I really loved. And so after having shouted this name, I got it out of me, shouting it into these rocks of sound, shouting her name almost desperately so that she'd listen to me and forgive me. This sounds a little melodramatic, but it's very true; it sounds marvelous, actually, and very abstract.

So I simply continued the low pulse of the Swiss chord with the breathing. It's a natural continuation for another nine minutes, and it's unbelievably long, but you don't even realize it, you're in suspended time. You listen to someone who's breathing aloud, coming from all the loudspeakers at once—it's a real mono situation, there's no longer a play with directions—so that in the middle, above the head, there are enormously big lungs, so to speak, breathing. We've performed the piece over 140 times in public, and many people in all different countries have said that it sounds as if all mankind were breathing. And I've felt that, too. It has kind of a cosmic feeling because it's so surreal, superreal. It's as if a thousand people were completely synchronous in their breathing.

THE HYMN OF PLURAMON

I've called this the hymn of Pluramon, who is a symbiotic being combining aspects of both a pluralist and a monist. And I say he lives in the Harmondie, which is a combination of harmony and mundus—the world. Harmondie is a region, let's say like Texas, ruled by Pluramon. It's a kind of utopia, a union of all the anthems, but they're still all together, they're not washed out—a union of the hymns. It's not one country that replaces all the others. Harmondie refers to the harmony in the world. And Pluramon combines the being of a pluralist, who really wants to keep the multiple and not destroy it, and the monist, who's always looking for the "one," for unification and integration.

And I'll tell you now what happened with the breathings. The next night I had a vision of inserting into this breathing brief memories of anthems that I'd used throughout the entire piece. But the anthems now occur in a completely different way. And I thought: I'll build a frame with these last "sound pictures," really make a rectangular frame. (These inserts into the breathing begin twenty minutes after the start of the Fourth Region.)

C: Perhaps sometime you could draw this series of "sound pictures" so I could visualize this process better when I listen to the recording.

S: I'd be glad to. Right now [Stockhausen finds a piece of paper and draws "Tracing Memories." See Fig. 2.]

First I made a picture without a frame—you hear a section of the anthem of Ghana with people dancing to very fast drum rhythms and one man's voice calling out "Ho-ah-ho-ho." Next, after some breathing, I make a stroke for the left side of the frame. This stroke is like a vertical line comprising many pitches, a cluster with a chord—very loud. And then you hear the Russian anthem chopped up with an electronic chopper—sounding like the scythe-bearing medieval figure of death (very ghostlike)—alternating with little sections of the Internationale; it sounds as if it were being played back by a transposition machine where the electric circuit is unstable.

In the third stage of the framing process you hear a stroke at the beginning (left side of the frame), followed by the Internationale which slips out of tune in its second half. And superimposed over it are the sounds of applauding crowds and horses and especially the clacking of the wheels of coaches as they go over cobblestones—I took these sounds from a recording of a reception given the English queen in an African town; and this is followed by another stroke for the right side of the frame.

In the fourth stage, after the left stroke, we hear an abbreviated version of the English anthem—the first and the final two measures—superimposed with sounds of children and large crowds and concluding with a loud soccer match cheer. And the bottom part of the frame is a sustained low sound. . . . In the fifth part, between the two strokes and above this low sound is the Indian anthem sung by a number of people in unison, accompanied by folk instruments; and along with this we hear rapid melodic passages played on the shenai.

Framing memories
(end of HYMNEN)

1 GHANA

2 UDSSR
INTERNATIONALE

To Jonathan

♡ Liebe
Stockhausen

(Pluramon(ster)o?o)

3 INTERN.
crowd

4 GREAT BRITAIN
children, crowd

5 INDIA

6 Signature
PLURAMON
(SLOW)

CHINESE SHOP (women, bells etc.)
STUDENT PROTEST

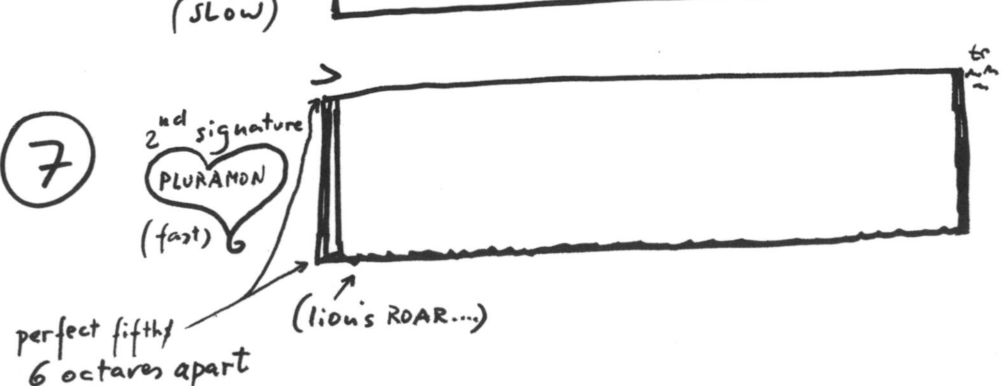

Now, during the "breathing" that separates this section from the next, you hear a voice speaking—my own voice—saying "Plu-ra-mon" very slowly—it's like an artist who signs his own painting. This is followed in the sixth stage by sounds recorded in a shop in China—the noises of women talking and of spoons on porcelain—superimposed with the sounds of a student protest at the Technical High School in Aachen. Here you find the two strokes, as well as a low *and* high sound; and the frame, which has widened along with the pitches, is now complete.

Just before the last stage you hear me saying once more: "Pluramon"—this time quickly—followed by the first stroke (the pitches between the top and bottom now make a perfect fifth six octaves apart). And then, after another section of breathing, we finally find the empty frame—which lasts ninety seconds. There's the breathing inside and this high and low sound. The low sound is really like a lion roaring, incredibly low and strong with all the harmonics inside trembling, very rich in timbre, and penetrating right into the stomach. Then we hear a few more breathings—very slow—and finally one last breath, a short inhalation and an accentuated exhalation shorter than the previous ones. Out, and that's the end.

DECOMPOSITION

C: Referring to your idea of the emptying of the frame, the psychologist David Cooper has written that what's first necessary in a therapeutic situation is the depopulation of the room. He means getting all the persons in the patient's and therapist's head out the door. Is this similar to your empty frame and the whole breathing section?

S: Yes. When I use the term "washing out," I mean it in the general sense: brain washing, cleaning out the brain. In this last loud section, you can't think of anything any more—figures, melodies, anthems—it's all gone.

C: It sounds as if you're decomposing the piece.

S: I've used decomposition many times before in the previous Regions, taking things apart and showing the individual limbs. For example, the German anthem is very interesting because it's a manifold division by two. Every second measure of this German anthem is alternatingly sung by a choir or played by an army brass orchestra. Every section played by the army orchestra is chopped up with an electronic chopper, in order to make half the music stutter. Then the whole German anthem, in its larger form proportion, is subdivided in the middle. And from the middle on, there's a synchronization first of several measures where choir and orchestra play in parallel, and then the orchestra goes faster and out of sync. You hear this very clearly because it's split into two loudspeaker groups on the left and right side. And you hear the ending twice. One comes later, it seems as if it can't come back to the tonic. And then I twist the whole meaning of the anthem several times; all of a sudden you hear ship horns—it sounds exactly like the christening of a ship, people are shouting, bottles are broken. And that turns again into a marching group, singing the anthem far away.

There's another way of subdividing. The choir sings "My heart and hand," and at "hand" I've discovered a trick to make the chord last more than two minutes, as if the choir has unlimited breath, and you don't notice how I did it. I then found a way to split this chord into two. Which means the chord itself goes downward and upward very slowly in glissando stereophonically; the one which ascends goes to the left and the other to the right. It goes through all the intervals and you hear all the combinational sounds and a lot of timbres coming out of that simple choir chord. These are produced because I go very, very slowly with all the possible beats through all the intervals. When I hit a major third, you suddenly hear the individual beats and it becomes more consonant. Then you hear the fourth, the tritone, and the fifth once more—again a great consonance. Just when it reaches the octave, the anthem continues. You hear it underneath, stammering.

MUSIC BORN OUT OF CHAOS

I decompose the anthem and recompose it afterward, but I *show* the process of decomposition. I don't do it secretly and then produce a new recomposition. I don't just present the chord itself, then the chord being taken apart in an octave, but rather the whole process—how it moves and what happens during this process. This one example explains to a great extent all the procedures of *Hymnen*. They're always different, but the spirit is very similar.

For example, there's an incredible movement in the First Region. You hear the Internationale, mixed up with all the shortwave sounds. It begins as if you're trying to get the news at midnight, but no matter where you turn the knob—you're a little too late—you get the national anthem and a good-night. Everything's distorted by the modulations of different radio stations, and that's the way the piece begins. Then in this chaos I've hidden little bits of anthems. One after another you hear people marching by; it sounds as if they're marching next door, but soon you realize it's in the radio, blurred by the sounds of traffic and other radio stations. In the course of fifteen minutes it becomes more and more the Internationale—sounds from all sides, five to six groups, young kids, old people all singing at once. Someone is saying "Don't come too late"—there are all sorts of inserts—already soon after the beginning you hear: "United Nations," just these two words recorded from the radio. And little by little you begin to sense how music is literally born out of the process of chaos. Next you have these individual words from roulette, which I talked about, and the developments of *rouge*. After this, the Internationale becomes completely clear and synchronous on all the loudspeakers.

This whole process has been interrupted several times by very strange, noisy low sounds which break upward in glissandos, almost like a volcano that wants to explode. After the Internationale has emerged clearly, this volcano opens—eighteen minutes from the beginning of the piece—and you hear an incredible roaring sound going upward in a glissando through the whole range of audibility, with a loud *bang* when it's reached its peak. And there it is, sounding exactly like little metal fillets being shaken in a box.

ONE BEING BECOMES ANOTHER

Then, bit by bit, the French anthem takes form, being interpolated with all the heads—beginnings—of other anthems. Three minutes later it becomes quite clear, and following this you hear it decomposed in a completely different manner. About eight minutes later, when this is over, you have a sudden entry of nine columns of sound, as if announcing a ceremony, and still this very high hovering sound—this is the beginning of the Second Region. I've described it on the record jacket, and I'd like to read it because it suggests the process of decomposition.

The first region merges into the second. The bridge . . .

It's just that hovering sound which is completely alone, high, and sounding like Indian bells, going slightly up and down.

> The bridge is the sharp "flood sound" that, at the beginning of the Marseillaise, hissed upward from a low, distorted tone and subsequently hovered over the whole first region.

In *Kontakte*, I discovered a way of making "flood sounds." You have sounds continually starting in speakers behind the listeners, and after a short delay the same sounds appear in speakers at the left and right, and, again a short time later, in the speakers in the front. Let's say one sound passes from the back to the front in one-third of a second; if it moves continuously—the sound with itself, in phase delay—then it gives the impression of moving floodlights. The sound really passes from the back to the front like water going over your head—and you're in the water.

> This "flood sound" now stands isolated for a long time, and then after being sliced by nine columns (with which the second region begins), it plunges downward . . .

Now something incredible happens. When this sound goes downward continuously and slowly enough, you discover at a certain moment that these are human beings shouting. All the shaking metal sounds we mentioned before were nothing but these voices —little boys shouting "Hi, come here!"—speeded up enormously.

I move this sound slightly up again in speed until it sounds like swamp ducks. At this point, I used an actual recording of swamp ducks, and you don't notice when the real ducks are continuing from the human voices. I then took one small duck—just a *Quack Quack*—and transposed her on the transposition machine, and she quacks the beginning of the Marseillaise: *Quack-quak-quak qua-qua, qua-qua, cah qua quaaa.* I take this sound down again, and once more there are human beings. These human shouts become lower and lower—*ai ao oh ou ahh*—and then, becoming dark and moaning without your noticing when it happens, they're completely transformed into very low brass sounds. These sounds, which are still mixed with the slowly speeded-down human voices, begin the Marseillaise—*waah-waah-waah wuâh*— very low and each time at a pace eight times slower than usual, until it seems like a funeral march.

Then I have this long summer day's airplane sound—a sound

I loved to hear when I was a child—lying in a meadow, watching the clouds and listening to this small plane—circling the room or hall for four-and-a-half minutes. You follow it as a line and you become very quiet. It's soft and tender and very pure. Afterward you have the continuation of the Marseillaise, so slow that you've time to listen into each chord. This is made with a flood sound; each sound moves from one side to another, and you get the feeling of being in an enormous hollow space.

C: Do most listeners actually perceive these transformational processes? In the States, many critics mistakenly hear them as some kind of pop art collage.

ALCHEMY

S: I test these transformations in the studio, and people can identify them very well. In France, audiences were laughing in amazement by what they discovered. It's just a question of having a public that knows how to recognize what's happening in music. . . . What I use is the mutation process of nature; that's what music is all about. It's an intermodulation so that one being can become another. I'm not interested in collage, I'm interested in revealing how, at a special moment, a human sound is that of a duck and a duck's sound is the silver sound of shaking metal fragments. All these sounds are interrelated very subtly just by the manner in which you listen to them and in the way that they're exposed in time and space; the basic material is all the same. This is what I meant when I talked to you about alchemy—transforming one substance into another. Many of the fairy tales are about this: the straw that the miller's duaghter has to weave into gold in *Rumpelstiltskin,* for example. This has been in my works from the beginning: transubstantiation. Like the mystical moments in religion when the water is transformed into wine. And that's the theme of *Hymnen.*

PLUS-MINUS: A COMPOSITION WHICH PRODUCES ITS OWN CHILDREN

C: Gaston Bachelard has written: "For each invented world, the poet causes an inventing subject to be born. He delegates his power to invent to the being he invents. We enter the realm of the *cosmicizing I*. Thanks to the poet, we relive the dynamism of an origin within us and outside us. . . . Melting into the basic element is a necessary human suicide for whoever wants to experience an emergence into a new cosmos."

S: Exactly. It's what the compositions I'm dealing with are all about. I create something that can recreate itself. Phoenix music. And in *Plus-Minus* I even thought for the first time in my life of composing a piece that would have its own children. In the score there's a note asking everybody who makes a version of it to send his last . . . well, I must explain the piece. In *Plus-Minus* there are seven so-called types. Each type is very characteristic: a central sound, accessory sounds, and ornamental elements. The types differ in that you have, for instance, sounds which are only in the center, then others where you have an accessory sound coming first, followed by the central sound. Or the other way around. The accessory sounds must be of a different nature—noisier and played with different instruments. It's like composing beings which have a different number of bodies and limbs—four legs, three arms. These types can grow or shrink, through the completely prescribed plus or minus process, in number of parts. They can, for example reach +13 units of themselves—if one type has accessory sound plus central sound, you must have this entity thirteen times. It can be completely renewed when you've reached thirteen times itself, but this then results in sound events that are terrifically long; you hear the same event repeated thirteen times.

You can also reach 0 by subtracting. [The amount you have to add or subtract is indicated in little flags on top of the individual type—see Fig. 3.] And when you reach 0, you have to represent the event, this type, by a negative sound. Which means you have a negative band of sound—a layer of breathing, for example—and when it's further subtracted to —1, —2, —3, —4 units of this type, you make an equal number of "holes" in this negative sound wall—the sound that's absent is represented by the silence that's broken into the sound wall. Here we might use radio sounds, which are fairly undefined, or whole choirs breathing—you can think of other possibilities. If the type is accessory sound first plus central sound, then you make a short hole, then a big hole, but it can't be transposed any more in pitch: silence is silence, it doesn't move up or down. When the type reaches —13 units, you've had a lot of negative appearances of this type. It may be only one of the seven types which at a certain time, through the subtraction process, is moving into the minus—the others may be very far in the positive, and growing—but when one type approaches —13, then it dies, and it can never be used again in the piece.

PUNKTE AND ANTIMATTER

C: This reminds me in a way of the idea of antimatter.

S: Very true! And in *Punkte*, too, at certain moments the sounds in the air are the music, but at other moments, the holes that I literally erase out of the sound wall are the music. [See Fig. 4.] Let's say I make a solid, chromatically closed sound wall —five octaves with string players. Then where I'd usually put a dot on the paper I now take an eraser and make a hole in this wall; and those holes are then the music. The wall becomes more or less transparent. These holes have certain shapes—they go up or down. And the stopping and starting of sound indicates the edges of such holes. . . .

If at the end of making a version of *Plus-Minus* you've reached, for example, for one type: +3 units, another +7, another —5, another +12—and three have died—then you've only four of seven types left. And you're asked to communicate the last status of your version to the publisher so that it can then be used as the starting point for another interpreter who wants to make a new version. The piece would then, like a living being, always generate new pieces, and one "family" branch would only die out when all the seven types had been brought to —13.

ASSASSINATING *PLUS-MINUS*

C: Has anyone ever tried intentionally to assassinate the piece?

S: In 1963 I spent a couple of weeks in Sicily by the seashore, and as I couldn't take a lot of paper with me I tried to hide in the shadow of a rock and think clearly about a new piece, and *Plus-Minus* is what emerged. (I'd discussed all the possible transformations of the seven "musical types" that occur in the score with Mary, and we drew them in the sand together.)

At that time I was thinking about "negative sound" and "colored silences"—silences that would have different shades— and I brought the piece to my first class at the Cologne Courses

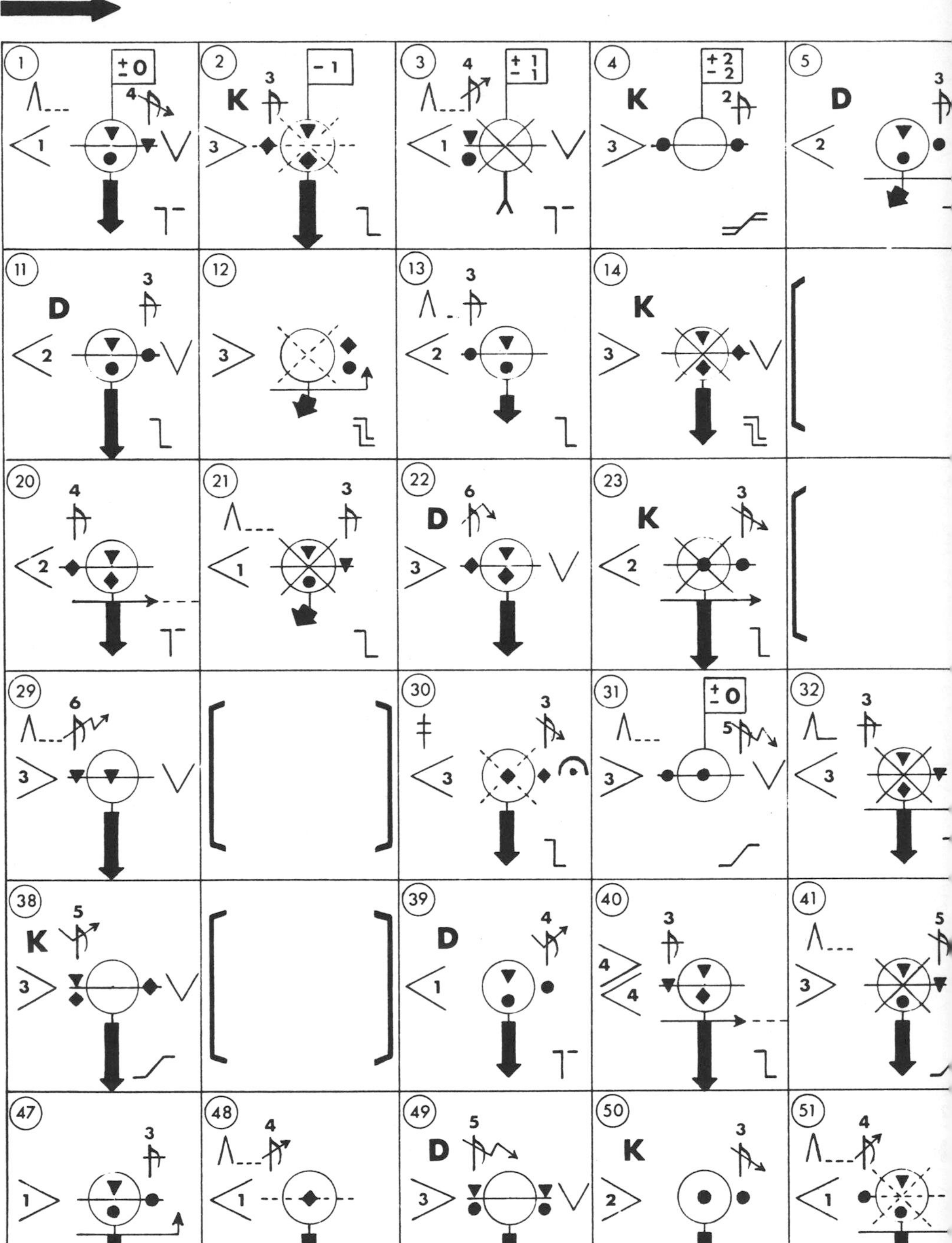

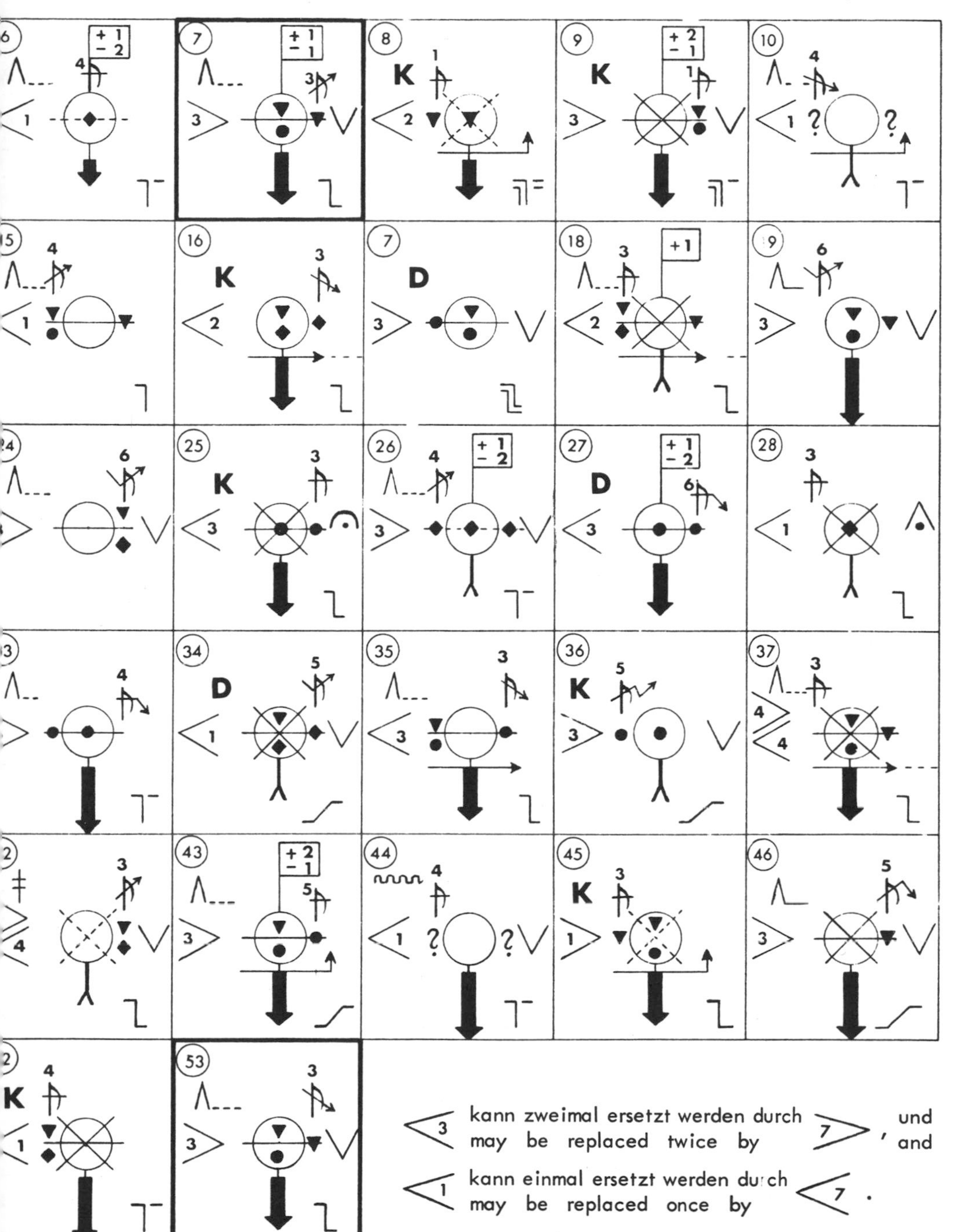

FIGURE 3: One of seven symbol pages with numbered events from *Plus Minus*

46
rit. molto
Kl. Fl.
Fl.
Altfl.
Ob.
Ob. d'amore
Engl. Horn
Kleine Klar.
Klar.
Baßklar.
Fag. 1
Fag. 2
Kontrafag.
Horn
Tromp.
wawa
subito pp
117
118
Vibra
Mar.
Marimba
Vibra + Marimba
ganz allmählich öffnen
allmählich schließen
Motor langsam
Spitzd.
Pos. 1
Pos. 2
Klav.
Harfe
Glockenspiel
alle normal
alle sul tasto
alle sul pont
Dpf.
Vl. I

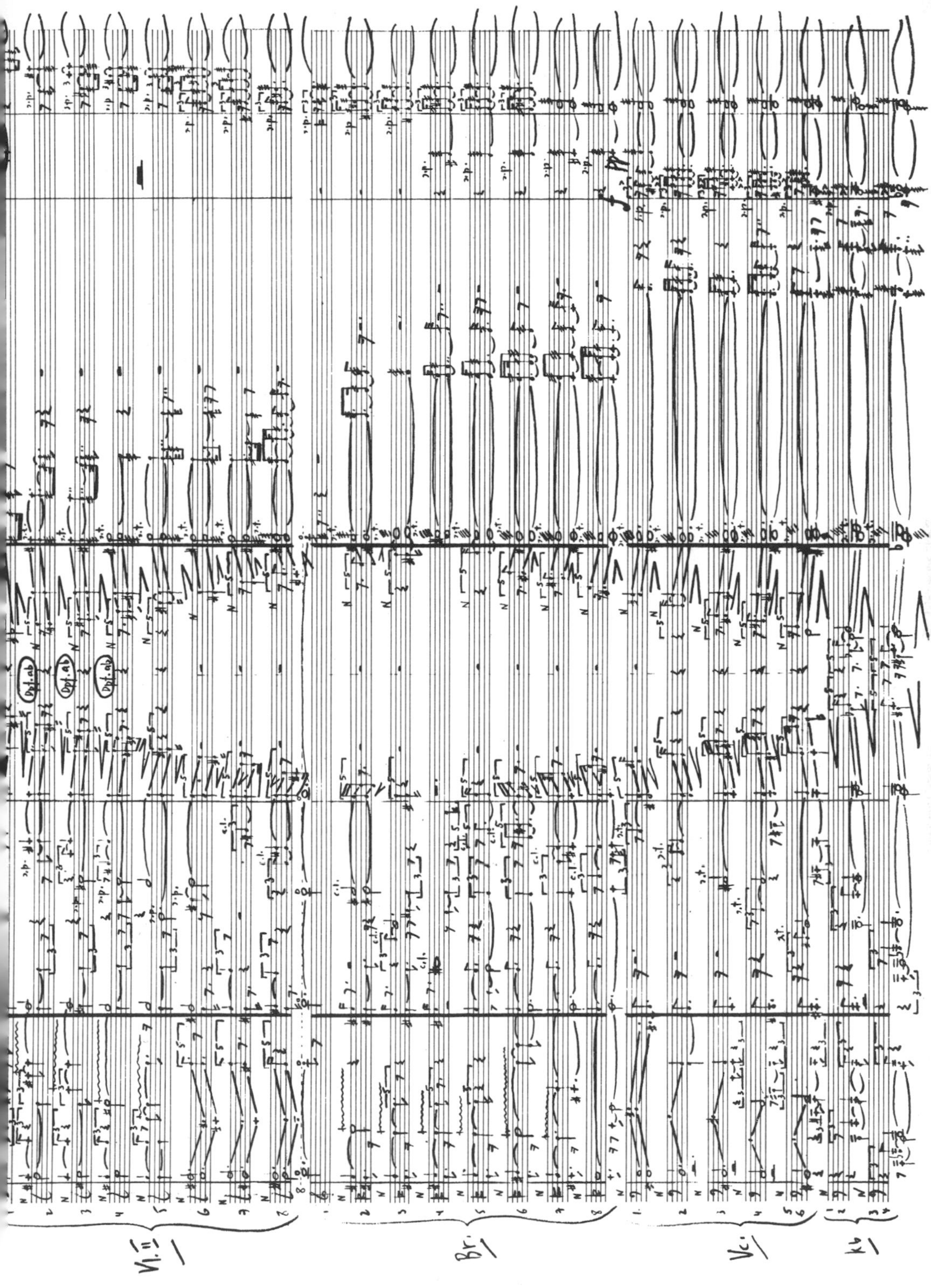

FIGURE 4: "Erasing" in *Punkte*

for New Music, proud that I'd made a piece that allowed for many different versions and which at the same time gave a very strict skeleton for the composing. Twenty-five versions were made during my composition courses for all kinds of instrumentation—one for four harps, another for recorders and children's choir, another for large orchestra, and so on.

And I remember there was an Icelandic composer who looked like the young actor in the movie of Jules Verne's *Journey to the Center of the Earth.* After he understood all the rules he left and returned two or three classes later. "How is it going?" I asked him. He said: "I've finished"; he was the first to have done a version—I think it was for percussionist and piano. And then I asked him what he had done, and he said: "It's short, really. I found a way to bring all the seven types in the quickest possible way to —13, and I killed them off." There were just a few blips and blobs and then lots of silences . . . that was it. And it reminded me in spirit of the Jules Verne movie in which the guy who's walking down through the caverns of stalagmites and stalactites is so curious—he's almost diabolically and yet at the same time quite naïvely getting himself into dangerous situations—that he's always losing not only his way but also his "girl friend"—a duck called Gertrude who seems to know the right direction. But the guy gets lost—the stones are rumbling in the hollow caves, water dripping—and in fright he calls out: "Gertrude! Gertrude!" and she replies: "Quack-quack, Quack-quack." [Laughing.]

Anyway, this Icelandic student reminded me of this character, always trying to do something very adventurous. Well, perhaps what was lacking in our course was Gertrude. But Gertrude did exist actually, because there's a woman named Gertrude Meyer-Denkmann who's a pianist—she lives in Altenberg and is quite well known now—who takes her hairbrushes and uses them in the insides of the piano in order to demonstrate how good a disciple she is of John Cage. And her students are always amazed to see their piano teacher brushing the strings! . . . Yes, she's the Gertrude of the story. That's Gertrude and that's *Plus-Minus.*

I wanted music that reproduces itself. And that's what music does spiritually anyway; if it's very rich then in history it reproduces itself in the brains of other composers. They make new pieces and they're not even aware that they're composing babies of Stravinsky, for example. Some composers are simply reproduction factories of a model composer who's created the basic substance.

Carl Orff, naturally, is such a case. He heard *Les Noces*, and that was it. He lived a whole lifetime from it. Penderecki lives from *Carré*. He was sitting in at all the rehearsals, and I knew exactly what he wrote up to that very day and what he started writing twelve days later. Since then he's taken just one aspect of *Carré* and amplified it.

C: Speaking of reproduction, the French biologist François Jacob has mentioned that "death is a necessity built into the egg by the genetic blueprint itself."

S: Death is necessary for washing out memory. It would be horrible if we contained all the memories of 60 million years. In order to start fresh and anew and on a different plane it should be all washed out. Death is just a little trick. It's like changing your means of transportation. You go from a car into an airplane. Sometimes, of course, people go from the airplane and start walking or crawling for some time.

C: Do you know of Otto Rank's observation that "the artist is his own mother"?

"CLOTHE YOURSELF WITH THE NEW MAN."

S: With every new piece that you discover intuitively it's as if you lose your skin like a snake. As it says in the Bible: Clothe yourself with the new man. . . . My old man produces a new man. Very few people go through many lives in one life, and they die and are reborn again in one, superficially speaking, earth life. Some have only one life in one life or don't even complete one life in this life.

C: Michel Butor points out that while Proust once compared the composition of *Remembrance of Things Past* to the construction of a cathedral, he also modified this, writing: "Pinning another sheet on here, we might say that I am building up my book, if not like a cathedral—that would perhaps be too ambitious—like a dress." And Butor suggests that in his great work, Proust is in fact recreating a mother for himself, in order to be reborn.

S: I once said: Let's not only pursue things of time past, but also of the time not yet found: to regain not only the subconscious and the unconscious layers within us, but the layers of time that are coming—the superconscious and supramental.

C: It sounds like forward dreaming.

S: That exists, and I do it very often. I completely anticipate experiences that come sometimes hours, weeks, years later. I've *been* to these places though I've never been there before. Vision is nothing else. Foresight. Or *forehearing* the future. That's what I did with *Trans*. I heard the whole piece in a dream and had to compose it for several months to realize it.

C: Chou Wen-chung points out that in the Japanese *gidayu* and the Korean *p'ansori*, "individual speech sounds are often transformed into musical events according to their timbral values as well as the dramatic context of the words." This striking musical use of phonology seems to exist in *Stimmung*, too, along with the breathing once again.

S: In several models you have to "whistle"—without the whistling sound—what you've sung before, breathing with the same formants—you hear the melody of the overtones with the sound of the wind. The breath goes through the same mouth position and produces the same pitch relationships that, formerly, you've heard in the overtones within the vowels.

A POEM FROM STIMMUNG: DIFFFF-DAFFFF-DIFFFFFFFF

I wrote several poems for *Stimmung*, and I'll read you one [see Fig. 5] which comes to mind on hearing your question. The singer, Mr. Fromme, speaks it a short time before the conclusion of the version which is on the record; this poem, in fact, gave him the idea of continuing for a while at the end with breathing. It must be read with the feeling of a big, slowly flying bird, one flapping of the wings per measure. (The *dif* and *daf* phonemes are sounds I hear when I'm an eagle or when I see other large birds gliding.)

I must say how it's written. It begins with *dif*, and I count innerly the number 5 which is written above the letters. There are five measures of *f*, so I count *dif* 2 3 4 5 *daf* 2 3 4 5—and then a measure of eight: *dif* 2 3 4 5 6 7 8. Then comes a nine-unit silence, which means I must count an *f* which isn't spoken nine times. Then again comes *dif* 2 3 4 5 *daf* 2 3 4 5 and *difdidif* 2 3 4 5 *daf* 2 3 *dif* 2 3 4 5 6 *füü* . . . and the *füü* goes with inward breathing. The number of *ü*'s is exactly prescribed: four times *ü*, *üü* twice, then four times *i*, and four times *ü*. Et cetera. The tempo is indi-

Stockhausen

STIMMUNG

Textblatt

mit dem Gefühl eines grossen, langsam fliegenden Vogels, pro Takt ein Flügelschlag

deutsche Aussprache

die Taktziffern bedeuten ♪

im Tempo ♪= 162

5/♪ 5 8 9
difffff dafffff diffffffff

5 5 1 5 3 6 7 — + — 4 + 4
difffff dafffff difdidiffffff dafff difffffff füüüüüüüüüüüüü

stimmlos atmen, mit Lippenstellung färben

einatmen aus ein

1 2 3 5 7 5
dif diff difff diffffff diffffffff dafffff

ruhig – zunehmend intensiver

4 4 4 6 7 > 7 — + — 4 — + — 5 4
difff daf diffffl daf difff daf diffffli daf diffffff fliiiiii gennnnuuuunn dichchchch

5 6 6 7 — + — 3 8 5
uuunn terrrrmm feeeeeder bauuuuuuchchch füüüüüüüü lennnnnn

stimmlos

dichtes [r]

2 5 6 7 > 2 8 19
ist mein himmmmmel liiiiiibes schreiiiiiii benn difffffffffüüüüüüüüüüüüüüüüüü

stimmlos

Figure 5: Poem from *Stimmung*

cated by the metronome marking of 162 units per minute. You can also see on the paper when to say *dif* higher and *daf* lower—when it goes up, then you go higher in pitch; and when it goes down, you go lower proportionally as it's written. Then it says *fü*—breathing in, out, in [demonstrates] . . . and so on until the *dif* with an accent, a little break. And from the *f* comes the flying—the German *fliegen* means "to fly." And I write the line of the flying movement [demonstrates with a voice soaring up and down], which literally means: "Flying and feeling you under my feather belly. *Ist mein*—is my—*himmelie* . . . I connect phonetically *Himmel*—sky and heaven—and *Liebe*—love. (It's my heavenly love.) *Schrei* means cry, as in "cry out," but I twist it with the next syllable and say *ben*, because *schrei-ben* means "to write" in German. In English the present participle would be *cryting*—it's untranslatable: "Writing into the sky, my love, because I feel you under my feather belly when I'm flying." That's the end of this poem except for *dif*—another flap of the wings. The breathing we talked about results from this poem and from the end of *Hymnen*.

[At this point on the tape, Stockhausen gives an extraordinary recitation of the poem which can be heard as rendered by Wolfgang Fromme near the conclusion of the recorded version of *Stimmung*. At the end of the final *füüü*, you can hear on the cassette tape what sounds like the first chirps of newly born robins, emerging from and magically extending the last moments of indrawn breath. Then silence.]

What is music, what is language? You don't know. We've spoken about flying, phonemes, and the transformation of musical intelligibility into verbal intelligibility, and vice versa. We've also spoken about the decomposition of any sound phenomenon, and it's all in such a little poem.

HOW STIMMUNG WAS COMPOSED

C: What does the word *Stimmung* mean and where did you compose the piece?

S: It means "tuning," but it really should be translated with many other words because *Stimmung* incorporates the meanings of the tuning of a piano, the tuning of the voice, the tuning of a group of people, the tuning of the soul. This is all in the German word. Also, when you say: We're in a good *Stimmung*, you mean a good psychological tuning, being well tuned together.

I composed *Stimmung* in Madison, Connecticut, during the winter when Long Island Sound was frozen. There were unbelievably strong winds, and I just watched the white snow on the water in front of my two windows. That was the only landscape I really saw during the composition of the piece.

What was important for the creation of *Stimmung* was the fact that I'd just come back from Mexico where I'd spent a month walking through the ruins, visiting Oaxaca, Merida, and Chichenitza, and becoming a Maya, a Toltec, a Zatopec, an Aztec, or a Spaniard—I became the people. The magic names of the Aztec gods are spoken in *Stimmung*. . . . And then the space. I sat for hours on the same stone, watching the proportions of certain Mayan temples with their three wings, watching how they were slightly out of phase. I relived ceremonies, which were sometimes very cruel. The religious cruelty isn't in *Stimmung*, only the sounds, the whole general feeling of the Mexican plains with their edifices going into the sky—the quietness, on one side, and the sudden changes, on the other.

Perhaps I'm still a child concerning this: I imagined a priest standing on top of the 108th step of a pyramid, shouting for the sacrificial victims to be brought up. In the end it was terrible how many people they offered. You get the impression that there were always ceremonies taking place. And it's this ceremonial aspect that's manifested in *Stimmung*, the way the singers sing and behave while they're singing.

C: Had you conceived of the piece before reading anything by Aurobindo? There are a lot of similarities to much Indian music.

S: I first read a book about Aurobindo in May 1968, during the period when I was writing *From the Seven Days*. I worked on *Kurzwellen* two months earlier and on *Stimmung* three months before that. . . . That Eastern feeling is a result of the timings which exceed by far those of Western pieces. Neither Bruckner nor Mahler has such dimensions of sustained sounds through which you can listen into the sound and hear such swinging periodicities—swinging in the literal sense. . . . Perhaps it might have something to do with my Japanese experiences. Perhaps you might find some atmospheric relationships between *Stimmung* and gagaku music, but only with regards to the Sho instrument. And even Sho music doesn't have this exactly.

C: What about *Stimmung*'s relationship to Gregorian chant, the feeling of [sings a Benedicamus].

S: Not to me. There the effect's basically melodic. That's really flying! Whereas *Stimmung* is standing still and vibrating inside. It's more like a butterfly sitting on a blossom.

C: Like some of Webern's early pieces.

S: Opus 7 and Opus 10 in particular. But if there's any comparison that can help us, I've been told about certain similarities to performances by Tibetan monks. . . . You see, when you try to discover new ways of making music, then every once in a while you obtain something that sounds like a music which already exists somewhere, even if you've never heard it. When working on *Stimmung,* I originally started out writing melodies in the beginning. And then when I emphasized the different overtones in the sound pulse I was singing, I gave up the idea of melodies and thought of one sustained spectrum and of basing everything on the precise changes of the overtones. Naturally, this has happened somewhere else in the world when people also discovered what you can do with the voice. That's what I meant when I said that when the whole approach to art becomes total—you experiment in order to discover new ways of making music, to discover the music all over again, to compose the whole history of music since the first sound of creation once again—then the already existing styles or objects simply occur as individual items among many others that aren't yet known—they become special cases, special solutions.

"TIME CANNOT BE SEPARATED FROM BEING."

C: Generally speaking, as Joseph Needham has pointed out, there are two traditions concerning the nature of time. One is the Indo-Hellenic tradition in which space predominates over time. And since time is cyclical and eternal, so the temporal world is less real than that of timeless forms and has no ultimate value. Pantheism (the deification of all space) and polytheism (the deification of particular spaces) tend to support and are nourished by this conception. In the Judeo-Christian tradition, however, time predominates over space, its movement is meaningfully directed toward the apocalypse. The world era is fixed on a central point which gives meaning to the entire process. And monotheism is the product of this world view.

Now *Stimmung* seems to combine both of these worlds.

S: It's as if you're reading my lips. The new concept is to combine these two because one is the other, it's just the way you look at it. There's a wonderful remark in a little book by Victor von Weizsäcker called *Gestalt and Time*. Traditionally, he says, it's been thought that things exist *in* time. People have had an abstract concept of time as if it were something in itself. But time only occurs if there's a being; and *by* being it manifests time. As something becomes a form it occupies a certain space; it has a form, a condensation, so as not to be scattered all over in particles—something personal and individual. Automatically, time occurs in a being, but the being isn't in time.

With the definition of astrological time, there was always one constant time and everything referred to movements of the stars; the movement of the sky was considered to be the clock. And all life that was changing and growing, decaying and being reborn on this earth was measuring itself according to astronomical time. But then man came to understand the organic concept of time by which every being, every star, every molecule, every atom has its own time. Which means that time and space, as we discussed it technically yesterday, are becoming interchangeable. Time occurs not just *in* space but in *a* space, which is a being. There's no such thing as time that can be separated from being.

And von Weizsäcker gives many examples of the concept of prolepsis. For instance, when a horse makes the first step, you can already see in its initial movement the entire process of how it will gallop or trot—it shows its potentiality in time and space. Concerning the concept of the matrix, on a very primitive level when you cut a worm into two or three, the remaining elements begin to have a life of their own. When in childhood we lose our first teeth, we grow others. The fantastic concept of the matrix is that in every atom there's a complete world. The more complex the species, the less ability there is to reproduce the limbs and parts of the body. But potentially, every cell of the body contains the complete matrix of the whole body—of you, not of someone else.

C: Musically, this reminds me of the idea that each motive contains the embryo of its fully developed form.

S: That's what happens in *Mantra*. The mantra of *Mantra* is a thirteen-note formula which is blown up to sixty-three minutes. It's always this mantra, whose largest proportions just represent the same proportions of the initial mantra. It's one seed which brings about an enormous tree, a whole world.

It's interesting, in reference to what we said about time and space, that every space creates its time; and this means its duration, also—how long it lasts until it disappears and becomes another formation. The way it occurs to you for the first time reveals to you its complete life, so to speak, its extension in time.

There's another very important book that you should recommend in this context called *The Genesis of Living Forms* by Raymond Ruyer. He's written a very wonderful essay on the concept of form and formation, in which he talks about how more and more we're concerned with the process of the *forming* of something. When we see an object like this vase, glass, ashtray, or tape recorder, it's important to think about how this particular ashtray came about. Why this ashtray? Why this tape recorder—the way it looks and feels and what it does? We should think about what it was before and what it will be afterward in order to understand it. We're so used to seeing the so-called objective world like a horse wearing . . .

C: Blinders.

S: The word's beautiful in English—making it blind to the true reality. There's just a very small window through which to look at the world. It's the same as when we look at an object—a flower or ashtray—with only the short amount of time that we usually give it. We should study the whole process of the ashtray not yet being the ashtray or no longer being the ashtray—it's all the ashtray, don't forget this—it's not the tape recorder. It's the process, and that's why Ruyer emphasizes so much the idea of formation in order to transcend the traditional predominance of form.

COMPOSING PROCESSES

When I found this book five years ago I was completely in the process of composing *processes*. Early in the sixties I said that what we had to compose was composition and not compositions. We have to compose the process of how to compose rather than composing pieces. You see this everywhere. At the beginning of the sixties, process planning became very significant. And being in Japan showed me that the Japanese, when they build a temple or an important house, always think that it's important what you see and experience when you're approaching the house, a thousand yards before you reach it, and what you experience when you've first glimpsed it through two bushes. There's a little bit of the house, it disappears again for several minutes, and then you see another aspect of the house because the path is winding around it; almost as in a spiral, you come closer to it. And when you finally reach the house—by constantly taking pictures with your eyes and imagining it when you can't see it for a moment—you've experienced it in a million forms, in a process. You've already lived in the house, whole dramas have occurred before you ever reached it. And when you leave, you're usually led down another path. When you've gone to the tea house at a Zen temple several times, the tea ceremony master will block certain paths that you've gone through before with bamboo sticks. He'll lead you down another path, and you must follow stones around which a string has been bound.

In the Japanese house everything is windows—paper windows. So a whole wall disappears, and you look into spaces you've never seen before because they've just arranged the windows differently. If you go from one room to another, the head of the house might just slightly move the paper window toward the other side so that when you returned to the first room you'd see another part of the landscape outside, differently framed by the window. There's a wonderful interplay between the inner and outer—you're in the house and you're looking outside all the time; you're outside and you're looking into the spaces within the house. And inside the house you find plants that duplicate the plants outside of the house in miniature or in different sizes. It's always mediation. It's what we were saying yesterday: mediation, mediation, mediating. It's beautiful.

STRUCTURALISM

C: Concerning your discussion of formations—ashtray, vase—structuralists believe that what we signify is a function of how we signify it. Are you at all interested in the structuralist method?

S: Certainly, but they repeat something that's become almost a banality, because when the physicists started diving into the atomic microcosms, they said: All we can say is determined by what we can measure with our instruments, so we're constantly describing the abilities of our measuring instruments and, finally, we really don't know what it is; all we know is what our instruments are. The means of analysis are all we can talk about, which finally means that we're always talking about ourselves—the matrix of our brain which has produced the tools to penetrate into aspects of existence. But the tools are just prolonged brains or arms. So we're constantly talking about the possibilities of ourselves when we describe something. And then again, the subject-object contradiction of the classical antinomy is dissolving because when I speak about the object, I'm really speaking about my speaking about the object. Only when I stop identifying with myself do things become exacting, because when I'm experiencing my abilities of experiencing, I begin to realize that I'm not myself, but rather this incredibly huge IT which is watching with its trillion eyes, of which I am one eye, O Jonathan . . .

C: It's interesting that Lévi-Strauss has seen the processes of myth as similar to those of music.

S: We've looked at this truth from different angles in our conversations, as when I said that a music like *Mantra* is nothing but a miniature model of the stellar constellations—of the forces of the stars and at the same time of the processes that occur in the micro. Yes, of course, but what's wonderful is that we can adapt these things that are too big or too small, too fast or too slow. We simply transpose or translate literally the universal forces and all their proportions into that very narrow range of the acoustical waves that we can perceive—we translate them into our bodily language.

C: Many structuralists try to translate phenomena into *language*, emphasizing a lexicon of permissible terms and binary functions.

S: In a way, they simply reproduce the brain rather than letting the brain discover something that's beyond the brain. . . . It's a closed system that makes variations, projecting itself on the outer world, but never trying to reach supramental regions where the brain itself is seen as being simply a device that can be started and stopped. The brain is a fantastic, very useful servant, and nothing else. We should be on very good terms with it and remember that most people let the brain work things out within itself, which means doing combinatoric work. Many pieces of art are simply the result of this kind of work and are very intelligently made. But we shouldn't forget when we carefully experience them —not just intellectually analyze, listen to, or compare them—that the newer, more astounding and more unknown something appears to be, the more it suggests the existence of something beyond the common combinatoric abilities of brain—there's definitely intuition coming into it.

Now we must be very careful when we talk about the structuralists' use of *language*; not using the term in the common sense. What do they think about Babel? God divided the people—punished them for their sins—by splitting the one language into many languages so that they could no longer understand each other.

C: They're generally concerned with basic, universally identifiable syntactic structures. And some structuralists have said that you can think only in terms of words.

S: Let's make a little jump even if people might say we're crazy. There are precise descriptions of Tibetan lamas who let their pupils build stone walls around themselves; they're in darkness for several months. One of the Dalai Lamas spent a year isolated in complete darkness, and he had continual communication with his pupils; he was teaching and talking to them through telepathy. So what is the language? They'd say it's the waves he emits. Why has the American army been secretly training people who have an exceptional degree of telepathic powers to communicate with submarines under the polar ice where radar doesn't function? Is that also language according to their terms?

If my intuitive experiences or my communion with the Divine is called a language, then I perfectly agree. Then everything is language that occurs through wave communication. And then—let me make one point which will probably sound humorous—our sun is the most intelligent creator of language in the whole solar system because it permanently communicates, it gives very precise information to every plant, human being, and existing element on this earth—what to do, and how to grow. In this sense it's language, too.

C: It's been said that the theory of nature and the world is contained within the perceived relations of actual objects.

S: All the words are relative, because what's perception? Can we say it's also ESP communication? Is perception bound only to our six senses or is it also allowed to all the other senses, the inner senses? What about the situation when a certain person comes into my room for the first time and I immediately know if I like the person or not? This is a complex decision which I make in an instant without having talked to the person. And in all cases I've found out later that my first response was best.

It's the same in composing. When I begin to think through

and reduce it to a language that's organized in a very abstract, intellectual form, then I realize I'm really atomizing many wonderful complete sound visions. Naturally, I need to do it most of the time because I have to write it, and writing is the compartmentalization of entire events and experiences. Our writing—especially the way we Western people write—is based on adding elements atomistically in order to get entities.

C: Language is seen as the Fall from that mythical time when words were music, and structuralists believe that we can only look back nostalgically to that age. . . .

S: That's ridiculous! We can only look *forward* because it will come again—and much better! The chaos of Babel is only a transition. Atomization is necessary, we split the atoms before they can re-form and unify on a completely different and higher level. The intuitive age is just coming now. Certainly. We are conscious of it, whereas what they're talking about isn't the Golden Age, but the Mythological Age, which means it's very dark. At that time beings were eating up and vomiting out each other. It's the lost naïveté. But it's far more important to reach for this unity and simplicity consciously. It's terrifying to be no longer naïve, yes. But how wonderful to be simple again and at the same time have a unified concept of the cosmos as a conscious unity and a conscious common language. Then it's really a question whether at that point we'll still have to talk about language because we'll understand each other completely, as certain beings do already. We will hear the fundamental of the universe and all its partials.

SYNCHRONICITY

Let me come back to a couple of things we were just talking about. The Judeo-Christian tradition fosters the concept of one initial explosion—creation—everything starting from the One that reveals itself in its multiplicity. The idea here is that of time being an arch, finally arriving at the last days and the last judgment—it's the cosmos coming to an end. With the idea of nirvana, however, we don't find that starting-and-stopping concept of time because, if I understand it correctly, nirvana means to be in all the times and everywhere at once—in an omnipresent state, *eternal* in the sense of reaching the timeless by incorporating everything.

C: It's similar to the idea of synchronicity.

S: Wonderful. Yes. It's the verticalism—everything exists at once. If you could make a clear cut through the whole universe, you'd see that everything that we define as "history" or "development" exists at once—you'd experience all the layers of sub- and supraconsciousness. It's just that we can't be everywhere at once at the same time because of the way we are. That's why we think of time as being a successive process—one thing after another—because we're simply unable to grasp this great truth. We have these blinders—in this case they're necessary—otherwise we'd just explode from the joy of looking through everything, at ourselves and the whole meaning of existence.

C: If you break down the phrase "I repeat myself," you find "I repeat my Self."

S: Who says I?

C: Well, that's the mistake, isn't it?

S: No, that's the truth. There's someone watching the I: the higher I is watching the lower I saying that it repeats itself. Who says "I repeat myself"? When I talk like this, who's saying that the I sees that the lower I repeats itself?

C: Who writes your compositions?

AN INFINITE SERIES OF THE I, THE YOU, AND THE IT

S: That's why I say that nothing belongs to me. There's an infinite series of the *I*, an infinite series of the *you*, and an infinite series of the *it*; and only these three make sense. In classical logic, as I've said before, the third always had to be excluded—that was the alpha and omega of Aristotelian logic. . . . So what I want to say is that in the new cosmology these traditions are combined. We spoke about the concept of the "ylem" occurring every 83 billion years: you have that Judeo-Christian evolution of time which comes to a standstill, contracts again, comes to an end, after which the whole universe is purified by fire. The universe explodes again, it breathes periodically. So you have both the unlimited and the cyclic—cycle to cycle to cycle, endlessly. And what's interesting is to begin to understand the spiral tendency of these cycles. That's not just a dull repetition or variation.

C: Some of the early Greeks believed that Socrates would reappear as Socrates in five thousand years—speaking exactly the same words he spoke before. This isn't what you mean . . .

S: But even if that were true he'd reappear, as you've said, five thousand years later. He couldn't live a second if he were exactly the same physically or mentally. He'd immediately blow up, he couldn't even breathe the atmosphere. Socrates is just a name.

A TERNARY SYSTEM OF LOGIC

C: You mentioned before the falsity of the object-subject duality, saying that you can't speak about something without speaking about your speaking about it; and you've also said that one's way of looking at something is itself transformed by what one sees. Aren't you suggesting that finally there's no distinction between your audience and your music?

S: Be careful. If you do away with dualism, you shouldn't level out everything. It would be more interesting to add a third force and begin with a ternary rather than a binary system of logic. We have the public, the musicians, the sounds produced, the waves perceived. All we can analyze now is what people manifest as their reactions: what they say, how they behave, the waves we feel in the hall which are emitted by the people themselves. So we can't speak about the music as such without speaking about these who are listening to or making the music. We can only talk about what we're able to describe concerning what we hear. How can you be aware of sound waves without your being what you are? The public becomes the music, and the music becomes the public.

C: Then why are there so many uncomprehending critics?

S: It's like asking: "Why are there clocks?" They're devices based on common agreement meant to facilitate an objective system of evolution or analysis. Let's say we all accepted the Platonic idea, described in *The Republic*, where certain sounds and instruments all had their precise functions. Plato gave very particular significance to what sounds do to man—what kinds of feelings, emotions, or thoughts they stir up in him. In Russia today or in Germany under the Nazis we find something similar to this. They tried to relate certain effects to certain sounds. In Nazi Germany they spoke about non-Aryan art, and they burned a lot of paintings and chased musicians away whose works deviated from the common denominator; those who were defining the aesthetic principles had a closed system of what was and wasn't good.

Now we have to ask another question: Shall we really accept the completely atomistic concept in which everybody has his own aesthetic? By that concept, communication is impossible. That's the other extreme, and we are really heading toward it. The so-called idealistic anarchists in America are envisaging a world where there's ultimately no group anymore that can agree—everybody is alone with his own canon of values. The other extreme, of course, is where you have a whole collective whose group ideal is affirmed by some power elite or unified by a myth like that of the ancient Greek gods.

THE NEW SPIRITUAL FAMILY

There are many possibilities in between, and I'd rather say: Let's not stay at either extreme, but rather constantly move from one to the other. What I'd like now is if people on the same wave-lengths, on the same level of consciousness—although it's almost impossible to measure this—if spiritual friends formed groups no longer bound by ties of city, village, family, blood, or race, but by the level of consciousness they've achieved—their consciousness of themselves and of themselves as being in the world and universe. If such people meet, they wouldn't need to talk very much about what music they like, about what's good or bad. It would become a global group structure like a network—as when you're flying over a city at night and you see these points or light which are like the synapses of the brain; it really looks like an enormous thinking brain. As Teilhard de Chardin said, if we were outside of the noosphere we'd feel the warmth of all these human beings. It would look as if our earth were *shining*, there'd be an enormous light emanating from this thinking activity. . . . So this group of beings, these spirits that have a common canon are scattered all over the globe now—a friend in Japan, one in Texas, Mexico, Alaska—*that's* the new group spirit. That's the only real underground, though I'd rather call it an overground.

C: It seems to me that many of the young radicals who are working in different kinds of collectives also have these shared values and don't seem particularly atomized.

S: Yes, there are strong countermovements already. They've found friends who aren't necessarily just from their home community or schools. It doesn't seem as if some of these young persons are atomized. I was of course talking specifically about aesthetic judgment, but it does apply to everything. I do think that a new nationalism is emerging, in the positive sense—being an individual in an expanded family. I don't believe, as we're being told over and over, that the family is gone—that's only the obligatory family where you had only a choice of those persons who you knew in your village, town, or where you worked. You had very little chance to discover unions which were spiritually clear and perfectly alive.

C: This is one way of saying that ESP is a metaphor for love.

S: Yes it is. Exactly.

THE SPIRAL: "THE CIRCLE WHICH LEADS TO ECSTASY."

C: I wanted to get back to your idea concerning the spiral movement of human consciousness.

S: I'm not saying the world is fine the way it is. The other day, for instance, I was in a taxi, and the driver pulled the car onto the pavement in order to park for a moment, and in doing so he almost drove into a young mother and her child. I told him to stop it. What did he think he was doing? "They're just foreign workers," he said. "They're human beings," I said. And as long as this kind of attitude exists, you'll never get rid of wars.

There are people who say we must change as little as possible, but this seems to me a ridiculous statement. I'm working all the time to construct things. But I have to recognize and use and transform the forces of destruction. Once, when I was verbally attacked during a discussion in Frankfurt, a man got up and said that I was a *Stehaufmensch*—a Stand-Up Man, one of those little plastic toy men with lead in his feet: you can throw him anywhere and he always returns standing up. The person who called me that really described my whole life. Whenever I lost the dearest things—things I had gotten too attached to—then after the shock of losing them, I turned this loss into something positive, I began to see what was "essential" again; I began to see the whole and to live for the whole.

I want a world where everyone can understand the total. Because then *understanding* is *becoming the other*, and by that is love. Love is accepting the most opposed things—you begin to understand the whole spiral process. Of course you have to take a side: I'm on the side of unification, construction, understanding, and higher consciousness. This is my law and I'd fight for it.

C: I've read the first draft of Jill Purce's book, *Spiral: The*

Cosmic Law and Man's Aspirations Towards Eternity, which I hope will be published soon.* This book exemplifies the ideas you've just mentioned.

S: Jill Purce showed me her book after she heard a performance of my *Spiral* in London. And her book is extraordinary. It shows the spiral going through all the different manifestations of life—art, music, literature, dance, religion, mythology, physics, biology, botany, and, naturally, astronomy. Everything is a spiral, she points to this unity in the cosmos, and with this one aspect she unifies her book and thereby acts as a counterbalance to the atomization in the world. Unlike myself, she never talks about herself; she transcends the egocentric. In her essay, "Eschatological Visions of the Universal Deluge in Leonardo and Turner," she discusses the theme of the deluge and the urge toward personal dissolution in order to allow for the new to be born. In her book on the spiral there are hundreds of wonderful photographs about which Jill gives a few comments in order to allow you to discover your own awarenesses. She just gives you the key—it's like the thread of Ariadne which leads you out of the labyrinth.

Aurobindo speaks of the spiral as the principle of the steady increase of consciousness—involution rather than evolution. The spiral goes in all directions, bringing us everywhere. In the spiral inside an electric bulb, the beginning is connected to the end, and these two electric circuits make light. This circular spiral gives light, and in this feedback, it rises. As I've said before, you always go through what seem to be similar situations, but they're never the same. You *remember* and you *expect*, but the instant is no longer the instant, it's now eternity—you are everywhere. And that's what the spiral brings about. It's the circle which leads to ecstasy.

* Jill Purce's essay "The Spiral in Art: Aspirations Towards Eternity" appears in *The Structurist*, No. 11 (1971), published by the University of Saskatchewan.

"And Los beheld his Sons and he beheld his Daughters,
Every one a translucent Wonder, a Universe within,
Increasing inwards into length and breadth and heighth,
Starry & glorious."

—William Blake, *Jerusalem*

THE KATARAGAMA RELIGIOUS FESTIVAL OF CEYLON

C: You told me that in 1970 you attended the Kataragama religious festival in Ceylon. Would you describe it?

S: Several days before it starts—even after it has begun—you can see lots of families with their kids on the road walking literally hundreds of miles to go to Kataragama, where every year there's a two-week festival for Buddhists, Hindus, and Muslims. For the Hindus, it's a festival of self-punishment; for the Buddhists, a festival of joy; and for the Muslims, of competition.

When you arrive you see the river filled with human bodies alongside elephants taking a bath. The water is considered holy, so there are many sick people, but others, too, pouring the water over themselves. . . . The first thing everybody does is to walk to the main temple, in front of which is a large stone and a hill of coconuts. Each person takes one, prays a little, stands there with eyes closed—an enormous tension building up in the face—and then all of a sudden he opens his eyes, throws the coconut on that stone, and then watches the result. If it splits exactly in the middle, the wish that he's just formulated in his mind will be fulfilled. And if it breaks with many little splinters, the wish is rejected. If it breaks in uneven pieces, the wish will be only partly fulfilled. And as you look at all the people passing by in line you can observe every imaginable human expression—the very happy face, the slightly disappointed face, the proud face, the sad face, the furious face—one after another.

There were saddhus running around, once in a while picking up pieces of coconut and putting them in their mouths. One whom I watched for several days always put his head over an oil flame—there were a lot of open oil flames standing around—and then he laughed and ran screaming all about the place. He came up to me with eyes that were smiling and angry at the same time, opened his hand, and I gave him some money which he put in a little shirt pocket, then he danced around and again put his head in the oil flame.

Soon I saw a very high wooden cart on wooden wheels being pushed along by several persons with an old woman in front holding an old stick like a witch, screaming and attracting everyone's attention. There was a naked man suspended horizontally, hanging by a string and six large fishhooks in his back [see page 106]. You could only see the whites of the eyes, and once in a while they stopped the cart, the woman screaming some words that I didn't understand, and all sorts of men as well as women with babies in their arms stood in line again and went up a four-foot-high platform in front of this man who was hanging horizontally. He held a trident in his hand and started talking automatically the moment they touched him, telling them the future, and again you saw all the different expressions on the people's faces. Someone waiting on him held out a little pot containing ashes, and the man took some, put them into the mouth of a baby, never opening his eyes and talking all the time, then placing some ashes into his own mouth. Literally, the skin on his back was pulled upward about five inches, but no blood was coming out—two hooks in the tendons and four in the back. People began to push him, and these hand-cut wooden wheels made this *dok-a-dok-a-dok-a* sound—he looked like a piece of rubber swinging up and down. I followed him for almost half an hour. And afterward, when I sat next to him, he looked at me and made a sign that I should take a look at his back. There were no really deep holes in the skin, only one small spot of blood, and he was very ashamed of it, he made a sign that I shouldn't look at it any further.

This man was a Hindu, but the Muslims who had a ceremony later in their own temple really put him out of business. These are special people—the fakirs—who do these sorts of things, the spirit completely dominates the body. And at the end of the festival, too, you can see the so-called fire walking—it has been studied by all sorts of doctors from Europe and America—a twenty-foot-long woodpile (I've seen the Trance Dance in Bali, but not on such an enormous pile), about four to five feet high, and the whole thing is set on fire. When it's really hot and all the wood's burning, then persons who have trained to do this run over the fire, with naked feet, and when they return to show you their feet, there's not the slightest trace of their having been singed. I've heard that some Westerners who have gone there have tried to walk on this pile, too, but they were badly burned.

When you walk down to the river, you can see people renting these round wooden constructions, colored very joyously, which they attach to their shoulders and then start dancing wildly until they fall into a trance. The wooden yokes are heavy, and they rub the skin of the back until it's raw. You see, this is what the Hindus do in order to punish themselves. It's all based on the story of a Hindu monk who was refused alms by a Hindu, but was given something by a Buddhist. And the king who converted from Hinduism to Buddhism ordered a fifteen-day-long festival, to occur every year before the full moon in July. So the Hindus punish themselves because of that story, while the Buddhists feel very proud of themselves. Every evening at six o'clock you have this fantastic dressing of the elephants; some holy bones are placed in a reliquary, and then a whole series of processional dances take place.

C: What kind of instruments do they use?

S: Several typical Ceylonese drums. And they also play these oboelike instruments that make high screeching sounds like the old Greek aulos—it sounds really crazy, like snake music—very penetrating and very sharp. And they also have little antique cymbals.

One beautiful moment occurred when I walked down to the river after I'd seen that man putting his head over the oil flame, and there I saw him again, walking into the river in his shirt and trousers as if he were drunk. He made very strange movements, looking up to the sky, his hands weaving. And then he let himself just fall backward into the water, laughing happily, and when he looked down at his body and saw in his pocket the money that I'd given him, he removed the bill and just threw it into the air—it fell in the water—and forgot about it.

There was also this very beautiful-looking saddhu always sitting in front of one of the side temples—there were three parts of the main temple, and he was sitting at the left side by the stone door. He never moved, he was continually in lotus position, holding his head a bit to the side. And he had a strange hat on his head which looked as if it were made of black strings mixed with cow manure. I always wondered what he was up to—most of the time his eyes were closed. I returned very early one morning . . . it was the third day . . . and I suddenly saw him stand up and walk very slowly to the center of the temple area, which was composed of soft sand. He sat down very gracefully, like a ballerina in the most fantastic ballet performance, aware of all the movements of his fingers and arms. First he made a sign—placing his two palms together he closed his eyes and bowed his head several times toward the sun. Then his hands went up to his hat, very slowly opened a knot, and loosened it. It was shaped like a large cobra, but as he unwound it like a spiral outward . . . I discovered that it was his natural hair. He laid it in a circle in the sand—it was lying in front of him like an enormous snake, much longer than himself . . . and he was a tall man. And then he started doing his meditation. I took several photographs of this fantastically beautiful person [see page 107]—he didn't pay any attention, I didn't exist for him. And you can see that his face is perfectly harmonious, his skin completely unblemished. I asked a Ceylonese friend who spoke the language to please ask some of the priests to find out this man's age. He came back and asked me how old I thought he was. I said, to be honest, I'd watched him a long time, and I thought he was about fifty-five. And he said: The priests say he's from India, and he's ninety-three. . . . And then, freely like a dancer with a very light step, he wound a wide toga around his body and moved away through the trees. It was a beautiful moment.

Now, the Muslims are the minority religion at Kataragama, and they really want to make a showing. One night I attended about a two-hour performance given by a dozen fakirs—who were sitting on the ground in a circle—and two high priests sitting up on a stage. The priests were wearing these green robes, and their eyes were almost closed—just a *slit*. The fakirs started drumming, kneeling in a circle, and in front of the priests were a lot of torture tools of all lengths and sizes—some long and sharp, some broad—all kinds of metal tools that reminded you of medieval torture chambers. . . . They began a very slow periodic beat on the drums, and once in a while you heard a collective yell, very low and rising slightly higher in pitch. They sped it up in a fabulously slow accelerando—musically, it was very well rehearsed. And when it was going very fast, the priest opened the slit of his eye just a bit, looked at a fakir, and made a small, sharp movement with his chin to one side. The first man put his head down and began trembling—he didn't want to perform. The priest made an angry face and then looked over all of them; they were already overheated and drumming very fast. He stared at another fakir, and this one made a movement: OK, he accepted . . . but he looked worried. He got up, made three bows to the ground in front of the priests, and chose a metal weapon. He held it and started moving slowly with it, took a piece of flesh of his breast and *slash!* he stuck the foil through the skin and danced with it. Next he pulled out his tongue: *slash,* through the tongue; then he made his cheeks firm and through both cheeks—*slash*—here in and there out . . . next, through the arm here, through the arm there. Now he had many lances in his body and danced more and more wildly with the drums while the others watched him, and one of the priests, a devilish smile on his face, looked very satisfied with that performance. It was a real event for the whole crowd. He danced until foam came to his lips. And as he tumbled down, another jumped up to help him get the knives out. And all they did then was to put a little bit of ash on the wound . . . but there *was* no wound, no blood came out. When all the knives were removed he made three bows, clapped his hands together, and the priest gave a very gracious sign of satisfaction. The drumming slowed down a little, then sped up again. And now the next fakir stood up, a very tall man who began to dance in slow movements. The first thing he did—and this I found the most shocking—was to pick up a chisel about eight inches long, put it right in front of his skull. Then he took a thick little wooden hammer and while dancing, he hit the chisel into his head. When he finally took his hands away, you saw that thing sticking in his skull as he continued to move.

These people want to demonstrate, like the Hindus who do it all the time, that the spirit can completely dominate the body, that you don't feel pain, and that you can control the blood stream—that you can do almost anything with the body that you like: you're master of the body. And people who can do this draw the crowds, they think they're supernatural beings.

C: What was your feeling about this afterward?

S: I found it a very good lesson, and I thought that if many people in the West were aware of the fact that they could be masters of their bodies, even on a much lower level, we wouldn't have all these pseudo-sick people running to the doctors every day with God knows that complaint. . . . I was told that before Kataragama begins, these men undergo six weeks of fasting. And the ceremonies go on and on—full of surprises. I have many photographs of unique people who seem to have stepped right out of a fairy tale: men or women, you can't divine their ages, they look incredibly transformed—the way they walk, dress, or behave. One of the saddhus, for example, who was completely shaved, was always blowing very very long sounds into a large shell. And if you do this three or four times you get completely dizzy and faint. But he did it *constantly*, and he did nothing but that. . . . So you see "originals," people who have a certain specialty, and that's their kind of religious worship.

I think attending the Kataragama is the best kind of schooling you can have—especially when you're young and very receptive—in order to see how far human beings can go in spiritual exercises and in their complete devotion to what they are doing. If any of the radio musicians or if the musicians in our group made their music with the devotion and energy we find in *these* people—they're really on fire!—then we would have some of the best music in the world.

THE OMIZUTORI CEREMONY IN THE TEMPLE OF NARA, JAPAN

C: When you were in Japan you mentioned to me that you attended the Omizutori ceremony in the temple of Nara. I'd like to ask you later about your own music-in-space compositions, but I know that this ceremony suggests many basic ideas about sounds moving in space.

S: In the Omizutori there are eleven priests who participate in the ceremony. And their "running"—in heavy wood clogs on a wooden floor—is an integral part of the music itself. Let me give you an example of how the movement of sound in space can't be separated from the quality of the sound itself.

At a certain moment late at night all the priests are sitting around the altar meditating, when one of them gets up, puts on these heavy clogs, and starts walking slowly and fairly regularly so that the sole and the heel fall with the sound: da-*tak*, da-*tak*. In this way he goes around the altar, and whenever he faces south he takes one of the laurel leaves he's been holding in his hand, throws it at the altar, and makes a shout. It sails down very slowly—this is beautiful to observe—and then the second priest begins running after him, then the third, the fourth . . . until all eleven priests are walking.

Can you imagine the unbelievable crescendo of twenty-two heavily wooden-clad feet on this resonant wooden floor! The altar is piled with rice cakes and oil lamps, and when the priests are walking around it the sound changes its color completely—coming toward you and then moving away. . . . They start running very slowly at first, then faster and faster, until there's the enormous thunderlike sound of all of them running and yelling as each throws a laurel leaf into the air. One leaf after another tumbles down, the first hasn't reached the ground when the next is thrown again, and while these yells are becoming louder at one place, the wooden sound is always moving—twenty-two heavy percussion instruments, wood against wood. When the priests reach their highest speed, the first one throws one of his shoes against one of the wooden walls, that surround the altar, and the second priest throws his at a different point on the wall, so you hear what sounds like twenty-two pistol shots in a decreasing decelerando, a fantastic space music.

You must imagine me now standing behind a thin wooden wall, looking and listening through little holes. I was the only "profane" person allowed even in the gangway, which is located just outside that wooden wall, and through these holes in the wall, as if in a confessional chair, I observed and listened to the priests. . . . As far as the public for Omizutori is concerned, the women aren't allowed to come into the temple itself; they have to stay in small rooms that are connected to the outside of the temple by little doors, and they listen to the sounds by sitting on tatamis and leaning their heads against the wooden walls—they can't see anything. A few older men sit and follow the whole spectacle behind a translucent white gauze curtain. They see the flickering lights of the oil lamps and hear the sounds, but they imagine rather than really see what's actually happening.

C: What does this event signify?

S: The consecration of water. It's a Buddhist ceremony that has occurred once a year over the past 1,200 years for six weeks, and the climax lasts three days and three nights. Eleven priests purify themselves during the six weeks by going into meditation, eating only one meal of rice a day, wearing paper clothes, and doing exercises all day long. . . . Did I ever describe to you how they time some of these events with a sand clock and the horseshoe nails? I really should sometime, it's fantastic—they get the information by chance operations, looking in one book which instructs them to check in another book for a certain constellation of a certain year. And then a third volume tells you what to do at 3:00 A.M. on the thirteenth of April 1966, you have to start burning a certain incense, for example. . . .

But let's get back to music-in-space. I mentioned before that the men sitting behind the gauze curtains hardly see anything, but at irregular intervals during the night the curtain opens very abruptly and one of the priests begins a very stylized walk around the curtain, then suddenly falls vertically down onto the floor. You hadn't observed it before, but there's a springboard on the ground which is constructed in such a way that when the priest falls on one knee and one elbow, he's pushed up again so quickly that you've hardly noticed he's been on the floor at all. It makes a short, terrific noise, you see him standing up again stiffly, then several seconds later he falls once more, stands up again, turns to the left, and very quickly walks away and disappears behind the gauze curtain. This event may occur at 4:00 or 5:00 A.M. so many of the men behind the curtain are asleep. And they wake up with this enormous noise and see this strange red- or green-cloaked being standing and falling in front of them and then running away. Can you imagine dreaming of this event later on? You might not know where it comes from—have you seen this in your childhood, this strange person? You open your eyes and there it is, that sound and that shock.

I've described the circularly moving sounds and how with decreasing speeds the priests throw off their shoes with twenty-two sharp accents against the wooden walls. And therefore, one after another, each is running in his stockings. So the tremendous roaring wooden noise is transformed into something that sounds very much like the wings of pigeons—twenty-two very light feet running on the wooden floor. . . . The priests are breathing very fast, and I should also mention that they run in the order of their sizes: the first looked like a tall sumo fighter, the smallest was a tiny little man. And running all together they seemed like a moving scale of organ pipes.

The tallest priest, now completely exhausted, let himself fall in one corner without making any attempt to sit on the floor; he took a large shell and, heavily and wearily, began breathing and panting into it. The next priest now threw himself into another corner at the opposite side and started making a lower-pitched shell music. One after the other fell down. And eventually the whole room was filled with new sounds—five higher in pitch at one side of the altar, and six lower in pitch at the opposite side. And all this time the running sound was continuing: the shell music was irregular in rhythm, whereas the running sound was a kind of regular ritardando. . . . Finally, the smallest priest came running like a little dwarf, panting, and *boom,* he fell down, too. So the music had been transformed from the wooden roar into the pigeon-wing sound, the sounds of rapid breathing into the slow shell music—three completely different constellations of sound in space in total transformations from one into the other.

"Scientists are the poets of today. 'Art' means keeping up with the speed of light."

—Edgard Varèse

C: What areas of musical composition do you think composers today might think of exploring and expanding on? I know that last year in your courses at Darmstadt you centered on just this question and that you structured your seminars around six areas or spheres, the first being the micro-macro continuum. We've touched on some of this before. . . .

NEW AREAS OF MUSICAL COMPOSITION

S: We've mentioned the historical hierarchy of the musical parameters—pitch, harmony, and melody; durations in rhythm and meter; and dynamics, which refers nowadays to something more complex than just the amplitude of the notes, classically being described by the Italian symbols, from very soft to very loud for every given instrument. Each instrument already has a certain energy by the nature of its construction. By this I mean that the flute has a different energy from a trumpet. The forte or piano of each will be quite different because of the complexity of the individual waves within a period; even if they had the same amplitude they'd have a different loudness. . . . We also talked about the emancipation of timbre. And then about the movement and direction of sound in space. These are naturally the "hot" items of current and probably future composition. And I also suggested the building of instruments which would allow for an equal differentiation of the diverse parameters. As I've said, I don't think there's an absolute hierarchy; parameters can take each other's function in polyvalent composition.

In Darmstadt I gave a résumé of the past twenty years and also spoke about the developments we can expect during and even after the next twenty years, because these last years have taught me that though I had a lot of concepts in the early fifties which I thought would be realized very quickly, actually everything is going very slowly, and I have no illusions about what can be practically realized within the next decades. In our electronic studio, for instance, we still have basically the same equipment we had ten years ago, and though it's a very well-supported radio station, we don't have the money to buy the extremely expensive materials needed for more sophisticated computers and converters. I don't foresee any immediate way musicians will receive the special equipment they need. In 1967 I thought that the most theoretically advanced concepts in the field of music synthesizing were being discussed at Stanford University. But they were all saying that while this is all theoretically possible, they'd need this and that and another few million dollars in order to obtain the whole available range of musical frequencies and the necessary binary information per second necessary to compute all the characteristics of nonstationary sounds.

So I spoke to the students about the future. And I mentioned that in various areas of science each scientist who attempts to make new discoveries tries to keep himself informed about the global status of his work. For example, I'm sure that Russian and American scientists, in spite of their countries' political hostility, make a point of reading each other's publications. And that's what musicians have to do. And in particular to have the concept that it isn't so important just to strive for one's own style in music in order to break through—to find something that no one else has explored. It's rather a problem of developing ways of integrating different musical parameters and suggesting these to everyone concerned with music—publishing houses and cassette and recording companies (there are attempts to combine these functions), critics, concert managers—even physicists who are interested in new developments in acoustic research. They should all be part of what we as composers or performers are envisaging for the next twenty years and even further on.

C: Did you give illustrations from examples of your own compositions?

S: Yes, and I explained the relationships between the structuring *within* the sound and the structuring *of* sounds in order to build larger entities, to construct larger musical formations that allow many solutions for a given process plan. I pointed out that the most important development of the last twenty years has been that of the transposition of discovered textures and structures and acoustical material into a *larger time* by expanding the proportions. And vice versa: constructing larger sections, realizing them, and making new sound material for that particular piece by condensing these structures. So that what's heard at one time as a structure with a certain rhythm and subdivisions is condensed to the point where it becomes a timbre of an individual sound.

The other day when you and I visited the Cologne radio studio, there was a young composer who was very frustrated because the studio didn't have the sawtooth generator he wanted—it had been broken. I suggested that he just get an old amplifier—there were plenty of them standing around particularly for that purpose—and then use it to distort a sine wave, let's say with sixty db, then get the amplitude down again in order to obtain a very rich harmonic spectrum. The resulting individual harmonics will even be much louder than those realized by a sawtooth generator which produces only a specific selection of the overtones of a spectrum, along with a decrease of amplitudes the higher the partials are—which anyway isn't very good for filtering in the higher regions. And I said: All you need to do is just to start the piece and make one or two minutes with the sound material you've already chosen. You can go on quite a while by cutting a certain section out of the material, putting it on a tape loop or a Springer machine, which condenses it in time, and then have new sound. You next superimpose it with another section of the piece that you also make continuous, and condense it until you again have a unified sound. In this way you can constantly produce new sound material from the music which you've already composed. Just by manipulating a small bit of initial material you can achieve enormous variety. The characteristic manipulation occurs by adding amplitude modulations on different levels which are then speeded up to such an extent that individual layers of sound are modified by different amplitude modulations. And these layers can then be synchronized again.

TAPING RHYTHMS

When I was working on my Kurzwellen-mit-Beethoven music (*Stockhoven-Beethausen Opus 1970*), I found new ways of starting with simple, and gaining completely new, sound material. For example, I fed a section of Beethoven music into several filters at once and kept the individual layers synchronous in phase—that's very important. And then I fed the individual layers into different amplitude modulators, or else into what we call pulse choppers, which superimpose a rhythm of open and closed electric circuits on the sound material which is in that particular layer.

C: I'm not too clear about this.

S: Let's say you have piano music and you feed it through four filters; each filter takes out a different frequency band, and you modulate each band in a different way: one, with a ring modulator which adds further frequencies with the sums and differences of the original frequencies; another, you lead through an echo chamber: the third, you chop with a certain rhythm—ritardando-accelerando—which means that with a pulse indicator, which also functions as a chopper device, you make holes into it, and only once in a while do certain durations of the original sound come through, the rest is silence; and then the fourth you rhythmetize with a loop that has a rhythm but no sound—which means you record it on tape to which is glued another tape in a certain rhythm so that this fourth layer is rhythmetized with the particular rhythm that you've prepared. And afterward the output of that loop is fed together with the other layers so the music in the synchronicity remains completely intact—you don't destroy anything, each layer goes a different way. One can also put one layer on a "Springer machine" which changes the pitch without changing duration, so that it always remains synchronous.

C: What do you mean by "taping rhythms"?

S: That's easy. You take white leader tape and with a special glue stick little pieces of magnetic tape on it, and the distances and lengths of these pieces now determine the rhythm. You let this tape loop run all the time: you record some music on it, and the music takes on that rhythm. In this way you can superimpose any rhythm on any music.

Also, as I've said, we have a special machine where you can prolong some musical event without transposing it downward at the same time. This reveals a completely different inner structure and timbre development. Slowing down and speeding up, to a degree where one goes beyond certain limits of perceptibility, enables you to discover a new region where rhythm becomes timbre and harmony and melody. Or vice versa. When timbre becomes rhythm and even *form*—you slow it down until the average proportions of the durations are longer than eight seconds—then you land in the region of formal sectioning and proportions (by that I mean the more architectural aspects of music). So between form, rhythm and meter, harmony and melody, and timbre composition there's a continuum, and it's very important to develop it further now.

TWENTY-ONE OCTAVES OF MUSICAL TIME

And also in composition itself, we find this constant flow between that instant when you listen into the sound and don't develop further formal aspects, and the instant when you go into another time—the rhythmic proportions between, let's say, eight seconds and one-sixteenth of a second. Just as the region of pitches has seven octaves, this rhythmic region also has seven "octaves of time": eight, four, two, one, one-half, one-fourth, one-eighth, one-sixteenth—this corresponds very well to our pitch octaves. And I'd also say that we have more or less seven octaves for the formal proportioning—which means seven times the proportion one to two. It begins with four-to-eight-second-long events—eight, sixteen, thirty-two seconds; then one minute, two minutes, four minutes, eight minutes, sixteen minutes. So sixteen minutes is, I think, traditionally the longest characteristically unchanging duration of what we could up to now consider to be a formal musical section—one movement. Between sixteen minutes and eight seconds we also use a field of seven time octaves. So in all, there are approximately twenty-one octaves of musical time. (Naturally, however, there are about two more octaves, at 6,000–12,000 cycles, above the pitch region for "brilliance"; and, if we consider the total length of works with several movements adding up to one hour for one composition, we would also have approximately two more octaves, of a half hour and one hour, below the region of formal sectioning.)

All these durations are based on our perceptions, naturally, and they can be enlarged. So it's very interesting to discover new processes of diminution and augmentation. And I hope you know what they are.

C: They're old musical terms, aren't they? If you turn an eighth note into a quarter note, you're augmenting it—you're slowing the duration and increasing the note value. And diminution is the opposite.

S: There you are. And the new processes I proposed applied not only to the coloristic aspects of the music and melody, harmony, rhythms, and forms, but also to what is within each of these regions, to the proportions between the macro and the micro. For instance, the other day we said: the noisier the sound, the larger the scale; and the purer the sound, the smaller the scale. We can now make a lot of experiments relating micro-intervallic proportions, that are linear, to relatively macro-intervallic proportions in the vertical. And very little has been done really to objectify all these new approaches.

I think every serious musician—no matter what his private aesthetics, his expressive desires or nondesires, or his social interests concerning what the music should be and for whom it should be written—should make a contribution to music in general, which can then be made available to every other musician. If a scientist makes a discovery, it's mainly important because it brings the whole field that he's working in further ahead, and all his colleagues as well.

(2) METACOLLAGE AND INTEGRATION

C: Your second lecture at Darmstadt was called "Metacollage and Integration."

S: Metacollage means, of course, going beyond the collage. I presented many examples from Varèse, Berg, and Stravinsky. In music they've always called this method the "citation technique," and it's a very old technique, it has existed since the Gregorian chant, which often integrated popular tunes. Famous folk songs were integrated into alleluia melodies which then became official Gregorian chants. Through collage, the composers of the first half of the twentieth century anticipated the enormous pluralistic spirit that appeared after the last war; the so-called global village and tourism helped purvey this spirit. And these composers prepared the people through their art for this *state* of collage.

Collage is *gluing together* and seeing what happens. It's not really mediation. And collage is exactly what's happening in society: New York is a social collage. The glue between the people is mainly the knife and mutual exploitation and hatred. But that's the first stage, naturally, because real love would go beyond this, it would create a metacollage. And then real mingling and symbiosis would begin. But we artists of the second stage have to announce that stage—to go far beyond the collage and reach the intermodulation of all the different forces that are combined in one composition. Our music represents models of elements that are very heterogeneous and seemingly unmatchable, where individual characteristics are very strong and there's mutual respect. These are complementary societies and structures in which one really supports the other by being very strongly what one is rather than becoming the same as the other. And the intermodulation goes so far that it ultimately creates new species, which aren't a synthesis in the old sense where the components disappear, but on the contrary, where the components are quite visible and complete each other. One thing completes the other, and that creates an ascending spiral movement and a cohesion—systems become coherent.

It's very difficult technically to go beyond collage, to modulate one event with another without destroying it, really discovering those original qualities of something which are the most characteristic and which are strong enough to be matched with the stronger characteristics of something else—leading to real symbiosis. It's necessary to compose strong subjects. In America the music that's most praised has done away with all musical subjects. Cage is the example of collage music where everything's just thrown in one pot and you see what happens. The famous anarchism is the "spiritual background" which allows a place for everything and everybody without taking account of the fact that a certain object that you use, let's say a triad, is not the same as any other sound object that's less common or less simple. There's a natural differentiation among things, and if you just leave them the way they fall then they function the way they are, which means some of these elements immediately oppress and dominate others, even acoustically *cover* others. What remains in your head after hearing such a piece are these few elements which are the most redundant. If there's no choice, then things create their own hierarchy. If you don't want to balance out something, you wind up with a nonintegrated situation.

C: You told me about the trees outside your house which were getting strangled by the vines. Do you think there's such a thing as natural selection in which the best weeds out the worst?

S: In music, the most redundant and the most familiar wins, the most commonplace sounds stick in the mind and the others you forget. So you get a very hierarchical music. I'm not so much interested in exclusivity, I want to integrate as much as possible. But you must give more time and space to a weak sound, otherwise the strong one just buries it. And I don't mean strong only in terms of dynamics, but of oldness, of being known. What is old is always stronger than what is unfamiliar, and what's simple is always stronger than what's complicated. Metacollage and integration mean setting up no exclusive systems, but rather really dealing with strong subjects and then trying to create balanced situations, mediating and intermodulating.

(3) EXPANSION OF TEMPO SCALES

C: Your third area was the "expansion of tempo scales."

S: After the last war, the notion of tempo disappeared. Composers got trapped by the fact that they composed with individual durations, whereas tempo is always based on periodicity, on the so-called "beats." And within these beats you have different velocities. During the course of a section with a very fast tempo the longest duration may occur in a fermata. Or the fastest ornaments might occur in a very slow tempo. In classical music the fastest melodic figurations appear in the slowest movements.

The expansion of the tempo scale means first of all that we work with a whole variety of tempi in a given composition. In my very first compositions I did away with movements. I said: a composition is a composition, and I don't want movements, one fast, one slow, one medium-fast, one very fast—like in a classical symphony; that's an old concept. These tempi should all be able to occur simultaneously, always relative to each other, unexpectedly in *one* completely integrated composition. The tempo should potentially change at every instant. In almost all the music that had been written up to that time there was one basic tempo in a movement, and the different speeds within the tempo were variations of it: there was a slow or a fast movement. This is also true of most of the music of the fifties; even nowadays you still find this. And in order to introduce relativity into the composition of tempi, you must be prepared at any given moment for the tempo to change, and you with it. Which means—using an example of a situation in space—that a person would have to move in space with his chair, rather than sitting and listening to the music with one perspective. And in pitch, too; in most compositions there's a certain medium pitch predominance, and therefore the extremes, very high or very low, are always heard in the music in one perspective, as if the point of reference were constant. But in a modern composition this point should be switched so that something in a very high register may, at a certain moment of the composition when you've well prepared this, assume a position from which everything *else* is made relative—at that point it can only be lower. You just remain in the highest regions for a long time, you settle there. Or you can make the very low regions the focus of your perspective for quite a while.

So the perspective in melodic listening must become mobile, no longer fixed. And the same with tempo: you compose it in such a way that a new tempo can become a new point of reference, and all the others then define themselves as being faster or slower in relation to it. In *Carré* or *Kontakte* I very consciously expanded the tempo scale—what was considered to be the "slowest or fastest possible" tempo. In the latter it goes so fast that you don't hear individual sounds anymore, the whole structure becomes statistical. What does this mean—*too fast?* It's reaching into a completely new region.

EXPANSION OF SCALE AND RANGE OF TEMPI

C: What about the subtle use of polyrhythms in the works of Elliott Carter?

S: That's the superimposition of different rhythmic layers, and it's very important. But expansion of the tempo scale means that we really want consciously to expand more and more toward the fast and the slow. There's that Japanese *timing* we talked about. And this average degree of change in time can be technically analyzed in works of folk and traditional non-Western music. What we must do in our music is to expand the scale and range of tempi. It opens a completely new dimension for listening because a person who experiences this music becomes as *much slower* and as *much faster* in his reactions and experiential time as the music. This expands man and also his awareness of what music can be. And it's dangerous at the same time. You can't just say; right now I'll make a tempo of metronome marking 2. Every thirty seconds you'd have a period that you'd refer the changes of a given structure to. You must be *able* to compose music which sustains itself in a tempo as slow as metronome marking 2. This is unheard of. What's interesting is to expand the tempo scale, but at the same time compose it so convincingly that the time doesn't just fall apart and everybody goes home.

C: Have you tried doing this?

S: Every piece I try to go a little further. And then they say, it's too long, it's too boring. I know, however, that the sound I put into such a slow tempo is interesting enough; you can have a wonderful time listening to the "innerness" of the sound. But if you make a whole music like this, then it's gone again. I don't think you should do away with the tempo concept. In most of Xenakis's works, or Ligeti's, for example, the tempo composition is neutralized. You can see in the score that the basic beat—even if people say you don't hear it because of irregularities of the rhythms that are placed into these measures—is just written two-four or four-four all the way through, and the conductor functions simply like a clock beating the measures mechanically, which results in an arbitrary coincidence of his movements with the rhythmic randomness of the music. No tempo feeling comes up. . . . Densities, yes. There are densities that change, but there's no feeling for tempo.

(4) FEEDBACK

C: The next thing you discussed at Darmstadt was *feedback*. You didn't simply mean acoustical feedback, did you?

S: I mean, for example, any kind of feedback between musicians who play in a group, where one musician inserts something, bringing something into context and then listening to what the next musician's doing with it when he's following certain instructions, transforming what he hears. I'm referring now to compositions of mine like *Prozession, Kurzwellen, Spiral, Poles for Two*, or *Expo for Three*, in which I've worked only with symbols that indicate at any given moment what kind of transformations you're supposed to make with what you've chosen—either your own previous event or an event that another musician is playing. You have to listen from the moment he's clearly started until he's completed the musical event with a certain duration, a certain register, a certain shape of dynamics, and a certain number of limbs—by which I mean rhythmic subdivisions by a certain melodic texture. After this you look at the next transformation sign in your score; this may be a plus or a minus or a star sign, etc. [see Fig. 6]. This last sign, for example, specifies that you choose one of the elements of the event and compare all the others intervallically with this one, thereby creating an alternation of structure, like 212523242. There are lots of different symbols processing the event that you choose. And the feedback that's established is just incredible. With the one single musical configuration at the beginning of the two versions of *Kurzwellen* on the Deutsche Grammophon record, for example, you can hear how the transformation signs operate. (I am referring to the station identification signs which the musicians picked up with the shortwave receivers; on both recordings the *same* signs are at the beginning, though the recordings were made a year apart.) A musician adds a few limbs to the configuration; he had a plus sign which he applied to the rhythmic segmentation. Another musician hears it and transforms it, transposing it in register and at the same time in duration. This same element is picked up by a third musician who transforms it, let's say, in dynamics with another envelope. So the *feeding back* really leads to incredible processes of transfigurations and, eventually, mutations.

Solo is a piece in which a performer makes a version using six note pages and six pages of form schemes, from which he chooses one. The basic principle here is that what he plays is partly picked up by microphones and fed into a special time delay machine. He has four recording assistants, the first of whom opens and closes the recording machine according to a formal scheme which has its own rhythmic instructions. He chooses certain elements of what the soloist is playing: here a sound, there a little section of melody. His score indicates when he should pick something out and record it. And what he records is all verticalized by a process of superimposition.

Perhaps you can imagine how this works: what he records runs along six tape heads, and the distances of these six heads correspond to six time differences. You can "read" what's just been played over tape head *two* or *five* or *six*, and what the head "reads," it feeds again on the same tape together with what the soloist plays anew. So he can sometimes play up to eighteen layers

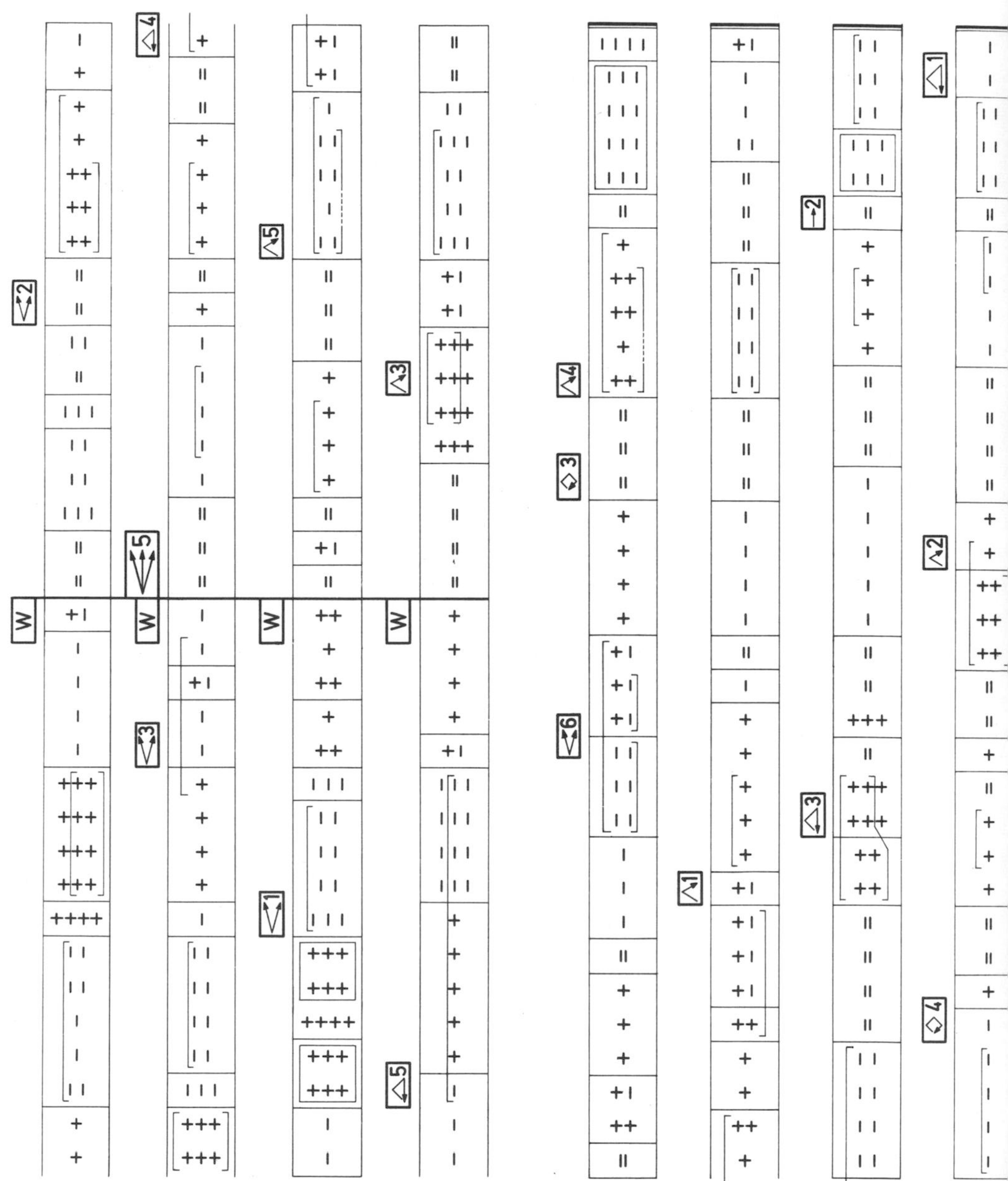

FIGURE 6: Transformation signs from *Kurzwellen*

with himself: a feedback's established, he thinks aloud, so to speak, because he reacts to the superimpositions of certain segments of what he's played before.

C: He feeds back what is fed back.

S: Yes, and that's an endless spiral. He reflects on his own reflections. It's an instantaneous decision based on stored memory. He interprets his own interpretation. And this is another process of feedback.

I can show you how we work in studios with several people at once. You give them individual instructions in order to use the different kinds of apparatuses: filters, modulators, recording machines, transposition machines, potentiometers. For a given section every person has a chart for the action he has to perform. You listen over the speakers to the total result of the collective interactions of these several people, which immediately affects your next decision; and what you decide you hear at that same moment. And that influences all the others, who react instantly to any movement that you make. Entire musical constructions can be the result of this feedback among several people.

C: During one performance of *Spiral* that I attended, there was one moment when a child in the audience cried. . . .

S: And the musician reacted to it. Yes, in such a process the musician reacts to everything he hears. And that was an amazing musical event because the audience could understand the process; they don't really believe that the performers react to instantaneous radio programs, they think there's recording involved.

C: Maybe you could suggest that the listeners contribute their own sounds.

S: It would be chaotic, like a kindergarten. It would be like what happens at the Tivoli in Copenhagen where people stand in front of the distorting mirrors and start making grimaces. . . . I have thought of inviting a small number of persons to a new kind of experimental concert hall whare everybody has a desk, as in a university, and pushbuttons that can produce sound material or influence the music that's made. But all the attempts up to now in this direction have resulted in very loud music because everybody wants to be heard, and within half a minute it's all forte fortissimo, except for some short moments when it becomes soft again. But then it begins all anew, horrible crescendi where everybody starts shouting in order to be heard and the music becomes too dense. . . . It's only possible with mutual communication among musicians.

C: What requirements do you think are necessary for an improvisational group?

S: In our group the musicians have had a lot of training with composed music, and they make a lot of qualitative decisions as to what to or what not to react to in order to create a really coherent organic music. You need self-education in order to go further, to integrate, and to make something interesting out of any uninteresting thing. (The main thing is, for example, to remain silent for longer periods.) Musicians who are pretty slow in their reactions can't participate in this music. And it immediately becomes clear who the best musicians are for this kind of approach. In traditional music the performer may work for half a year, rehearse, and be a brilliant musician. But in this kind of music it's not really possible. He must react very quickly, on the spot, and, even with a sixth sense, anticipate what the other musician does and integrate any heterogeneous elements that are thrown in. Very few have developed this skill to transform them so that they become part of the whole and are no longer thorns in the flesh.

And for this, musicians must always go back to composed music which is very carefully worked out and the result of a lot of filtering. It lacks a certain spontaneity and this high quality of intuitive feedback, but it provides and proposes new ways of working with certain musical formulas. The musician should always alternate between this free kind of intuitive feedback playing and faithfully studied determinate music.

C: So there's also a feedback between these two processes.

S: That's very important, between a situation where only an individual is responsible for the result and that in which the group is working together. I think basically it's all a question of time, since in the instantaneous music with a high degree of feedback, the time of preparation is zero and the tension of realization is maximal. Whereas in determinate music, the time of preparation is infinite, but the instantaneous feedback is minimal. And both are necessary and complementary. And that's why I think it's ridiculous to say that we're finished with determinate music and should now create only aleatoric music, or just let the machines make the music while we have a good time, push a few buttons, and simply feel amazed and pleased by what results. (This is one way of discovering certain combinatoric results which we can't think out.) Or else we can all sit around playing, and it doesn't matter too much what sounds we make, we're all having fun together. This has a therapeutic function, getting it out, making no demands, saying everything is fine, no matter what it is. But there's no challenge, and you become very lazy, actually. That's why musicians should switch between these two aspects, and composers too—zero time and infinite time.

In a "composed" score, six months of thinking and intuiting can be condensed into a thirty-minute performance. When we play intuitive music in our group, thirty minutes are thirty minutes. But in these minutes, the particular tension of now or never—because we know we win or lose, it will be beautiful, extraordinary, or just mediocre—creates something very special that you never attain when you sit at a table, smoke a cigarette, look out the window, answer the telephone . . . you never have that now-or-never tension. While composing a score there are sometimes beautiful moments late at night when you've worked all day long and all of a sudden everything falls into place. These are fantastic moments. But it has nothing to do with the tension of sitting in the hall, the people are there, and you know you can't erase anything.

Every once in a while I compose pieces like *Mantra* and *Trans* which are completely determined and which condense a lot of time and musical imagination and thinking into the actual performance time. But when I've done this for a while, I must go back to group playing where the new experiences I've become aware of during the composing can now add many new aspects to our playing together. We should have many ways of making music, not just one.

And parenthetically, I think that if free jazz musicians also played "composed" new music their technique and their sense of coherent musical entities and unities would develop even more.

C: Eric Dolphy and Cecil Taylor, among others, certainly have developed this sense.

S: Yes, several feel it now. But they should also have the possibility of playing on stage like the soloists in the so-called classical field. Musicians should go diagonally through all the possibilities of *music*, no longer restricted commercially by terms like "jazz."

(5) SPECTRAL HARMONICS

C: At Darmstadt you also talked about *spectral harmonics*—I think we've gone into this.

S: Yes, that's *Stimmung*, for example—to work within the spectrum of the sound with completely new techniques, emphasizing certain formants and harmonics, but not necessarily only the whole number harmonic relationships. Let's say you have many sounds at once and then dynamically bring them out of that wall of sound one after another. You have the concept of musical reliefs which have different layers, one behind the other rather than one above the other. . . . And as I said before, new instruments must be built which permit many more subtle ways of going into the spectrum of the sound and by that enlarging the whole field of what can be composed. And new musical material, new vocal techniques like those used in *Stimmung*, can change the method of composition.

(6) MUSIC-IN-SPACE

C: The last subject you discussed at Darmstadt is a large one—*Raummusik* or music-in-space. You've been concerned with this area of composition in works from *Gruppen* and *Carré* to the recent *Sternklang* park music.

S: For twelve years I've made all kinds of different approaches to new situations of music in space. *Gruppen* for three orchestras, for example, requires a hall which is wider than it is long and in which most of the listeners are surrounded by the orchestras—one at the left, one in front, and one on the right. I originally wanted to write a normal orchestra piece, but when I started composing several time layers I had to superimpose several metronomical tempi, and it was impossible to find a solution by which one conductor would be able to lead the three sections of a large orchestra in different tempi. So I finally concluded that the only way was to split the diverse time layers and put each group in a separate place so that one didn't get distracted by the signals of the other conductors. Once I had the idea of separating the three groups—each consists of thirty-six or thirty-seven musicians—I began to think in terms of alternations of sound movements: triangular rotation—one, two, three . . . one, two, three—with accelerando-ritardando; then alternations between two groups; and moments when one group would add only short sound events to the continuous alternation of the other two groups. I also thought in terms of moving timbres: there's one spot that led to something I hadn't expected myself—a chord is moving from orchestra to orchestra with almost exactly the same instruments (horns and trombones) and what changes isn't the pitches but rather the sound in space. Each orchestra, one after another, makes a crescendo and a decrescendo; at the moment when one starts fading out, the next orchestra begins to fade in, producing these very strong waves of revolving timbres.

In an earlier electronic work like *Gesang der Jünglinge* I'd used five loudspeaker groups, but because nobody had five-channel machines I made a four-channel version later on. I think it's in *Kontakte* that I've succeeded best in really integrating the movement of sound in space. There, a whole series of sound movements is differentiated as much as timbres, rhythmic values, or pitches. I used a particular system based on the degrees of change from zero to a certain maximum. "Degrees of change" means the following: let's say a sound, which is in one of four loudspeakers set up in the four corners of the hall, occurs afterward in one of the speakers next to it (while it is continuing in the first speaker)—this is the first degree of change. Next, a sound in one speaker stops and at that moment begins in another speaker either to its left or right—this is a stronger change and it's degree number 2. In number 3, a sound in one speaker occurs afterward in two other speakers, but remains in the first. And so on.

Next I dealt with the speed of that movement—how fast the sound travels from one spot to another. And naturally this already overlaps with the rhythmic construction because changing the position of a sound in space automatically creates rhythm. You can have a continuous sound and let it revolve in four speakers with a certain speed. If it's periodic and revolves once in a second, then what you hear is four distinct events in four corners of the room.

ANYTHING CAN FUNCTION AS RHYTHM

C: In this case, rhythm is a function of the space.

S: Exactly. That's why I've asked: What is rhythm? Is it the rhythm of the timbres, of the spatial motions, of the pitches, of dynamics? Anything can function as rhythm. Rhythm simply indicates intervals between changes, no matter what the changes are. And the same is true of harmony and melody. When I speak now in composition seminars about *spatial melodies* I mean particular sequences of points in a given space where sound can occur.

Once you start doing this you can discover how to make sounds go vertically or diagonally up and down a wall without having speakers at the different levels.

C: When you were describing the Omizutori there seemed to me something really special about those three particular sounds—wood, wings, and the breathing of shells.

S: Yes, didn't there? And that's what I mean: we have to find out which sounds can and cannot move. I naïvely started to try to rotate any sound I produced, but it didn't work at all. I found that only certain rhythms can be moved in rotation or at certain speeds; and, as I was saying, if you want to go up and down a wall without having the speakers at different levels, then you must experimentally find out what kind of sounds can do it. I can say in general that the sharper the sound and the higher the frequency, the better it moves and the clearer its direction. But I'd also say that the more a sound is chopped—let's say in the region between three and twelve pulses per second—the better it moves in space. And the sharper the attack of each segment of a sound event, the better it moves. Whereas a continuous or harmonious sound or a spectrum of vowels doesn't move very well.

TOPOLOGY OF SPACE: PROJECTING AND DRAWING SOUNDS IN SPACE

C: You seem to be talking about a kind of topology of space.

S: Yes, any point in space should be precisely defined with respect to where the sound occurs and how it travels from one point to any other. At any given spot in an auditorium we should be able to project the sound, but this isn't possible nowadays because we don't know that much about it yet. As I said, there are many principles that we're discovering now. And I've already described to you my experiments with the rotation table.

The topology of space you mentioned necessitates the development of new systems of notation. I once investigated the notational procedures of air and ship navigation in order to find out what methods they were using. . . . You see, the ultimate goal for me would be a situation in which a musician who's performing on stage has a radar device or an electromagnetic field surrounding his body. If he has a certain magnetic center on, let's say, a part of his face, then wherever he goes, so will the sound, and the space through which he moves will designate and delimit the sound he's producing with his instrument.

Another way of accomplishing this might require that every musician have an assistant who writes with a light pencil on a three-dimensional radar space and in this way describe where he wants the sound to be heard in the hall. But the problem here is that he's limited to the speed of the movement of his arm, and since you'd want to go faster sometimes, you'd probably have to have someone working the knobs of an accelerator device: you'd need one person producing the sound and another projecting it in space. . . . If you wanted to do it yourself then, God knows, you'd probably have to make music like the astronauts in those rotating chairs in space labs. What I want is a kind of radar screen so that the musician can drive in space with the sound. He doesn't himself need to fly, it would be fairly complicated to have a hundred musicians flying in an auditorium. . . .

C: There'd be a lot of crashes.

S: A lot of intentional crashes, I'm sure, and they'd probably crash the conductor all the time. . . . But what I have in mind is a situation where you'd sit and project your sound in space with any given speed and draw the musical configuration of the sound in the air. That is what I want to come to: I think that the time when a musician is bound to his body—when the sound is bound to a body which cannot fly—will soon be over, and should be over. We have to make the sound move in any direction with any given speed and in any given space. This is technically what we have to develop next. And then you'll see: music will be great fun even if people don't understand the really intricate qualities of the given composition; at least they'll have the experience of living with the sounds which will surround them and pass by.

WALKING AND RUNNING MUSIC

In our concert hall situation today we've gotten so used to the lack of almost any kind of movement that you could easily replace a musician with a loudspeaker, put a dummy in his place, and you'd hardly recognize it. There are some spiritual aspects involved here, but if the intuitive current isn't present, and if the musicians are only executing a beat, then you really *can* put a dummy there.

We've even thought of putting the musicians on swings in order to make the sound move, but this becomes too complicated. In the mid-fifties I conducted a seminar in Darmstadt where we produced walking and running music—the instrumentalists and singers made movements while they were producing the music, going out of and coming into the room; they composed several pieces in which a sound or a group of sound makers would remain in the same place *only* in a specific situation. And we split the public into separate groups in order to give them different listening perspectives.

The physicality of the production of sound is changing all the time. Already in *Zeitmasze* I wrote arrows over certain sounds in the score, signifying that the clarinet or oboe or English horn player had all of a sudden to raise his instrument way up into the air, blow the sound, and then put it down again—like a goose which lifts its head and makes a shrieking sound. From the very beginning I've thought about where the instruments would have to be placed, I didn't want simply to have an automatic spacing of the sound. And, for one piece after another, I specified different and particular spatial arrangements. We should also realize that even a classical score can become more transparent with a different placement of the musicians. All this is leading to a situation in which the designation of the movements of the body will be one very important and specific aspect of the ceremony of making a sound: we have the example of the cross-legged position of the Indian musician or of Japanese musicians who sit on their heels when they perform.

C: Could you describe some of your own music-in-space projects?

ENSEMBLE

S: *Ensemble* was the first public presentation of a piece of what I call my "process planning" collective music. And it was the result of three weeklong seminars of four to six hours daily in 1967 with twelve composers whom I selected from twelve different countries. I composed the overall "plan" and each composer worked with one instrumental soloist—I'll explain this in a moment. The four-and-a-half-hour performance took place in a large gymnasium in Darmstadt, but the event actually began before the people came in, and it ended in a very particular way: one composer after another left the gymnasium with his accompanying musician; as they drove away, the instrumentalists kept on playing in the back of the open-roofed cars or through the open windows—we'd arranged to meet at 2:00 A.M. about twenty miles outside of town. And this "farewell" music was an integral a part of the event, as was the situation when the audience, approaching the gymnasium earlier that evening, could already hear a whole house of music—a sounding box.

Now every composer was responsible for composing something for one soloist; he fed this soloist information, either with gestures—based on a certain predetermined signifying system—or by placing small cards in front of him, on which music of a more or less determinate kind was written out. The musicians would know what kind of symbols to expect, but the composer could surprise the soloist during the performance by changing the order in which the cards would appear. Every musician was amplified over two speakers which were placed in a diagonal direction, and these speakers were sometimes opened by another four musicians, each one manipulating the soloists' movements of sound in space. I had composed nine inserts which unified the whole ensemble by verticalizing—harmonically and rhythmically—all the musical events.

So it was a pluralistic, a soloistic, and a collective situation all at once. You had a multiple perspective—everybody chose his place, people walked outside to the terrace and met friends; some sat listening to the music inside, while others talked outside. And because of this continual movement I had to create the right conditions for the performance. I found special rubber mats that could cushion the noise of people walking about, and I arranged the locations of the podiums on which the instrumentalists performed and of the speakers. It was an example of an entirely new topology that we had to design ourselves.

MUSIC FOR A HOUSE

C: The next year, 1968, you set up the *Music for a House*, also at Darmstadt.

S: Yes, this was an expansion of the one-room concept. I

don't think it's absolutely necessary any longer to experience music in only one room. The polyphony of music—music of many layers—should find its correspondence in a polyspatial situation so that in one building—and I'll talk about my ideas for such a building later—there would be a room like the control center in the unmanned spacecraft complex at Caltech. And in such a room the public could hear and see over a multiple speaker and television system everything that's going on in the many rooms of the house at once. And if they wanted to listen more carefully to the details, they'd just have to walk into the individual rooms—they'd go through the music. And in *Music for a House* this center was located in the basement in which four speakers were set up—one for each of the four rooms of the house.

Music for a House was another collective composition in which I again made the process plan and gave examples of how to compose individual text compositions. There's a wonderful book written and edited by Dr. Fred Ritzel which describes the whole seminar [*Musik für ein Haus,* published by Schott in 1970]—I wish it were translated into English. It's like a detective story describing the birth of a new concept. You see, traditionally we're used to hearing one composition played after another in a concert hall. But what I wanted to come close to creating here was a performance of twelve works at once. Actually, they weren't really taking place all at once—sometimes there were five or four or two. There was even a situation in which all the musicians gathered together in a room in order to perform just one piece.

Every instrumentalist carried a time plan and watched the clock—each had a ten-minute break between performances. So the public would sometimes meet different musicians with their instruments walking around the rooms on their way to perform somewhere else. In a given room you could see a trio all of a sudden re-forming into a quintet—two musicians were leaving while four others entered from different places: there was a continual exchange of performers. People really experienced a whole house vibrating. It took place in Darmstadt at a Masonic lodge with large glass windows, and we played in four halls which had traffic signs and arrows pointing to the different entrances. And I gave names to the halls: Sound Attic, for example, was one; Zeng! was another (it has simply an onomatopoetic meaning); Echo, a third; Vibratorium, a fourth; and Sound Box was the name of the control studio I talked about before.

Just to describe briefly what happened in one room: At a certain time during the evening, a trio was performing in the Sound Attic, and what the musicians played was amplified over speakers which were located in the corners on high stands. The composer who had provided the material for the musical process sat at a control desk with potentiometers and then moved the sound of each instrument throughout the room. He also had a second small control desk with another four potentiometers. And by opening up one of them he could listen over separate speakers to any of the other rooms, and if what was going on there seemed interesting he just left it on and gave certain signs to the musicians in his room in order to show them how to react to this—through imitation, expansion, transformation, or synchronization.

C: Could the other room now open up their speakers to hear *their* sounds being transformed?

S: Exactly. When the other room opened up their speakers, then the feedback began; the musicians there realized that another room was reacting to them and there was a real dialogue.

This system gave us a chance to have a wonderful ending for the event. We had recorded the day before for four hours—we didn't rehearse the performance, we just went through this four-hour process from beginning to end. And at about eleven o'clock of the night of the performance, we started playing these tapes in two of the rooms. The tape recorders were also used to add electronic music or recorded shortwave sounds to the instrumental music of the actual event—this was part of the whole composition and so it wasn't unusual for the tape to play over the speakers. But the music recorded from the day before was now being played back, the musicians were beginning to leave, and the people thought: They're going on to another room! You see, nobody knew exactly when the music would be over. The whole house was sounding with the same kind of music heard earlier on, but no instrumentalists were around. People went into the next room, thinking: Here they are, but no one was there. The music was still playing, so they walked into another room: no one there, either. And so the public was left wandering through the house completely alone while all of the participants were eating at a distant restaurant. [Laughing.]

C: You once told me about a man you met who lived in Hobart, Australia—a town in Tasmania—who made plans with you to use Telstar and have groups of musicians in Australia,

Central America, and Europe who would watch each other on television screens and perform together. This is the *Music for a House* idea on a universal scale.

S: It would have been the first global music. I would have composed a piece for several groups which weren't together in just one city or country. And everything they played would have been immediately communicated to anyone in the world who was watching television or listening to the radio.

VARÈSE'S ESPACE

C: Did you know that Edgard Varèse planned a multilingual work called *Espace* with "voices in the sky, as though magic, invisible hands turning on and off the knobs of fantastic radios, filling all space, criss-crossing, overlapping, penetrating each other, splitting up, superimposing, repulsing each other, colliding, crashing"? And Varèse imagined *Espace* being performed and broadcast simultaneously in different parts of the world, the choirs singing in their own languages with a "humming, yelling, chanting, mumbling, hammered declamation."

S: I visited Varèse in his home in New York City, and we met in Europe several times. I operated the potentiometers at the first Hamburg performance of *Déserts*. I liked him very much. You know, Schönberg as well as Varèse had great ideas that went far beyond the available means. And when I was with Varèse we talked about some of these things. During his last ten years or so he was apparently more interested in astronomy than in music. He went to see a scientist friend of his in an observatory in order to watch the stars. Varèse's concepts went really far beyond his technical means. And I always felt as if he were a good father.

CONCERTS IN THE CAVES OF JEITA, LEBANON

C: I've seen photographs and also the film taken of the amazing concerts that you gave in the caves of Jeita, Lebanon, in 1969.

S: The lower caves were discovered at the end of the last century. And only ten years ago a man named Sami Karkabe came upon the upper cave which is more than a mile long and filled with stalagmites and stalactites. Three years ago they built a 100-

yard-long tunnel connecting the outside of the cave to the inside. There's a remnant of a human bone encased in stones at the entrance—and fossils, too—almost 40 million years in the layers of the mountain!

We performed *From the Seven Days* and several versions of *Spiral* on the first night. There were 180 small speakers hidden in the rocks, and as the audience walked through the cave, we very softly played *Stimmung* over the speakers. Everyone became silent —it was like entering the womb of existence; or, as I said to someone there, it was as if there were a fantastic hole in the stomach of God.

It took about twenty minutes to walk to the inner section which opened up like a grand cathedral; a Lebanese architect designed a concrete snakelike path between the stalagmites and stalactites. And you walked up several staircases until you arrived at the upper dome, which is where we made the music. Everyone sat against the walls on this path—there was an audience of about twelve hundred persons each night. The musicians were somehow in the center on a circular platform, about 150 yards away from some of the listeners. And the speakers, as I said, circled us in the rock walls about 80 yards distance from the musicians.

We performed *Stimmung, Hymnen, Telemusik,* and *Kurzwellen.* And we had a hard time getting shortwaves there; we had to lay a mile-long cable through the cave in order to reach the outside. What was fantastic was that the reverberation time for a loud sound was seven to eight seconds, but when the next sound occurred, the reverberation time came so much later that it didn't destroy the music, though each sound had a long tail, so to speak. I had a control desk which enabled me to move the sounds which were flying through like prehistoric dragons—I could make a sound cross several hundred yards from left to right. We had spotlights on the musicians—the rest of the cave was dark—and when you looked down from the circular platform about a hundred yards deep you could see through a hole an underground river which was lit by several projection lights. The caves made the music sound both prehistoric and also like something out of science fiction.

André Masson and Max Ernst came to the concerts. On the first night I shouted their names, and the musicians answered and started transforming these sounds: *Ma*-ax. He later told me that at that moment it seemed as if he had died and was hearing his name on entering a new world.

C: It sounds like Charon taking you across the river Styx.

S: Yes, it was like that. I was shivering on the outside and hot inside. The audience was transported. People said that it sounded like the music from Atlantis or of a distant star. They looked at the musicians as if they were ghosts in some supraconscious dream. . . .

OUTDOOR CONCERT AT ST. PAUL DE VENCE

These concerts remind me of an event I set up the same year outdoors in the Giacometti courtyard—surrounded by the large sculptured beings by Miró—of the museum of the Maeght Foundation in St. Paul de Vence in France. We played *Unbegrenzt* (Unlimited) from *From the Seven Days* and inserted into it three versions of *Spiral*. Musicians were sitting on the roofs, in the courtyard, and on the wooden ramps which were constructed for the audience. We started at 6:30 P.M., and when the people began arriving throughout the next hour they could already hear the music from far away. We played until about ten o'clock, integrating not only our instrumental and vocal sounds but also those of the frogs and cicadas and all the other animals which woke up to the rising of the late summer moon. And then, one after another, each musician started walking off, continuing to play, into the forest. (Every once in a while a musician would run back from the forest through the courtyard, only to disappear again, echoing in the night.)

We had built a special small wagon with an almost invisible string for Bojé and his Elektronium, and he was pulled away while he was playing through a little gate close to Miró's "Cosmic Egg" into the Labyrinth of Miró. Michel Portal had two saxophones around his neck, Diego Masson walked around banging a tam-tam, and I had a large sliding bird whistle and car horns. And then, one by one, all disappeared further into the pine forest—there was now a full moon, cicadas whirring, dogs barking. After a long time of not knowing what to do, the people tried to follow us, but when someone approached us we hid until he or she passed by. And then slowly they started dialogues of sound signals with us. . . . When the people decided to go home they began walking to the parking lots. The last thing I remember occurred about 2:30 in the morning—a twenty-minute-long dialogue with car horns. I started it but then all the people who hadn't left began making horn music with each other; and as one after the other drove off, they exchanged sounds for miles down the road. . . . The instructions for *Unlimited* were: "Play a sound with the certitude that you have any amount of space and time." . . . At least some of us were almost certain that we had an unlimited amount of time and space.

STERNKLANG IN BERLIN'S TIERGARTEN

C: What about *Sternklang* (Star Sound)?

S: *Sternklang,* which took place at night in the Berlin Tiergarten in June 1971, was something different. You had to walk to discover the five groups of musicians who were separated by bushes and trees. As you approached one group the sounds became more transparent and louder; and if you were in between two groups, you could hear sounds coming from afar and mixing—this change from one sound area to another was very important.

There were "sound runners" of each group who, at particular moments, had to sing or play a certain sound model while they were running from one group to another—which picked up this "model," transforming and integrating it—while the runner went off to a third group. The runner was accompanied by a torch carrier who lighted his way. The musical material included the singing of the names of the star constellations with a technique I used in *Stimmung*: a certain constellation of pitches are held for a long time and you listen to the subtle timbral changes. And here, every musical event was determined in all its proportions.

It was like being in a Japanese temple—you'd approach and stay with a group for some time and then walk over to listen to another one. Most of the thousands of young people at the event were just lying in the meadows, many couples embracing each other. Most of them chose a place where they could hear the music of two groups—there was one group on a small island in the middle of a lake and another at the edge of a meadow by the shore—and they just stayed there listening and looking at the stars.

C: Debussy once wrote about his ideas for an open-air music which, he said, would allow the composer to get away from arbitrarily fixed tone values and forms. He talked about a harmonic dream in the soul of the crowd . . . breezes, scents, flowers, leaves . . . all united in music.

S: I didn't know Debussy wrote about this, but it's wonderful: he was right. You have to compose differently when you know that the listeners are coming and going—you shouldn't write music that goes too fast, it's better to let the listeners dive into the sounds and follow them. While these sound runners were running in circular movements from one group to the other, singing and playing their "model" for the next group, they made connections between all of them. They picked up new "models" as they went along, and in this way the music was shifting and rotating very slowly.

C: Varèse once said: "Art means keeping up with the speed of light." And as early as 1928 in Berlin he sketched ideas for a piece to be called *L'Astronome* in which an astronomer who receives extraterrestrial signals and answers them is taken up into other worlds. It's interesting that forty years later you performed *Sternklang*—also in Berlin—in which star constellations are "read" by the musicians . . .

S: Yes, the notated "model" refers in the intervals and the rhythms of the notes to the stellar constellations. I drew them from star maps, but the musicians could see the same constellations from different positions—upside down, backward—depending on where they were sitting.

C: You also wrote that *Sternklang* was intended as a preparation for the arrival of beings from other stars.

S: I wanted to make music which was a real spiritual ceremony and which provided a musical atmosphere of vibrations such that beings who visited our planet would really be pleased by it and would understand it: it would be a kind of greeting music to receive them. You see, people don't understand that beings from other stars are what the Spanish were to the Aztecs, and vice versa—not more and not less. They're not only further ahead in technology; we'll also meet beings who are like Australopithecus.

C: I mentioned the Debussy and Varèse ideas because I sometimes feel that in some way you're instinctively manifesting and fulfilling a number of previously "imagined" musical events.

S: When you mention these ideas, I'm reminded of something I really don't like to talk about. Since I started composing, I've once in a while had the physical experience in which a dead composer was standing behind me while I was working. This has happened to me with Schönberg, Webern, and also Bach and Beethoven, and Mozart. I can't explain this, and people will think I'm insane, but when I've been very tired or when I was struck with a problem, then somehow I received help. Whether people believe this or not, I have experienced this . . . and I've also gotten help in my daily life from my parents, who were both killed when I was young.

PAINTING AND MUSIC: RAUSCHENBERG AND JOHNS

C: The discussion of music-in-space reminds me that we haven't talked much about painting. You've mentioned Klee in terms of multiperspective and Grünewald's transparent angels. I'm interested in knowing what relationships you find interesting between certain of your compositional ideas and those of painters with whom you've discovered some kind of affinity.

S: When I was working on *Kontakte* and *Gesang der Jünglinge* I found that Robert Rauschenberg had developed a fabulous scale in one given composition in his use of the found, almost untouched object that revealed usage—time which had crystallized in an object like a worn-out tire, an army jacket, or whatever. It was what he did with it, brushing it and drawing it together with the gesture—it's more a gesture than a real intermodulation by which a tire would have been mediated with another section of the painting. Rauschenberg used such a large brush that you could look between the individual brush hairs and by that observe the gesture of an artist who wanted to pull things together and unify them through movement. . . . Or when he painted both the stuffed chicken and the photograph in a box, he showed—by means of the specific color he placed over them—that they had something in common.

The maps of Jasper Johns, too, seemed to me comparable to what I was doing in *Hymnen,* in which the national anthems might be related to the map of the United States: everybody can recognize the names and shapes of the states, so the artist can play with the individual letters, drawing each one differently and in a very particular way. Because people know what to look for, you can distort or transform the name or the individual letters. Or you can even paint over the whole map so that many parts disappear, but people can complete the painting because of their common knowledge. . . . And the same recognition idea works in Jasper Johns's famous beer can: when you saw it standing there it looked just like a real can, but it fell out of your hand when you touched it because it was so heavy. The weight transformed it. As

Picasso once said: If I take a cup in my hand, it's a new cup because of the way I hold and present it.

C: Works like *Telemusik* and *Hymnen* remind me of Uccello's perspectives through which the spaces seem to move.

SIZE AS A MUSICAL PARAMETER

S: That's because I like to change the ordinary perspective. When the Marseillaise in *Hymnen* is heard eight times slower than normal it sounds like funeral music. And it's like putting in the same landscape painting a tree next to a man with the same height so that the dimensions don't seem quite right anymore. Or when you present a car which is ten times higher than a normal tree. When you change the normal size of things you create a completely new world. And this reveals the fact that *size* is a musical parameter—a car can also have the dimensions of another object; it can be small as a mouse, and a mouse can be as big as a skyscraper. These things were always considered surrealistic, but it has become possible by expanding and contracting the size of an object to show size as a parametrical possibility. And in this way you come back to the source of magic in all fairy tales where all of a sudden a mouse starts speaking or where Gulliver can be seen as relatively small or large. This is a technical device that allows you to bring things together which are out of the ordinary in terms of size, expansion, time, space, and color, too. . . . But we'll talk about this more fully if we discuss *Mantra*, because this is what that composition is all about.

BRUEGHEL AND BOSCH

C: I couldn't help thinking of Brueghel's paintings when you were describing all the activities taking place in *Music for a House*.

S: Brueghel has been one of my favorite painters for many years. But for another reason. I'd discovered the relevance of his work when I was composing *Gesang der Jünglinge* and when I was studying chance operations in my seminars with Meyer-Eppler. I was reading about social statistics, and Brueghel, of course, was always representing large crowds, every person in a different position, but here and there you could see an individual standing away from the group. And when working with the idea of the masses, with what for me were the new characteristics that emerged with the development of mass society and collective thinking and analysis, I realized how important Brueghel was with regard to this kind of experience.

C: And Bosch?

S: Bosch had a fantastic ability to make concepts of past, present, and future relative. He anticipated the future—submarines, rocket ships—like Nostradamus, while at the same time placing prehistoric creatures in modern times. It's like being in a time machine. He showed beings who were half animal, half plant, or half object, half man. He's a "faithful" painter—faithful to what we spiritually really are. When I think of an object, I become that object, otherwise I'd never understand what it is. And these beings which are strange crossings of animals, plants, and objects of different periods of time can be seen to represent the man of the future, a man who can become more and more omnipresent and omnidimensional, who realizes that he *is* everything else. In me is every animal, though I'm not conscious of it. The animal a person loves most is the part that's most awake in him. We *are* this, and in Bosch we see this.

C: I've thought of the history of cave paintings, many of which—from different historical periods—were supposedly superimposed in a way that the earlier drawings were never deliberately erased or mutilated. And I've felt this somehow similar to the effect of *Mikrophonie II* in which parts of your older compositions are heard without disfigurement.

DEGREES OF PERFECTION AT A GIVEN MOMENT IN A COMPOSITION

S: In one of the composition seminars I gave in 1959—and which I continued in 1961—I asked every composer to work with a scale describing the degrees of perfection. And I said that up to now only works which were complete and perfect were considered to be good compositions—where the composer had written the best possible solution at any given moment. But I said that what we should do is to work consciously with different degrees of perfection at different given moments of the composition—working with different degrees of the beautiful, not just with what is completely harmonized, but with the whole scale of the beautiful: with the ugly, with the so-called ugly, the no-longer beautiful, the not-yet-quite beautiful, the completely beautiful—in one given composition. And in this way you'd begin to understand the process of life. Because garbage might now appear as important, if not more important, than a new object since it incorporates time: it shows you a long span of time *condensed* into one moment. An old chair speaks, and the more you meditate on this chair, the more it becomes a vehicle by which to see the people who may have passed by or who once sat on it. A new chair makes you creative with regard to the future: you imagine what may happen to it, who may sit in it one day.

So the old-as-the-new, then, can be seen as an important compositional aspect that might stimulate the creativity of a person who deals with these different states of perfection and who listens to them and becomes himself more or less perfect. That's why I liked Chamberlain's auto parts: he made very beautiful sculptures in which the lines of the compressed parts of bashed-up cars revealed a wonderful artistic quality—it was so much more than an abstract object. The artist lifts up everything that has a banal function to a level where he discloses the spirit that has allowed for this object's birth as well as its decay in order to give place to something new. And this whole process should become the subject of art rather than a small segment of the historical process of frozen objects.

C: It has been suggested that the burning bush in the Bible is a kind of art event.

S: Art in the sense of being out of the ordinary, first of all; second, revealing the unknown; and third, being a medium to the eternal, having this transcendental quality. Yes, all the basic conditions for a work of art are given.

C: It seems to me that many of your works reveal just this numinous reality.

S: I can't reach any grand realization of it because the means aren't available. I'm giving a direction, and the seeds are important, but I think that other composers in the future will explore these phenomena in much more depth. We're at the beginning of a new era, and I can only have glimpses of this new spirit. What I'd love to create is a music which would always be available in a music house, a place where you could go at any time and where the music was always renewed.

C: Would you describe your ideas for such a music house?

S: There would be certain rooms in this music house where you'd be able to hear very quiet, meditative music. In other halls you'd have new music—the most recent works of contemporary composers. And then rooms in which you could hear older works. This historical function—reminding us where we've come from—is today mainly exercised in concert hall situations where you can't easily come and go as you want. The type of music house I'm talking about requires a special kind of architecture; and there should be soft carpeting on the floor and heavy curtains in front of the doors as in old movie houses so that you can come in or leave without disturbing anybody.

C: Are you thinking of having Renaissance music in the basement and contemporary music in the attic—a kind of musical archaeology?

S: I know what you mean, but this isn't just a house with many floors and rooms. What I'm talking about is a house which has several auditoriums, each of which must have specific acoustic conditions. Up to now we've had this concept of objectivity: there are acousticians who speak of an ideal hall of 1.3 or 1.5 seconds reverberation time. They start shooting with pistols and measure the amount of distortion, or the distortion of steady waves in the room, and what they have in mind is a certain ideal hall which permits clarity, transparency, and enough warmth for the sound. But then we have to ask what kind of music they're thinking of? Is it very slow Renaissance choral music? Certainly not. It's more likely to be classical symphonic music. And then everything that's fast is slightly blurred, while the extremely slow is too dry.

It's possible technically now to have halls with flexible reverberation time, but I'd prefer to build different recesses into a hall so that there would be, for example, two orchestral areas, divided by a wall, and you'd have mirrors at the two sides of the hall, effectively placing an acoustical shell around each orchestra and allowing only the conductors of the two orchestras, not the players, to see each other. Or on one floor there could be four orchestral or four sound sources, and this hall would have the shape of a four-leaf clover. You could also build a typical kidney-shaped room. But not square boxes, which are only interesting for very specific kinds of music.

C: Have you made any designs for these new halls?

S: Yes, quite a few. One, for example, is for a kind of large lighthouse tower, inside which the public would climb up in a spiral. There'd also be a lift in the middle. You'd arrive at a platform on which are housed several halls separated by gangways. And from these gangways you can see the wonderful composition of city lights through the glass walls. The four halls I imagined on this platform have room for not more than four or five hundred persons each. I don't really like enormous auditoriums. I think the music gets ruined if you have to push sound until it's loud enough for six thousand people to hear it. And, conversely, sound waves become too soft and then they no longer reach the audience. My idea is that each hall would be of a different size and would have different acoustics so that you'd get a particular feeling in each and also different sounds—I don't want this "neutral" acoustic.

"WALKING FROM ONE HALL TO ANOTHER
'AS IF YOU WERE GOING
THROUGH AN ENORMOUSLY ENLARGED SCORE.'"

We shouldn't look for just one solution: the unifying coefficient should be that of a multiple concept. For certain musical projects, these four or five halls could be combined for a performance of one composition so that a multispatial concept is brought together with a polyphonic time concept. More and more we're beginning to think that every sound and every musical layer has its own time; we're no longer only thinking of a polyphony of voices, but of a polyphony of musical characters, even a polyphony of styles. And in order to make them clearer we should have the possibility of experiencing them in separate halls. But then people immediately say that this is no longer polyphony—you go from one hall to another as if you were going through an enormously enlarged score. Let's say you had a score which was made out of wire —a wire construction—and you'd literally walk through and really experience physically the polyphony—you'd meet a big ball which would be a musical note. And this is what I meant when I've talked about wandering in space through the polyphonic multilayered composition.

C: But you can't be everywhere at once.

S: But you never can anyway because I think that when you listen to polyphony, even the most sophisticated persons can really hear only three layers and listen precisely only to one at a time;

the others just seem to be "background." So it would be easy to listen in each hall to one layer while at the same time over the speakers you'd hear, mixed in, what was happening in one or several of the other halls. And when you wanted to, you'd just go out and walk a few yards into the next layer. In each room, you'd be able to see—over television screens—and to hear what was going on in the other rooms.

I also suggested in my drawings a special use of gangways for the musicians, similar to what you see in Monte Alban, Mexico: when the priests were performing a ritual there were often half a dozen altars quite far away from each other, and since the priests didn't want to pass through the crowd on their way to another altar, they'd just disappear through a gangway, walk down the steps, run underground to the next altar which they'd climb up, and then continue the ceremony. So this permits a minimum of musicians to re-form in many different concentrations; even the instruments could be carried underground.

C: This sounds like a kind of mise-en-scène.

S: Yes, this music house will permit all sorts of visual choreography. And I think more and more that musical events should also be choreographed—should have this liturgy—organized in such a way that what you see is artistically as unique and beautiful and harmonized as what you hear.

> "Now I'm opening out like the largest telescope that ever was! Goodbye, feet!"
>
> —*Alice in Wonderland*

MANTRA:
AN ANALYSIS OF ITS CREATION AND STRUCTURE

C: I just listened to the tape of the first performance of *Mantra* given by Alfons and Aloys Kontarsky in 1970. I think it's an extraordinary work, and I'd like to talk to you about it.

S: Wonderful. Let me get the sketches for the piece.

C: It's written for two pianos, ring modulators, and antique cymbals . . .

S: Yes, I'll talk about the ring modulation later. On each pianist's music stand is a wooden plate with thirteen antique cymbals, fastened down with screws, which he hits with beaters.

C: I suppose that each of the mantra's thirteen notes is matched by a cymbal corresponding in pitch.

S: That's very precise. The mantra itself has thirteen notes, and each cymbal sound occurring once in the piece indicates the large sections—you hear the cymbal whenever a new central sound announces the next section of the work. . . . And there are wood blocks, too, which have the function of marking and emphasizing certain attack and decay accents.

Now, the first piano has these thirteen notes [goes to piano and plays: A, B, G♯, E—F, D—G, E♭, D♭, C—B♭, G♭, A—see Fig. 7]. The thirteenth note is identical with the first, and the second pianist plays the same melody mirrored. This is what I call the mantra—I couldn't find any word in my language which had a similar meaning—and this formula is repeated all the time

FIGURE 7: *Mantra*'s mantra

in different degrees of expansion and contraction. It's not varied, only *expanded.* This procedure differs from those in traditional music where you develop a theme or add or leave something out: it's expanded in duration—in time—and in space, which means in its intervals. So the first major second, for example, can become a minor third or a major third or a fourth, etc. I have all the transformations here in my sketches, just to show you what happens to the mantra.

C: Within this mantra, are there symmetries, analogies, and groupings?

S: Do you really want to know everything about it? It's a real miracle. I'll get to the analysis, but let me first tell you how the idea for the piece came about. . . . One day I had to drive from Madison, Connecticut, to Boston—it was September 1969. There were four people in the car, I was sitting next to the driver, and I just let my imagination completely loose. Shortly before this, I'd traveled to Los Angeles in a plane, and the same thing happened. On the plane I made a few sketches for a piece for two pianos that had come into my mind. And now, on the way to Boston, I was humming to myself . . . I heard this melody—it all came very quickly together: I had the idea of one single musical figure or formula that would be expanded over a very long period of time, and by that I meant fifty or sixty minutes. And these notes were the centers around which I'd continually present the same formula in a smaller form. In going from the very large to the small I wanted to leave a lot of empty spaces with which to indicate the connections between the individual sounds of this formula by means of very quick movements of glissandos or trills, all the time showing the connections between the points. You see, you can go from the first to the second or the first to the fourth, the second to the seventh, or the second to the fifth, etc., making all kinds of linear connections. So that the whole music would be nothing but this formula. It's like when you draw star constellations in the night sky with your eyes: you go from one point to the next and your eyes make the relationships, jumping from one point to another. When I view a figure like Leo, for example, I look at it in many different ways, always drawing lines between the points with my eyes.

I wrote down this melody on an envelope. Then a year later, in February 1970, I went to Bali for a month and after that to the World's Fair in Osaka. I'd told a friend of mine that I'd thought of a composition for two pianos, that I'd very much like to compose it, so I started working it out in Osaka, but decided after a time not to complete this first piece. Instead, I came back to the melody that I'd heard on the drive from Madison to Boston. Perhaps the influence of the daily performances in Osaka of our intuitive music—working with a few instructions and then playing completely freely—brought me to *Mantra,* which is entirely notated. I hadn't written any entirely notated piece in over ten or twelve years. And I felt that I wanted to develop further a kind of music that only I was responsible for and not only make music with our group or with other musicians where I proposed rather than "ordered."

C: *Mantra* is so rich in surprises that it seems to have an improvised quality.

S: You *are* right, but on the technical level of construction it's impossible to improvise such a music. Imagine all the synchronism, the polyphony, and the fact that you always have the same formula without the slightest deviation—this just can't be played freely. *Mantra,* as it is, can only exist as a piece that's entirely determinated, it's constructed like the stellar constellations, and you can't simply let the sounds happen at random as in the music that we performed in Osaka. There's such a strong verticalism, every interval can be heard as part of a sequence; you can't interpolate something into or permutate it, you'd ruin the shape of the figure.

As I said before, I gave up my first project—a kind of theater piece for two pianos—which was entirely based on the idea of having the pianists perform certain hand and body gestures. (I described the kind of gestures to be made, but not the resulting sounds. The gestures were to be made on the keys, naturally, but also in the air. You imagined the music that the pianists were playing, and then later on these sections that you first saw in the air were repeated on the keys so that you could compare what you imagined with what you could now actually hear—it's exactly repeated. This piece was called *Vision for Two Pianos,* but I gave it up in order to compose *Mantra.*) I came back to the idea of constructing a piece in which one formula is spread over a very long time span and where every detail is just a different dimension of this same formula. The formula has very interesting characteristics.

C: Before you describe these characteristics, I wanted to ask you about the *idea* of the formula. In Greek, the word *nomos* can mean both "law" and "melody." Webern once mentioned that he arrived at his "row" by means of "certain secret laws," and he talked about the difficulty of choosing such a row. Is this at all similar to what you had in mind with your mantra?

TRADITIONAL VERSUS NEW MUSIC

S: Yes, except that I don't use the mantra the way Webern or Beethoven would have in developing the original "seed" formula—it has no thematic implications. At the beginning of my career, I pointed out that in traditional music—Webern also included—musicians always showed the same figure in different light. This is the kaleidoscopic idea of variation, transformation, and development; and all these dramatic forms were based on this principle. It's like the idea of theater which derives from the Greek drama where you have the figures—characters who go through the whole play, through all stages of dramatic situations, until they die, at which point the play is over. (In classical sonatas, the recapitulations presented the material unchanged from the beginning—and then the movement was over. But of course the development sections became more and more important.) All the early twelve-tone composers treated the series as a *theme* to be developed. They transposed it, added sounds, showed it in mirror form, but they always had a thematic concept. And composers like Boulez, Pousseur, and myself criticized this when we were young, pointing out that though the serial concept might have given birth to a completely new musical technique—by getting rid of thematic composition—composers like Schönberg and Berg still couldn't get away from it. What I said then was that in traditional music you always see the same object—the theme or the motive—in a different light, whereas in the new music there are always new objects in the *same* light. Do you understand? By the "same light" I meant a set of proportions—no matter what appeared in these proportions: the relationships became more important than what was being related. In this way you could constantly create new configurations by working with a series of proportions and, as we've said the other day, the proportions could be applied once to time, once to space. This created completely different musical figures, allowing us to move away from the thematic concept. And in *Mantra* I composed a melody that I wanted to work with entirely throughout one composition, not always creating new ones.

C: In German, the word *durchführen* means "to develop."

S: Yes, to "lead through."

C: Webern said that "to develop" means "to lead through wide spaces." Wouldn't this be the bridge between what he was doing and what you're doing now?

S: Well, technically speaking, Webern reduced the themes and the motives to entities of only two sounds—the interval. That was almost an atomization of the thematic concept: single ascending or descending intervals really were meant to replace an entire *theme* of classical music. So you have to listen very carefully to these two sound intervals in his music: they're the smallest possible entities of musical composition. He approached . . . very closely . . . and that's why we could start with Webern's concept in order to go in a new direction.

MACBETH BECOMES LADY MACBETH AND THEN AN ANIMAL; NEW PEOPLE APPEAR AND DISAPPEAR, NO ONE CHARACTER GOES THROUGH THE ENTIRE PLAY

Let me just say something else with regard to the comparison I made to the dramatic situation—the plotting of, let's say, a king, his brother, a queen, and the servants through all sorts of dramatic situations—the contrasts, battles, confirmations, killings, etc. These figures are like thematic material. But I say that you can take configurations in the same light and write, for example, theater pieces where one and the same actor is for some time Macbeth and afterward Lady Macbeth, then an animal—I mean that he really *changes:* always new people appear and others disappear, nobody goes through the entire play. But the way they behave, the way they're related to each other, the tensions or the constellations of these beings—*that* is the constructive element, rather than the figures, the *personalities*. The analogy to what I've done in my own compositions since 1951 would be the construction of a drama in which persons who have a certain relationship to others appear and then never show up again. But these same relationships that you've felt, these certain tensions, occur again and again, always between other completely different persons.

C: Let's say you see Macbeth and Lady Macbeth, and then each becomes the other.

S: That's the simplest.

C: But if Macbeth turned into a wolf . . .

S: That would be stronger. Or if, for example, you'd all of a sudden see two objects—a square box and sort of an imaginative, surrealistic animal—and the same kind of dialogue and tension existed between both of them. You see, it's the proportion, the interval, that you're concentrating on, but the beings are always changing.

C: Perhaps sometime you'll have a chance to see Robert Wilson's *Deafman's Glance*, which comes close to this idea.

S: I've never seen such a drama. But there must now be poets who have caught on—as apparently Wilson has—who have understood what's happened in music and are creating works in which you have the same people taking on lots of different roles. And that's like the same *pitch* taking on lots of different timbres or durations. The development of interchanging parameters will naturally reveal new attitudes of construction.

C: Let's get back to the mantra.

S: OK, now we have this thirteen-note mantra [see Fig. 7]. It's segmented into four parts which are separated by different pauses of different lengths. The first has four notes—A, B, G♯, E—an ascending major second, ascending major sixth, descending major third (you'll see that all the intervals occur in the mantra). Then a pause of three time units. . . . Let me speak about these pauses. They have the proportion of three, two, one, and four time units. The first segment—or what I call *limb* of the mantra, like the limbs of a body—has four notes; and the second, two. But these two notes are repeated three times—which makes six. The third section again has four notes (G, E♭, D♭, C), also with different intervals between these notes; and the fourth section has three notes (B♭, G♭, A). That makes thirteen.

The durations of the individual notes are different in each limb. In the first, the first note has a duration of one time unit, the second of two, the third of three and the fourth of four: like [singing: 1, 1–2, 1–2–3, 1–2–3–4]. Then a silence of 3 time units. . . . In the second limb (F, D, F, D, F, D) we have 1, 1, 1, 1, 1-with-a-dot, and ½, which, if we now reduce it to the smallest unit, makes it 2, 2, 2, 2, 3, 1—a proportion of 2–3–1. And then we have a silence of 2 units after the second limb. Next, in the third limb (G, E♭, D♭, C, and C is repeated) we have the durations of 5 plus 2 plus 1 plus 3 plus 4, followed by a pause of 1. And finally (B♭, G♭, A) we have a duration of 4 plus 2 plus 6. If we consider the total durations of the units I've just analyzed, then the first limb lasts 10 units; the second, 6; the third, 15; and the fourth, 12—so

10, 6, 15, 12. These are the different total durations of the four limbs. And the pauses separating these four limbs are, as I said: 3–2–1–4, there being a pause of four between the last limb and the first. The total duration is 53.

MANTRA MIRRORS

Now we can observe something else: the mantra is always presented in its original form with its own mirror: we have an upper and lower layer of the mantra—the lower one being the mirror of the upper, or vice versa. But it's not as easy as it sounds. The first limb is combined with a mirror form of the second, whereas the second is combined with the mirror form of the first. The same applies to the relationship between the third and the fourth limbs: the third upper layer is combined with the mirror form of the fourth limb, and the fourth with the mirror of the third. I've indicated this with the green, red, blue, and yellow colors on the record cover of *Mantra.*

EACH NOTE WITH ITS SPECIFIC FORM

Again, something else is very interesting: each note in the mantra has a different form. The first note (A) is a periodic repetition, and later on in the piece, when this character of the first note becomes predominant for a whole section of mantra repetitions, then *all* these notes will have this kind of periodic repetition in all different speeds. So it's the seed for its own amplification over a long section. . . . The second note (B) has an accent at its end—very short and loud. Every sound, as you know, has a head, a body, and a tail, or, as we say in technical terms, an attack, a development, and a decay. The characteristic of this sound is that of an accent decay—the thirty-second note. The third note (G♯) is "normal," with a duration of 3, as we've said before. And the fourth note (E) has an appoggiatura—a grace note in front of the note, but it's always around the center, occurring twice before it's finally sustained. . . . Let me just say before we continue that the repeated first note is poco marcato—it has a special characteristic: ta-ka-ta-*ka.* The second note has the forte accent at the end, the third note is mezzo piano, and the fourth one is piano again.

In the second limb, the two notes I was speaking of before

(F–D) are repeated three times. And this is actually the seed of a tremolo, sometimes resulting in a whole tremolo section. We were speaking yesterday about the democracy of all the elements participating in a musical society, so to speak. And there always comes a moment in my works when one characteristic has its time; it takes over and becomes predominant. But this requires a very specific, very characteristic, and very *personal* appearance of each note. And here we have the tremolo—it's pianissimo. And the last note occurs with a chord; it's accentuated mezzo forte, whereas the repeated F and D are pianissimo. You'll hear, later on, whole chord sections which are the result of that single note. And this particular chord is just the verticalization of the melody which was played before—the five lower layer notes of the first half of the mantra. It draws it all together.

Then in the third limb the first note (G) has an accentuated accent at the beginning: *TA* ta. Both in the mantra exposition and later on in the piece, this characteristic will become very significant. The next note (E♭), the eighth note of the mantra, is chromatically combined with the previous one—you have the intermediary note between the previous one and itself. You'll see later that if, for example, the eighth note of the mantra is an octave's rather than a major third's distance from the previous note, then because it's expanded you'll get lots of notes connecting these two in one direction, almost like arpeggios between central notes. . . . The ninth note (D♭) is played staccato. The tenth (C) is repeated once: its repetition has a different duration. And this note, irregularly repeated, is the smallest possible seed for Morse code rhythms. At a certain point in the composition, in fact, there's a moment when the performers actually use Morse code from the radio. It's one climax, so to speak, of the irregular repetition, and they use the realistic Morse signals of a shortwave radio in order to make the connections to this surreality and also to transcend the mantra and make it as general as possible.

Then, with the fourth limb, we have the eleventh note (B♭) which, just at the beginning, is the seed of a trill—the shortest possible trill. And later on you'll hear sections where whole groups of mantras occurring with trills will result from this atom. . . . The next note (G♭) has a sforzato characteristic, meaning a forte piano on the same note—loud-soft, it's the beginning of an echo, and all sorts of echo textures or echo structures can be derived from this single note. . . . Finally, the thirteenth note (A) has *together* with the lower notes a real arpeggio. It's not a chromatic connection, as we had with the eighth note, but an arpeggio which leads to this note itself. As you see, it goes from the A♭ to the G♯; the A which is next to the G♯ is already there and will continue to resonate. . . . So every note has a different character. And these thirteen different characters occur in thirteen large sections of the piece as the predominant characteristics.

TWELVE MANTRIC EXPANSIONS

The mantra itself, as you've pointed out, doesn't repeat any note except the thirteenth; it's a twelve-tone construction with the thirteenth note identical with the first. You can even hum it easily like a tune. . . . Now something very interesting happens. I have used twelve different *expansions* of this original mantra. And in order to explain what I mean by expansions I have to say a few words about the so-called scalar composition of *Mantra.* In all my previous pieces I've only used the chromatic scale. And when I had a twelve-tone series, the absolute identification of a note of the series with a pitch was self-understood. Whereas here in *Mantra* I'm working with thirteen different scales.

Let me explain this. Normally we have eighty-eight chromatic notes on the piano; that's what the first scale of *Mantra* is made up of. And in this scale the mantra always sounds the way I've just analyzed it with these thirteen different pitches. The mantra itself has an expansion of a major ninth. Now imagine that you have a piano on which every second note is missing; you'd then have a whole-tone scale. There would only be forty-four keys on the piano, and if you played this mantra, you'd have a major instead of a minor second; a tritone instead of a minor third; a major ninth instead of a fifth—always a double of the interval. But the whole-tone scale doesn't really occur among the thirteen that I've used. You see, my second scale leaves out certain steps of the chromatic scale, and if you look at it carefully [see Fig. 8], you can see that the lowest note of this scale is an A♯ or B♭. The first note of the next scale is a C—a major second higher; the first note of the following twelve is a D—also a major second higher; the next note, an E—a major second higher. Then an F♯, and, finally, a G♯. So there we have the whole tones as the first notes of a scale of twelve, but the octave is no longer an octave—it's become a major ninth—the octave is stretched, which means that once in a

FIGURE 8: *Mantra*'s scales

etc.
~ Frequenzen
von 330 Hz (e1)
ORIGINAL

while we have a major second in place of the minor second. This is what we've called a mode, a modal scale to be precise. You can analyze this to observe where the half tones and the whole tones are.

Let's say we play the same mantra we've heard before based on the chromatic scale, but now expanded. You can see, for example, that certain minor seconds or major thirds become fourths, and certain minor sevenths become major sevenths: they're stretched. . . . If you make a wire construction and then press it in irregularly, you get all sorts of different forms, though all the connections remain the same. This somehow happens with the mantra now. And in the third scale [see Fig. 8] the octave here becomes an octave plus a major third. So what in the first scale is an octave will here occur as an octave plus a major third, and the other intervals are stretched as well. It's as if you had a piano with rubber keys so that what was once seven octaves now becomes nine, or one—all the intervals become larger or smaller. What really occurs here is the stretching of this one chromatic scale. So the mantra might occur in any of these twelve scales.

And this naturally brings us to the twelve different expansions of the mantra itself [see Fig. 9]. The first four notes of the first scale [plays them on piano] become [plays first four notes of the twelfth scale]. This shows you two extremes, and you can compare the others yourself. And so in every one of the thirteen given sections of this piece there's one scale at the basis of each section—though not in the order as they're written in the illustration—and all the mantric presentations occur within this scale. In this way we find very characteristic widths and expansions and sizes. It's like a being that can enlarge to become a giant and then a mouse right afterward; it no longer has a fixed size.

ALICE IN WONDERLAND

C: It's like Alice in Wonderland—she drinks a liquid and becomes small and eats some cake and becomes enormous.

S: Ah, that's what *Mantra* is all about. Music critics who think this is old hat—just a variation form—really don't know what they're hearing. If you, Jonathan, start getting taller, as in the example of Alice, and all of a sudden you're standing in front of me a hundred yards high, then it's still Jonathan—it's not a variation of Jonathan. There's nothing varied, really, it's just that the complete Jonathan has many different ways of presenting himself. And that's what happens here. The mantra has twelve different "sizes." And the same applies to "time." When the mantra itself is based on the smallest time unit, it is compressed to three-and-a-half seconds; and when it's based on the longest time unit, it lasts for almost four minutes. I've made a complete plan of the composition, in which you can see the whole form; that is perhaps the nicest secret of the entire piece.

FORM SCHEME

Here's the form scheme [see Fig. 10]. It's like a family tree which designates the durations. The largest time expansions of the mantra last 212 seconds, and they occur here as the two columns of a bridge; the central one is 106—the half duration. So if the unit of the mantra that we have here on the paper is a quarter note and if the total mantric durations are 53 quarter notes, then when you have 106 it means that the quarter notes all become half notes, and the half notes, whole notes. With 212, each quarter note becomes a whole note—it's four times as long. And the fastest exposition in time of the mantra is just 7 units—what in its original form lasts 53. So you can see that what happens in space, in the intervals—the expansions and the different sizes—also happens in time. You can see exactly how a duration of 27 or 53 occurs in the composition. It's like the difference between a fly that lives one hour and a tree or rock that lives several thousand years. That's the concept of this piece: the mantra itself expands in time and space in very distinct degrees.

MANTRA AND ORIENTAL MUSIC

C: When I started listening to *Mantra* I got lost in the pitch terrain. I first thought it was recognizable because of what seemed to be recapitulations of or momentary similarities to different kinds of Western piano writing, as well as to certain kinds of Asian music. And then I realized I was in a foreign world until the end when everything came together.

S: That's very natural. Since I'm working with these different scales, there are moments when what you hear sounds modal and you immediately have some Balinese music in the room.

FIGURE 9: *Mantra*'s expansions

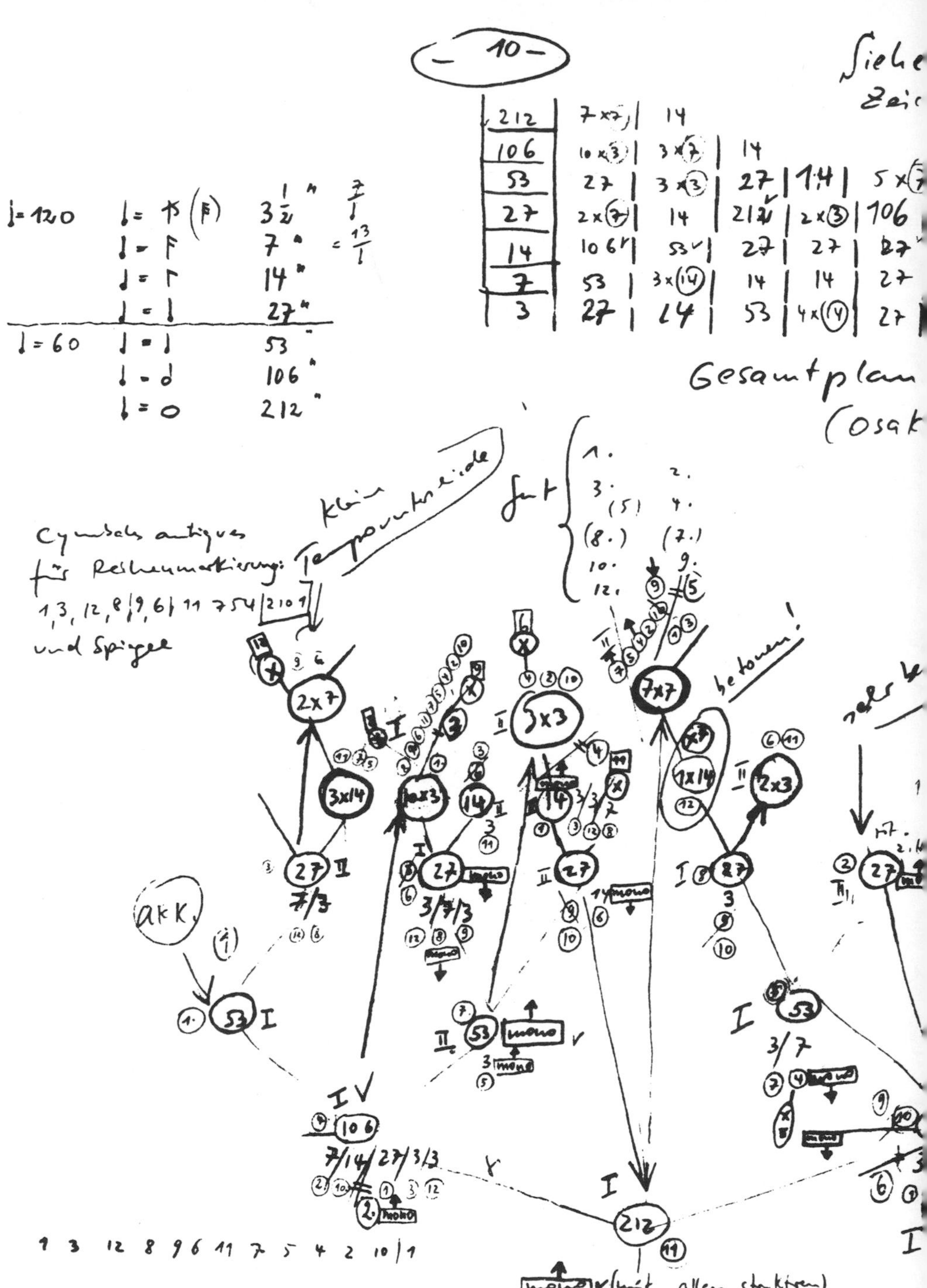

FIGURE 10: *Mantra*'s form scheme

umseitig
erläutern!

6 × ③ | 2 × ⑭ | ⑭ | 53 | Ende
14 | 212 | 7 | 53 | 3 | 15 × ③ | 27 | → 212 | 106 | 53 53 | 27 27 27 27 | 14 | 7 | 3 3 |
27 |
106 |

MANTRA

C: But also Mussorgsky, Bartók, and Thelonious Monk.

S: Exactly, because when I concentrate on the two notes of the tremolo, when they occur slowly enough, or add a certain speed together with a forte and with accents, then it does sound like certain parts of Bartók, as you say. Which means that all those different aspects that contributed to the "style" of a person or of a whole country can now occur automatically when you have these variable changes; they can occur because the parameters become so flexible and are based on a system of wanderings through the different scalar dimensions. But they disappear, too, and there are many new things which you've never heard. It's this same mantra which produces all the worlds—it wakes them up. By the expansions and contractions of one figure, you create all the different styles, and these occur among others. *Mantra* is very polyphonic. You always have several layers and, by that, several characteristics at the same time—up to four. And this contributes to the suggestion of the different styles or countries. Several colleagues have mentioned to me that, though there's no exact resemblance, the whole Orient is in it.

C: You haven't spoken about the new harmonic system of the sound transformation, the ring modulation which creates that sense of just intonation—the microtonal Eastern sounds.

RING MODULATION

S: The mantra is not only expanded, as I've explained, in the twelve forms, but by means of the ring modulation it's also contracted, so that the whole mantra is sometimes enlarged by only a fourth or fifth when it would normally expand over a major ninth.

C: Would you say something about the use of ring modulation—you're obviously doing something different from John Cage's "prepared piano" pieces.

S: It's totally different. In Cage's works you're presented with a given timbre world through the preparation of the strings that give it a certain unique color. And that's it—it's a static concept. In order to make different sections or areas in a piece you automatically have to use other pitches; if you used the same ones you'd always have the same timbres. Now this is perhaps an embryonic form of what later on became the *Klangfarben* composition of electronic music. Cage is interesting in that he composed his own sound world—as when he collected only metal instruments and set them up in a special orchestra for *Music in Metal.* In such a manner the sound world of the composition became as original as what was done with these sounds. And this was a new concept in twentieth-century music.

Now ring modulation, which is a technical process, does the following: you feed any sound into a ring modulator along with a second sound; this, too, could be any sound, but I use sine waves —the purest sound. What then comes out of the ring modulator is the sum of the two frequencies and the difference of these frequencies—the original sounds are suppressed. If I take the note A, for example, in the middle of the piano—440 cycles per second— and if I feed this A and a sine wave into the ring modulator, I get 880 cycles, which is the octave, and zero: this comprises the sum and the difference. Which means that when the output of the ring modulator is heard through loudspeakers, you're hearing the added octave of the original sound. Now since the octave is the second harmonic, I'm altering the timbre of the piano sound which is heard at the same time as its ring-modulated variety in the speakers; the second harmonic becomes louder because it's doubled.

To take a more differentiated example: if I have a 440-cycle sound and add its upper fifth into the ring modulator with the sine wave, then I get 440 plus 660 which, since there's a 2:3 relationship, produces a fifth harmonic—the major third 1,100. And then I get 660 minus 440 which is 220—the octave below the original note A. So we again arrive at a new timbre: the fifth harmonic [two octaves and a major third above the original note] is reinforced and there's an added octave below the fundamental piano sound. Another example: When I have the 440-cycle sound and feed 880 into the ring modulator, then what results is the sound itself, 440; and 880 plus 440, which equals 1,320—again the fifth. What's interesting is that when I slide my 880 sine wave very slowly upward or downward in a glissando, the original sound in the speaker begins to move away from the note that's being held on the piano, thereby producing beats and micro-intervals; I have 441-, 442-, 443-cycle sounds coming through the speakers along with the original sound. So, depending on what sine waves I put into the ring modulator, all the micro-intervals next to any note played on the piano can be produced.

Concerning *Mantra*: thirteen different notes for the thirteen sections of the piece are fed into the ring modulators, and these notes are the exact frequencies of the mantra itself. And they become what we call the "mirror frequencies" of everything that's heard in this section, which is always the mantra with its expansions and contractions. This leads to a new concept of cadential harmony; when the first note of the mantra is played, the first note of the mantra is in the ring modulator, producing a complete consonance—the octave or the sound itself. If I now move a fifth away from it, you'll then hear the second degree of consonance coming over the speakers. The major third produces a third degree of consonance, and, ultimately, the minor second or the major seventh produce the sharpest dissonances—this timbre sounds the furthest removed from the piano sound.

C: It suggests the gamelan effect.

S: Yes. The metal instrument sound emerges, and this is due to the fact that the "difference" produces subharmonic spectra that are heard along with the harmonic spectra which are always the "sums." And when I return to the thirteenth note at the conclusion of one mantric exposition, the extreme consonance always reoccurs: the intervals of the mantra itself are composed such that they move away from the central note, produce increasingly more deviations, micro-intervals, and noise components—what we call dissonant components—and then return. So that each mantra, from the first to the thirteenth note, is like a cadence that opens and closes. And there are intermediary closures: the fifth of the original note at the end of the first limb, the fourth at the end of the second, the minor third at the end of the third, and the note itself at the end of the fourth limb—a complete consonance. It leaves the central note, sounds even stranger, then becomes more consonant with the half closures of different degrees in between, until, at the end, there's that closure again. In "classical" music this process was realized by means of triads and harmonic relationships like sevenths or ninths. But here it happens through the mirror concept of the ring modulation.

C: You give each mantra its own life.

S: Yes. That's it. It's breathing. And the lengths of the breaths differ according to how much I've stretched or subdivided the mantric durations. It breathes through the ring modulation away from and then back to the central note. The ring modulation is like the middle line in a Rorschach test when the paper is folded; it's the axis of symmetry.

C: There's that amazing section at the end of the work that goes by incredibly fast. . . .

S: Some people think of Liszt at this point. But what you're hearing is an extreme concentration of the entire piece with all its notes—and I can check to tell you exactly how many notes there are because I know how many mantric expositions I've made in the different forms. The whole piece is condensed to the fastest possible speed: all the differences of durations disappear while all the notes with all the intervallic expansions are compressed into two minutes.

C: Why did you do this?

S: Well, it was wonderful to do. I remember the moment when I thought that I really should have the whole piece condensed. The original idea was to stretch one formula over an enormous time span, each note being so far away from the two others before and after that there would have to be all kinds of connections between them. And then this compression was the opposite idea.

C: Is this similar to the effect of the bombardment of atoms in radiation labs?

S: Is your comparison correct? If you bombard them they explode, they fall into pieces and the energy is freed. Oh, I see, yes. What happens here is like what I've mentioned before—the whole cosmos expanding, exploding then contracting again until the densest matter is reached, and then exploding once more. That's what really happens in *Mantra*. And so in a sense you are right, there is the effect of an explosion.

C: At the very end of the piece—it almost sounds like a coda, but perhaps that's too traditional a term. . . .

S: No, it's the simplest and most modest way of describing it. After everything that's happened it's almost nostalgic.

C: It moved me very much and reminded me again of the conclusion of *Hymnen*.

S: It's like someone who's humming a melody of music which he's heard ages ago. It reminds him of his childhood; his whole life has passed and at the very end he still remembers this very simple tune without all its complications—it's just the notes without the initial characteristics that it once had, just the simple naked notes. It no longer just goes ahead straightforwardly as it always did. It's really like someone taking breaths in between, like a wind that has blown through a melody that's no longer sticking together. . . . Memory.

There are those bell-like sounds—those arpeggios played on the highest octave of the piano after this very strong "explosion"; you can't go any further. And you're right, it's very similar to the end of the Fourth Region of *Hymnen.* It sounds like a large bright bell, then the mantra itself occurring in the very low octaves with its last characteristic—a broad arpeggio which suggests the *throwing* of the individual note somewhere . . . and then thrown back, like a farewell.

SATPREM ON SRI AUROBINDO

C: In your program notes for the first London performance of *Mantra* you quoted a beautiful section from a book about Sri Aurobindo by Satprem [see Fig. 11].

S: It's fantastic, isn't it? And you must read the book, too.

C: Satprem writes: "For true poetry is an act, it makes holes in the consciousness—we are so walled in, barricaded!—through which the Real can enter: it is a mantra of the real, an initiation." And I know that Sri Aurobindo talks about the descending *divine* meeting the ascending *human.* How does all this relate to *Mantra* itself?

MANTRA AND THE GALAXY

S: To say it as simply as possible, *Mantra,* as it stands, is a miniature of the way a galaxy is composed. When I was composing the work, I had no accessory feelings or thoughts; I knew only that I had to fulfill the mantra. And it demanded itself, it just started blossoming. As it was being constructed through me, I somehow felt that it must be a very true picture of the way the cosmos is constructed. I've never worked on a piece before in which I was so sure that every note I was putting down was right. And this was due to the integral systemization—the combination of the scalar idea with the idea of deriving everything from the One. It shines very strongly.

> "It's for a later period to discover the closer unifying laws that are already present in the works themselves. When this true conception of art is achieved, then there will no longer by any possible distinction

between science and inspired creation. The further one presses forward, the greater becomes the identity of everything, and finally we have the impression of being faced by a work not of man but of Nature."

—Anton Webern

Sunday Evening 2nd May in the Queen Elizabeth Ha

Concert in Association with Allied Artists

ALOYS and ALFONS KONTARSKY two pianos

Introduced by
KARLHEINZ STOCKHAUSEN

Mantra KARLHEINZ STOCKHAUSEN
(British première) (b. 1928)

Sound equipment by Hugh Davies

Mantra STOCKHAUSEN

There exists in India a secret knowledge based on the study of sounds and the differences of vibratory modality according to the planes of consciousness. . . . As each of our centres of consciousness is in direct communication with a plane, one can thus, by the *repetition of certain sounds* put oneself in communication with the corresponding plane of consciousness. . . . *The basic or essential sounds which have the power of establishing the communication are called mantra.* The mantras, always secret and given to the disciple by the Guru, are of all kinds (each plane of consciousness has a crowd of degrees) and they may serve the most contradictory ends. By the combination of certain sounds one can, at lower levels of consciousness, generally at the vital level, put oneself in relation with the corresponding forces and obtain many strange powers: there are mantras which kill, mantras which attack with precision a particular part or organ of the body, mantras which heal, mantras which kindle fire, which protect, spell-bind. This kind of magic or vibratory chemistry proceeds simply by the conscious manipulation of the lower vibrations. But there is a higher magic which also proceeds by the handling of vibrations but on higher planes of consciousness; this is poetry, music, the spiritual mantras of Upanishads and the Vedas or the mantras which the Guru gives his disciple to help him enter consciously into direct communication with such or such a plane of consciousness, such or such a force, such or such a divine being. Here the sound carries in itself the power of experience and realisation—*it is a sound that makes one see.*

Poetry in music which is an unconscious handling of secret vibrations may then be considered a powerful means of the opening of consciousness. If we could succeed in composing poetry or music which is the product of a conscious handling of higher vibrations, we would create great works having an initiatory power. Instead of a poetry which is a fantasy of the intellect and a nautch-girl of the mind as Sri Aurobindo says, we would *create a mantric music* or poetry to bring the gods into our life. For true poetry is an act, it makes holes in the consciousness – we are so walled in, barricaded! – through which the Real can enter: it is a mantra of the real, an initiation. This is what the Vedic rishis and the seers of the Upanishads have done in their mantras which have the power of communicating an illumination to one who is ready; this is what Sri Aurobindo has explained in his Future Poetry and this is what he has done in Savitri.

The mantra or great poetry, great music, the sacred word, comes from the overmind. This is the source of all creative or spiritual activities (it is not possible to distinguish between the two: the categorical divisions of the intellect vanish in a clear air wherein all is sacred, even the profane). We may hence try to say in what lies the particular vibration or particular rhythm of the overmind. And, first, for anyone who has the capacity to enter more and more consciously into relation with the higher planes – poet, writer, artist – it is quite evident, perceptible, that after a certain level of consciousness it is no longer ideas that one sees and tries to translate. *One hears.* There are literally vibrations or waves, rhythms which lay hold of the seeker, invade him, then clothe themselves with words and ideas or with music, colours, in their descent. But the word or the idea, the music, the colour, is the result, a secondary effect; they just give a body to that first terribly imperious vibration. And if the poet, the true one, corrects and recorrects, it is not to improve upon the form, as one says, or to express himself better, but to catch that vibrating thing – and if the true vibration is not there, all his magic crumbles, as that of the Vedic priest who has badly pronounced the mantra of the sacrifice. When the consciousness is transparent the sound becomes clearly audible, and it is a seeing sound, a sound-image or a sound-colour or a sound-idea, which links indissolubly in the same luminous body the audition to the vision and the thought. *All is full, contained in a single vibration.* On the intermediary planes (higher mind, illumined or intuitive mind) these vibrations are generally broken up – they are jets, impulsions, pulsations – whilst in the overmind they are vast, sustained, self-luminous, like those great notes of Beethoven. They have neither beginning nor end, they seem *born out of the Infinite and disappear into the Infinite;* they do not "begin" somewhere, they come into the consciousness with a sort of halo of eternity which vibrates ahead and continues to vibrate long after.

Selected by Karlheinz Stockhausen from *Sri Aurobindo or the adventure of consciousness* by *Satprem* (India Library, New York).

catalog of stockhausen's works*

1950/51	"Early Scores"
	THREE CHORUSES, after Verlaine for a cappella chorus
	CHORAL for a cappella chorus
	THREE LIEDER for alto and chamber orchestra
	SONATINE for violin and piano
1951	KREUZSPIEL for oboe, bass clarinet, piano, and three percussion groups
1951	FORMEL for orchestra
1952	ETUDE, musique concrète
1952	SPIEL for orchestra
1952	SCHLAGQUARTETT for piano and 3 x 2 timpani
1952/62	PUNKTE for orchestra
1952/53	KONTRA-PUNKTE for ten instruments
1952/53	KLAVIERSTÜCKE (Piano Pieces) I-IV
1953	STUDIE I, electronic music
1954	STUDIE II, electronic music
1954/55	KLAVIERSTÜCKE V-X
1955/56	ZEITMASZE for five woodwinds
1955/57	GRUPPEN (Groups) for three orchestras
1956	KLAVIERSTÜCK XI
1955/56	GESANG DER JÜNGLINGE (Song of the Youths), electronic music
1959	ZYKLUS for one percussionist
1959/60	CARRÉ for four orchestras and four choruses
1959	REFRAIN for three performers
1959/60	KONTAKTE for electronic sounds
	KONTAKTE for electronic sounds, piano, and percussion
1961	ORIGINALE, musical theater
1962/64	MOMENTE for soprano, four choral groups, and thirteen instrumentalists
	MOMENTE, "Cologne Version"

* Published by Universal Edition.

1963	PLUS-MINUS, 2 x 7 pages for realization
1964	MIKROPHONIE I for tam-tam, two microphones, two filters, and potentiometers (for six performers)
	MIKROPHONIE I, "Brussels Version"
1964	MIXTUR for orchestra, sine-wave generators, and four ring modulators
1967	MIXTUR for small orchestra
1965	MIKROPHONIE II for twelve singers, Hammond organ, and four ring modulators
1965	STOP for orchestra
	STOP, "Paris Version"
1965/66	SOLO for one melody instrument with feedback
1966	TELEMUSIK, electronic music
1966	ADIEU for wind quintet
1966/67	HYMNEN (Anthems) for electronic and concrete sounds
	HYMNEN, version for tape and soloists
1969	THIRD REGION OF HYMNEN with orchestra
1967	PROZESSION for tam-tam, viola, elektronium, piano, filters, and potentiometers
1968	STIMMUNG for six vocalists
	STIMMUNG, "Paris Version"
1968	KURZWELLEN (Shortwaves) for piano, elektronium, tam-tam, viola, microphones, filters, and potentiometers
1968	AUS DEN SIEBEN TAGEN (From the Seven Days), fifteen compositions May 1968
1968	SPIRAL for one soloist and shortwave receiver
1969	FRESCO for four orchestral groups, wall sounds for meditation
1969/70	POLE (Poles) for two
1969/70	EXPO for three
1968/70	FÜR KOMMENDE ZEITEN (For Times to Come), 17 texts of intuitive music
1970	MANTRA for two pianists
1971	STERNKLANG (Star Sound) "Park Music" for five groups
1971	TRANS for orchestra

discography

KONTRA-PUNKTE Soloists of the Rome Symphony Conductor: Bruno Maderna	RCA VICS 1239*
KLAVIERSTÜCKE I-XI Aloys Kontarsky	CBS (International) S77209
KLAVIERSTÜCK VI David Tudor	Vega C30 A278
KLAVIERSTÜCK VIII David Burge	Candide 31015*
KLAVIERSTÜCK X Frederic Rzewski	Mace S-9091*
KLAVIERSTÜCKE IX and XI Marie Francoise Bucquet	Philips T.C. 6500 101
STUDIEN I and II	DGG LP 16 133 (European) out of print
ZEITMASZE Conductor: Pierre Boulez Conductor: Robert Craft	 Vega C30 A139 Odyssey 32160154*
GRUPPEN Orchestra of the Westdeutscher Rundfunk, Cologne	DGG 137 002*

* Asterisk indicates that designated recording is commercially available in the U.S.A.

GRUPPEN (*continued*)	
Conductors: Karlheinz Stockhausen, Bruno Maderna, Michael Gielen	
GESANG DER JÜNGLINGE	DGG 138 811*
New stereo version, 1968	
ZYKLUS	
Christoph Caskel	Mainstream 5003* (Formerly on Time 58001)
Max Neuhaus	Columbia MS 7139*
Caskel and Neuhaus (2 versions)	Mace S-9091*
Sylvia Gualda	Erato STU 70603
Yasunori Yamaguchi	SONC 16 012-J (Japan)
CARRÉ	DGG 137 002*
Chorus and Orchestra of the Norddeutscher Rundfunk, Hamburg	
Conductors: Mauricio Kagel, Karlheinz Stockhausen, Andrzej Markowski, Michael Gielen	
REFRAIN	
Aloys and Bernhard Kontarsky, Caskel	Mainstream 5003* (Formerly on Time 58001)
Aloys Kontarsky, Caskel, K. Stockhausen	Candide CE 310 22*
KONTAKTE	
Electronic music	DGG 138 811*
Electronic music, piano and percussion: Aloys Kontarsky, C. Caskel, K. Stockhausen	Candide CE 310 22*
Electronic music, piano, and percussion: David Tudor, C. Caskel, Stockhausen	Wergo 60009
MOMENTE	Nonesuch 71157*
Chorus and Orchestra of the Westdeutscher Rundfunk, Cologne	Wergo 60024
Soprano: Martina Arroyo	
Conductor: K. Stockhausen	

MIKROPHONIE I Aloys Kontarsky, A. Alings, J. G. Fritsch, H. Bojé, K. Stockhausen, H. Davies, J. Spek	Columbia MS 7355*
MIKROPHONIE II Members of the Westdeutscher Chorus and the Studio Chori for New Music, Cologne	Columbia MS 7355*
MIXTUR Ensemble Hudba Dneska, Bratislava Conductor: Ladislav Kupkovic	DGG 137 012*
SOLO Vinko Globokar, trombone	DGG 137 005*
TELEMUSIK	DGG 137 012*
HYMNEN	DGG 139 421/22*
PROZESSION A. Alings, R. Gehlhaar, J. G. Fritsch, Aloys Kontarsky, H. Bojé, K. Stockhausen	Candide CE 310 01*
Same performers, different version	Fratelli Fabbri Editori mm-1098 (Vox)
STIMMUNG Collegium Vocale of Cologne Wolfgang Fromme: director	DG 2543 003*
KURZWELLEN A. Alings, R. Gehlhaar, Aloys Kontarsky, H. Bojé, J. G. Fritsch, K. Stockhausen (2 versions)	DGG 2707 045*
"SET SAIL FOR THE SUN" (FROM THE SEVEN DAYS) H. Bojé, A. Alings, R. Gehlhaar, Aloys Kontarsky, J-F Jenny Clarke, J. Fritsch, M. Portal, J-P Drouet, K. Stockhausen	Harmonia Mundi "Musique Vivante" HM 30 899

"UNLIMITED" (FROM THE SEVEN DAYS) V. Globokar, C. Alsina, J-F Jenny Clarke, J-P Drouet, M. Portal, J. G. Fritsch, K. Stockhausen	Shandar SR 10,002
"IT" and "UPWARDS" (FROM THE SEVEN DAYS) Aloys Kontarsky, H. Bojé, J. Fritsch, A. Alings, R. Gehlhaar, K. Stockhausen	DGG 2530 255*
"COMMUNION" and "INTENSITY" (FROM THE SEVEN DAYS) J. Fritsch, A. Alings, R. Gehlhaar, Carlos Roqué Alsina, J-F Jenny Clarke, M. Portal, J-P Drouet, K. Stockhausen	DGG 2530 256*
SPIRAL	
Michael Vetter, electric recorder	DGG 2561 109
Heinz Holliger, oboe	Wergo 325
STOCKHOVEN-BEETHAUSEN OPUS 1970 Aloys Kontarsky, H. Bojé, J. G. Fritsch, K. Stockhausen	DGG 139 461*
MANTRA Alfons and Aloys Kontarsky	DGG 2530 208*
STOCKHAUSEN: FESTIVAL OF HITS (Includes excerpts from *Gesang der Jünglinge, Kontakte, Carré, Telemusik, Stimmung, Hymnen*)	Polydor 2612023

about the author

Jonathan Cott attended Columbia University, the University of California, Berkeley, and the University of Essex. He has produced programs on contemporary music for WNYC, New York, and KPFA, Berkeley. His poems have appeared in *The World* anthologies and *Young American Poets,* and Angel Hair books has published his meditative gloss on Goethe's *Elective Affinities.* His essays on film, rock, contemporary music and poetry have appeared in several books, as well as in magazines and newspapers like *Ramparts,* the *New York Times,* and *Rolling Stone,* of which he is a contributing editor. He has just completed editing an anthology of Victorian fairy-tale novels, stories, and poems.